D1621554

MERMAIDS
& MARTINIS

Celebrate in Color!

— Hilary

MERMAIDS & MARTINIS

Turn Your Party Into a Memory

Hilary Pereira

DUNHAM
books

For information about bulk purchases or licensing of *Mermaids & Martinis,* please contact the publisher:
Dunham Books, 63 Music Square East, Nashville, Tennessee 37203
Printed in the United States of America

Trade Paperback ISBN: 978-0-9851359-1-1
Ebook ISBN: 978-0-9851359-2-8

Jamie Malkin contributed ideas, themes and lots of love to this book.

Illustrations by Anna Yakhnich
Edited by Emily Prather
Book design by Mary Sue Englund
Copy edited by Brittany Costa
Proofreading by Lauren Zerboulis

Photography by Nina Choi, Clark Mitchell, Kellie Sliwa, Daniel Movitz, Brian Friedman, Michael Paniccia, Jamie Betts, Abby Liga, and Dennis Pereira

TO MERMAIDS EVERYWHERE:
May you find a reason to celebrate every day.

TO MY PARENTS:
Thank you for giving me my roots and wings.

AND TO MY DEAREST FRIENDS:
Thank you for inspiring my "fins."

Welcome Mermaids!

FROM SPECTACULAR-and-swish social soirees to cheap-and-chic celebrations, from gracious gift giving to elegant etiquette, *Mermaids & Martinis* is *the* destination for all things fabulous and fun. If coming up with creative party themes and favors excites you, if making others feel special is gratifying to you, or if serving fantastic food and creative cocktails to giddy guests lights you up, then you've come to the right place. This book is designed to be a source of new ideas and tricks of the trade to help you really enjoy entertaining. This book will change the way you think about parties: it will teach you to worry less, laugh more, and discover *your* best hosting talents. *Mermaids & Martinis* will help you rediscover your Mermaid attitude, a la "Life's a piece of cake!" But be duly warned: soon everyone will want to pull up a chair and share a slice with you. Just make sure to save me a little frosting. Marzipan, if you could, please.

"The best way to pay for a lovely moment is to enjoy it."—**Richard Bach**

"Love, and do what you like."—*St. Augustine*

Some people are just born hostesses. Creativity, originality, and inspiration roll with ease off of their party-planning fingertips. You are probably thinking of someone who fits this bill at this very moment. She (or he!) is that thoughtful kitten who proudly proclaims that shopping for the perfect swizzle sticks puts the wind in her sails. If that person is you, welcome! It's always nice to meet a party-planning soulmate. But if this book is a nifty little nudge for you to exhale, and learn to start enjoying entertaining a little more (here's your first lesson: everything doesn't have to be perfect!), then in your hands is a guide to show you that parties are a creative expression of you, and the very best way to make other people feel great. This book can change the way you think about parties altogether, as a hostess *and* a guest!

It's high time to shrug off those pesky worries that can accompany party-planning and discover your best entertaining talents yet. You have been given unique hostess gifts, whether you fancy yourself a distant cousin of Martha's

Mermaid Memory
Mermaid Hilary

A few years ago I was enjoying one of those enchanting weekend afternoons in New York City. You know the kind—when there is nothing to do but follow the fun until the sun goes down. My friend Alvina and I met for lunch at a tapas bar in the East Village and ended up camping out over a delicious pitcher of sangria. The conversation turned to brainstorming ideas for a mutual friend's upcoming birthday party. From there we moved on to planning another friend's elaborate engagement party, then on to a budget-friendly bridal shower, a swanky summer cocktail party and, well, you get the picture.

A few hours passed, and Alvina exclaimed, "Hilary, you should really write all of these ideas down! People are always looking for great party ideas on any size budget."

Maybe it was a premonition, maybe it was the sangria, but I immediately visualized two Mermaids toasting martini glasses, and with that, *Mermaids & Martinis* was born.

or not. So write a poem for the guest of honor, build a tricked-out grill station for the next block party, bake a cake from scratch (or from the box) to honor the birthday boy, or create the almighty budget spreadsheet that saves a ton of money. Whatever your special skill may be, just be a part of the party. Honor someone in your life through your unique contribution, and it will come back to you ten-fold. You have already made the wise decision to bring this book home. You are now poised to become the Duchess of Hospitality, the Queen of the Welcome Mat, the host that undeniably throws the most unforgettable parties again and again.

What Can You Expect to Get Out of This Book?

Readers, rejoice! Within the pages you hold are creative, easy, and *affordable* ways to host a party with some serious soul. As we Mermaids believe, *Meaning is the new money.* Everything you need to throw a party like a pro, without breaking the bank, is right here, along with tips from other Mermaids, celebrities, and fabulous folks from Chicago to both coasts. This book has it all: guidelines on when to send save the dates and formal invitations, how to stockpile your "Mermaid Treasure Chest" for parties in a pinch, how much wine to serve for a dinner of any number of guests and tips on choosing your wines, how to stock your bar and set up a buffet, hunting and gathering tips, memorable gift ideas, how to give the perfect toast, how to perfect your party favors, floral arrangements and creative centerpieces, how to avoid and navigate party faux pas, party recovery, and much, much more. Designed to be read cover to cover or to be used as a quick reference guide, *Mermaids & Martinis* is your go-to source for all things celebratory.

In short, this book will be the difference between a "rubber chicken" event and an unforgettable memory. What's a "rubber chicken" event, you ask? When I first came to New York City, I worked for *Newsweek*. While walking the halls, I often heard executives and editors alike mutter, "Ugh, I have a rubber chicken lunch today." I was confused, and a bit shocked. I mean, these lunches were being given at the best hotels in the city, the kinds of places where zillion-dollar weddings were hosted for royalty from around the world.

Puh-leese, I thought. *I'll break out my violin for you people as I head to the cafeteria for my fourth chopped salad this week.* I brushed these comments off as smug, jaded talk from folks who just couldn't appreciate grand affairs because they had spent too many years going to them. I vowed never to become someone who would be bored by the idea of putting on a pair of heels to go to cocktails at The Plaza.

Then, the day came when I started to get invited to these lunches and cocktail hours too— sometimes as often as once a week. And, much to my surprise, I discovered that my colleagues were right! I finally understood what they meant. These lunches were indeed hosted in the most beautiful venues in the world, but all the gilded walls and stunning stained glass windows could not save these events. They had no soul, no magic, no energy. From the cloudy crystal to the bland cuisine, it all seemed so empty, so fake. Just like a rubber chicken.

Since then I've spent more than a decade creating some fabulous fetes with some of the most creative people on the planet, and I've been able to utilize my limitless imagination on some pretty big budgets to develop buzz-worthy parties and events for large corporations, celebrities, and magazines. But in my personal life, I have had to learn tips and tricks for resourceful, affordable hosting. When I started using *those* ideas at work, I was surprised by the response, and it led to a revelation: guests aren't always impressed with the over-the-top, expensive parties. But events where there is meaning in every small thing—where every dollar counts—will always be the real sensations. Trust me, I really had to use my inner Mermaid to make some of these events exciting! But the lesson learned was invaluable: spending extra time on the small bits really makes for the biggest hits. What matters to guests is the personalization of the party.

Mermaid Memory: *Mermaid Hilary*

A few months ago, on a very ordinary Saturday morning, I was sitting at one of my favorite coffee shops in the West Village, working on a chapter for this book when my cell phone rang. It was a friend and celebrity talent wrangler from Los Angeles.

She was in a real bind. A last minute emergency in LA prevented her from getting on a plane that morning to come to New York City to work the red carpet at an event that would host thousands of guests and celebrities galore.

"Hilary, I NEED your help!" I heard panic in the voice on the other end of the line.

"Um, ok . . . what can I do?"

After a short conversation, I enthusiastically agreed to help my friend host the event. My friend said she would email me everything I needed to know to prep for the event, and as soon as I got off the phone, the email appeared in my inbox. Attached to the email was a book of headshots of the celebrities who were scheduled to walk the red carpet in just a few hours! Yes, a *book* of headshots. I felt like Anne Hathaway's character in *The Devil Wears Prada* when she has to memorize every face and name of VIP guests at a gala. The problem was, I hadn't even heard of some of the celebrities in my look book— underground rappers, up-and-coming TV stars, and entertainment moguls—and I had only a few short hours before the event started.

Feeling excitement and a good deal of pressure, I went home to take a calming (and quick!) bubble bath. Visualization is one of my favorite ways to calm my nerves and keep my energy elevated. Closing my eyes, I visualized happy guests, a happy host (me!), and even a happy Kanye West, who would be the lead performer that night.

In just a few hours, I went from coffeehouse casual to red carpet glam and, in true Mermaid fashion, I jumped on the subway—to be cheap-and-chic (plus I was short on cab fare!) —and booked it to the venue. Soon enough, there I was, front and center, greeting celebrity after celebrity on the red carpet. Of course, with only so much time to prepare, I did have one Mermaid mishap. I called a beautiful television actress by the name of the character she played on the show *Lipstick Jungle* rather than by her real name. When I realized my blunder, I found there was no better way to recover than with a big smile and sincere apology, and we both laughed.

The night went swimmingly, and a personal high-light was when a well-known rapper said to me, "Hey, I really like your energy, girl." Well, that ended up being the key to it all. Even though I was not as prepared as I usually like to be, I had good *energy*. And it made all the difference.

> **RULE OF FIN:**
> *Energy is contagious. A positive host is a magnet for positive guests. Whatever you are doing, do it with energy! A small dose of enthusiasm will cover up any imperfection.*

What Is This "Mermaid" Thing All About?

"She was one of those happily created beings who pleases without effort, makes friends everywhere, and takes life so gracefully and easily that less fortunate souls are tempted to believe that such are born under a lucky star." **—Louisa May Alcott**

Who is a Mermaid? She is someone who enjoys the moment and celebrates the people in her life. Mermaids ride the waves of every year with delight and have a passion for experiencing life—in Technicolor! My friend Vanessa perfectly described a Mermaid when she said this about our friend Raina, *"She's such a Mermaid. She really takes a bite out of life!"*

Mermaids love hunting and gathering for that perfect gift, scouting ideal venues, searching for the most amazing places to visit for inspiration, and working to make their next event even more memorable than the last. The Mermaid is the main character in this book—and she is YOU! From imagination to execution, a Mermaid learns tips and tricks to guide her to throwing the most fabulous fete. So embrace your inner Mermaid and get ready to shine!

"There's a star in my eye and the room is alight. They don't want to be anywhere but here tonight."
—The Mermaid Mantra

> **RULE OF FIN:**
> *Don't be a flat tire at another person's party! If you can't be a best guest, then guest on outta there, sister! If you do find yourself feeling blue at a party, overly stressed, or a bit "unglued" while hosting your own event, use some of the tips and tricks in this book to help bring you back to happy. Because life is your party and you can cry if you want to, but I really hope you don't.*

Mermaids have discovered that the secret to happy guests is a happy host! Mermaids are allowed (and highly encouraged!) to have fun at their own parties. Like bees and dogs, guests will always sense if a host is nervous, stressed, or distracted. If you find this starting to happen, just recite the Mermaid Mantra. You can even pair the words to the tune of whatever song makes you happy and silently hum it at your next fete. Remember—being fully present is the best present you can give your guests. So, **start walking around like you were born under a lucky star**. It's contagious.

> **RULE OF FIN:**
> *If you get lost along the way, don't be discouraged. Instead, recite the Mermaid Mantra and you'll be back on track in moments.*

Mermaid RULES

In general, Mermaids hate the idea of having to stick to a strict set of "rules." Instead, we prefer guidelines that can be stretched and changed based on our waves of creativity. It's really all about living in the moment and making people feel special. So, with that in mind, let me present the Mermaid Rules. Our R-U-L-E-S are:

R: Respect. Respect your guests and their time—remember that *you* invited *them*. Don't assume it's their privilege to attend your party. If you are the guest—respect the party venue and treat it as if it were your own home.

U: Understand. Understand that things can always go wrong; handle yourself with grace when the unexpected happens.

L: Listen. At your event, make eye contact with your guests. Care about the conversations you are having with them, and be present in every moment. The event will go by in a flash. Don't miss it.

E: Entertain. Entertain with generosity, fun, authenticity, and an open spirit.

S: Smile. When all else fails, remember not to take it all too seriously.

Mermaids & Martinis is part party manual, part journal, and always a place where you can be my guest. So kick off your shoes and stay awhile. I'll share some of my favorite tips that I have learned through personal experience and from other great Mermaids along the way. When creativity is partnered with the right tools, every moment can be the ultimate party.

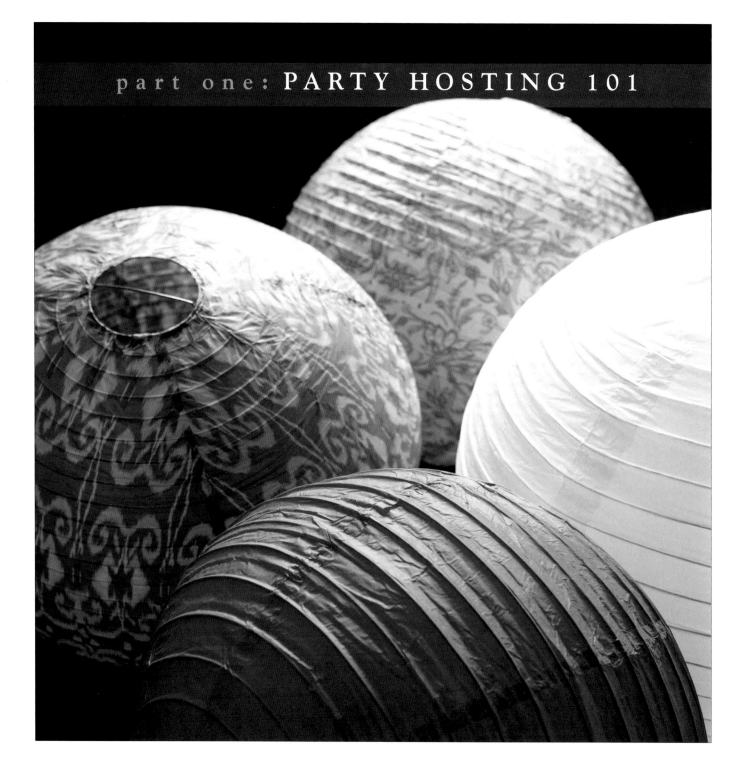

part one: PARTY HOSTING 101

Everything You Need to Know to Throw a *fin*Tastic Party

MERMAIDS, LET'S BE HONEST. Being a great host can be intimidating, right? There's so much to do and remember that sometimes it feels like you are never going to get it all done before your first guest arrives. It can make even the most committed Mermaid want to throw in the kitchen towel.

But it doesn't have to be this way! With a little help, you can easily master the basics of party hosting. And once you have the basics covered, you are free to be as creative and imaginative as possible. You can focus on the small details and nuances that really make a party special. Let's get started, because these next several pages are chock-full of everything you need to know to throw a *fin*Tastic party.

Mermaids & Money: Big Budget or Tiny Budget, Every Party Can Be Priceless

Mermaids know how to throw a memorable event on pennies or millions. Little bits and mini-moments separate a Mermaid party from just another catered event, because Mermaids

know that it's the *small things that make life big.* The first thing I do when planning any event, whether I have $50 or $500,000 to work with, is create a budget spreadsheet. I know, I know. I squirm a bit whenever I hear the word "spreadsheet," too. But it is so important. I have been burned many times by a budget. There will always be things that pop up that you have to pay for, and the budget spreadsheet will help you anticipate those costs and avoid the burn.

The Mermaid Motto: It's the Small Things that Make Life BIG!

Here's a sample budget spreadsheet to help you create your own. The most important thing to remember is to prioritize your budget. Decide on the most critical aspects of your party, and allocate money to those things first. In order to do this, ask yourself questions like, *"Do I really need the Beluga, or will the band offer a better experience?"* Once you set your priorities, filling in the blanks is easy. Start with the big items and work your way down. When you run out of money, you are finished. Don't forget to keep your spreadsheet updated as you plan the party. Should something cost a bit more than you budgeted for, you can easily adjust the amount of money you have left to spend in other categories..

VENUE
Site rental fee $_____
Permit(s)/licenses $_____
Additional labor $_____
Projected tips $_____
Subtotal $_____

RENTALS
Furniture (tables, chairs, lounge seating, highboys, etc.) $_____
Props/tenting/canopies $_____
Linens, glasses, utensils, plates, serving platters, specialty glassware, etc. $_____
Labor $_____
Projected tips $_____
Subtotal $_____

FOOD & BEVERAGE
Food/catering $_____
Beverages/bartender $_____
Equipment (ex. chocolate fountain, popcorn machine) $_____
Labor/staff $_____
Projected tips $_____
Tax $_____
Misc. charges $_____
Subtotal $_____

A/V & ENTERTAINMENT
Overhead projector $_____
DJ/sound system $_____
Music fees/licensing song fees $_____
Videographer $_____
Subtotal $_____

DECORATIONS/TABLETOP/FAVORS
Event/table decor $_____
Flowers/vases $_____
Specialty linens $_____
Chair covers $_____
Party favors $_____
Labor/seamstress/assistants $_____
Subtotal $_____

STAFF
Photographers, check-in staff, cleanup crew $_____

MISC.
Party "Sugar on Top": i.e. Photo booth, Karaoke machine, etc.

Extra supplies $_____
Guest transportation $_____
Hotel costs for guests $_____
Subtotal $_____

STATIONARY/PAPER/EVENT SIGNAGE
Invitations $_____
Paper/envelopes/stamps $_____
Specialty items: Drink tents/blow-ups/signage $_____
Photocopies $_____
Menus $_____
Place cards $_____
Thank-you cards $_____
Calligrapher/printer $_____
Subtotal $_____

Grand Total $_____

By the way, try this great, time-saving budget tip: address envelopes ahead of time to your venue, hired staff or hostess helpers and place their payments and tips in the envelopes. That way you won't have to deal with writing checks or counting cash at the end of the night.

A Spark of Inspiration

A Mermaid is *always* searching for inspiration, and she does not rule out anything as a possible source. It's amazing some of the ways we can wake up our inner Mermaid . . . you see something fabulous at a flea market, and, flushed with a feeling of excitement, you buy it. When

you get home and unpack the lovely catch, try to remember how you felt, what you first thought of when you saw it, and those sparks that lit you up. The object itself or how that object made you *feel* can induce creativity.

I believe everything and everyone is connected in some way. It always seems like we are drawn to things that somehow lead to the *bigger picture*. It's as if all the people, places, and things we are inspired by are lighthouses leading the way to the bigger destination of whatever we are working towards at that time.

"A flame begins with just one tiny spark."—**Aristotle**

A small example of this was when I went on a trip recently to Paris and I visited the famous flea market in the northern part of the city. Before I left for the trip, I had been looking for the right Christmas tree for my apartment. At the French market, I spotted these beautiful teardrop chandelier crystals in different colors—soft hues of pinks, greens, and sky blues. My inner Mermaid immediately envisioned how they would look strung throughout my apartment at my next cocktail party, so I purchased a bunch of them. When I got home, I realized I could do even more with my purchase. The chandelier crystals ended up looking beautiful as they dangled from branches I had spray-painted winter white. I loved my unexpected pastel Christmas tree that year.

One of my go-to muses is the almighty catalog! There have been countless times where I experienced a spark just by flipping through my mail at the end of a long day. The great thing about catalogs is that not only can the products themselves inspire creativity, but so can the photography. The way a photo is shot can help the reader envision themself right there on the page; sipping a cool lemonade on a great ocean deck decorated with lobster pots—doubling as ice buckets—filled with cool drinks and white seashells aglow with tea lights. Before you know it, *spark* comes an idea for your next great party!

When you start to look closer at the little details of your life, you may find that the simplest thing reveals a greater message. Inspiration can strike anywhere and at any time. Next time you're in a restaurant, shopping at the market, or even running weekend errands in the car, look around for little sparks of inspiration, and make a quick note of what it was or snap a picture on your camera phone. I've been inspired by everything from the name of a new restaurant to a conversation with someone I sat next to on an airplane.

You just never know. These little nuggets could help you when it comes to planning your next event.

Sometimes we feel stuck or uncreative—a type of "writer's block." When that happens, go out and do something you love or try something completely new. For example, since I live in New York City, I may make an impromptu trip to see a Broadway show after work one night. Or, I might stroll through a museum during my lunch break and invite my imagination in. Even if it's as simple as trying a new recipe that I saw on the Food Network, just reconnecting with my soul's pleasures always seems to bring a flood of good ideas soon thereafter.

Someone once described me as "sponge-y," and I took it as a great compliment. I think it's so important to soak up life. I spent most of my youth growing up in a house on School Street. Life really is a constant education, isn't it? Ask questions, listen well, and absorb all life has to say. If you stopped learning because you thought you knew it all, what would be left that was worthwhile and interesting? To grow always until your last breath is a wonderful way to live, and of course, to celebrate!

"You create your own universe as you go along."
—**Winston Churchill**

Vision Boards

One of my very favorite things to do to rev up my inspir-engine is to create a vision board. Just taking a few hours (or, better yet, setting aside a whole day with friends) to focus on what you want out of life or your next celebration really helps to "reset" where you may be at that point in your year.

I am involved with a great group of women called "Ladies Who Launch," and my dear friends Karla and Stella and I hosted an event that taught women entrepreneurs how to make vision boards themed "Launch into your best year yet!" Here are a few tips for creating your own vision board:

What you will need:

* Buy a bunch of colored or white poster boards if you are hosting a group, or just one or two poster boards for yourself. You can also use a large bulletin board. I've seen people frame their vision boards or drape fabric around them for a more polished effect. Collect a big stack of different magazines. It's usually best to go with your favorites. For instance, I always have *Real Simple, Travel & Leisure, O: The Oprah Magazine, Coastal Living, Veranda, House Beautiful, Food & Wine* and *Vanity Fair*, but then I also collect other magazines from places like train stations and airplanes. These might be financial, epicurean, or even kid's magazines. The more variety, the better.

* Make sure to have glue sticks, tape, or thumbtacks to affix your images to the board, and make sure to have a great picture of yourself.

* Create a playlist of inspiring music and listen to it while you work on the board.

What to do:

The general idea for creating a vision board is to pick images that "speak" to you. Be open to colors and photos of homes, places, and people that seem to jump off the page as an intuitive "yes!" The following example illustrates how to create a vision board for your next party.

STEP 1: Before you begin, take a few minutes to think about the event, the person you are hosting it for, the people who will attend, and the perfect theme. If you don't know the theme yet, no problem. After you create your board, you will probably have uncovered the theme. With these things in mind, go through your magazines and tear out images that "speak" to you. Place the tear-outs in a folder or over to the side. Let yourself be free to have fun looking through magazines and pulling out pictures, headlines, colors, or images of prints and fabrics that strike your fancy.

If the party you want to throw is casual and chic then maybe you will find your inspiration from casual magazines. If it is more formal and fancy, then those types of magazines may contain the best content.

STEP 2: Paste the magazine images all over your board. You can also add textures, swatches of fabrics, and color palettes that inspire you. As you lay the pictures on the board, you'll get a sense of how the board should be organized. For instance, you might assign a theme to each corner, such as guests, menu, music, and décor. Or it may be that the images want to go all over the place. Whatever seems most natural to you.

STEP 3: After everything is glued to the board, it's time for the "sugar on top!" Add words or phrases with paint, colored markers, glitter pens, or whatever you like.

STEP 4: Last but not least, leave space in the very center of the vision board for a fantastic photo of yourself where you look radiant and happy. Maybe it's a great photo of you that represents how you want to be seen at your party, with that star in your eye and the room alight!

STEP 5: Hang your vision board in a place where you will see it often, and make sure to look at it daily before the event.

> **RULE OF FIN:**
> *When a wave of inspiration comes rolling in, a Mermaid grabs her surfboard (or at the very least, her notepad)!*

Vision boards are a great way to prepare for a party and certainly for life. Keep your energy aligned with all the greatness that is headed your way.

Hunting and Gathering

Part of hosting a memory is the willingness to spend time creating it. For me, one of the most fun parts of hosting a party is the "hunting and gathering" stage. It's when you are on the search for that perfect *something* to really put your next party over the top. Or it could be just opening your mind and having that

> **RULE OF FIN:**
> *Enjoy the process.*

perfect *something* find you. This kind of search can range from hunting for that unique set of salt and pepper shakers to finding yourself carried away by a fabric or print you see in a store window.

> *"There is no way to happiness; happiness is the way."*
> —**Wayne Dyer**

So where do Mermaids hunt and gather? Anywhere from exclusive luxury fashion houses to thrift shops, major department stores, street bazaars, fabric stores, paint shops, flea markets, the Internet, a local farmer's market, souvenir shops, eBay (I love it!), hardware stores (one of my all-time favorite places), and city markets.

In New York, I often go to markets to hunt and gather for events I am planning, and I strike gold almost every time. Many times I will also walk away with some fabulous piece of vintage jewelry or a great, meaningful gift that I can save for the holiday season to give to a friend. I just love the idea of going into the same market on a different weekend and having absolutely no idea what is waiting for me.

I remember one of my weekend jaunts where I was happily rewarded (and a bit shocked)! For months I had been seeking a random assortment of things—an oversized seashell for an event, a coral necklace (for me), and a white quartz centerpiece for a dinner party. Well, I went into a flea market late on a very sunny Saturday, when most New Yorkers were frolicking in Central Park or lingering outdoors at a café, and I found all three, for under $100!

There can be magic like this all over the world. I have found some of the most unique and cool pieces at The Flower Market in Cannes, vintage lace at an antique market in Belgium, hand-carved relics at the bustling bohemian "hippie" market in Ibiza, and a beautiful set of flatware at the Wellfleet "Flea" in Cape Cod. When I can't travel, I use my laptop as my passport to foreign markets. I love shopping online at places like eBay, Etsy, One Kings Lane, 1st Dibs, Gilt Groupe, Oriental Trading Co., Luna Bazaar, Costplusworldmarket.com, Open Sky, Centurynovelty, foryourparty.com, and stores like Williams-Sonoma, Anthropologie, and Target. Here's a tip: if you go online with a short list of what you are looking for, it will help you stay focused and be less distracted by impulse buys.

Yard sales are another of my most favorite places to hunt and gather. Want to keep up with the Joneses? Rummage through their stuff! No matter how much green you glean from your paycheck, people from all walks of life love yard sales. Yard sales in affluent neighborhoods or elite vacation destinations usually exceed expectations. (I've hit the junk jackpot in the Hamptons, New York, as well as in affluent suburbs of Boston and Connecticut.) Take a mini road trip to a town near you, or, maybe it's just down the block from the fancy zip code you already live in. Either way, be adventurous and follow your nose to those homes that say, "Of course we hired a decorator." Then, leave a thank-you note in their mailbox for saving you a bundle along with your cell number to notify you of their next yard sale!

"A non-Mermaid's trash can be another Mermaid's treasure." —Mermaid Tracy

So how do you master the art of hunting and gathering? Let me share some tips.

Move Forth with Intention. When you go to a flea market or bazaar, set an intention before you go that you will be open to whatever "hits" you, but also set a budget. You don't want to go home with a bunch of things that will collect dust.

Be Willing to Go with the Flow. Hunting and gathering can take lots of focus, energy, and passion, but the most important aspect is being willing to change direction. I can't count the times I thought I was going to host one type of party and then the entire theme turned around on a dime. For example, last October I was planning a traditional wine and cheese party for some friends. But while shopping at a market for the party, I fell in love with a creative pumpkin beer label. Inspiration struck, and my wine and cheese party quickly turned into an Oktoberfest beer tasting. On another occasion, I was planning a party that started as a 1940s "Supper Club" event and quickly evolved into a 1970s-themed party hosted in the woods, complete with bonfires, Joni Mitchell guitar sing-along's, and a "Peace Path" through the trees. The only way to let in something new is if there is an opening for it. Being open always takes me to a better place, even if it seems easier to just stick to the original plan. But it's never going to be easier if you are not truly, deeply feelin' it.

Use That Pretty Head, Mermaid! You don't have to own a private jet or be enrolled in the million-mile club to be inspired. If globe-trotting is not your thing, something else is! I remember meeting a lovely waiter at a dinner once, and I was telling him about a trip I just returned from. He said, "You know, I've never been west of the Mississippi, but I have a really big imagination." We all can access our imagination at any time, anywhere—and what's better than a trip around the world when you don't have to deal with airport security and jet lag?

Best Places in the US to Hunt & Gather

- Brimfield Antique Show, Brimfield, Massachusetts (brimfieldshow.com)

- Alameda Pointe Antiques Faire, San Francisco, California (alamedapointantiquesfaire.com)

- Brooklyn Flea, Brooklyn, New York (brooklynflea.com)

- Santa Monica Airport Outdoor Antique & Collectible Market, Santa Monica, California (santamonicaairportantiquemarket.com)

- Marburger Farm Antique Show, Marburger, Texas (roundtop-marburger.com)

- West Palm Beach Antiques Festival, West Palm Beach, Florida (festivalofantiques.com)

"I'm the pink sheep of the family."
-Alexander McQueen

"Entertaining is the new black."

—Overheard by a Mermaid during Spring Fashion Week, New York City

"Over the years I have learned that what is important in a dress is the woman who is wearing it."
–Yves Saint Laurent

Like most Mermaids, I love a little luxury. There has not been a time when I have walked into a spectacular-and-swish shop and haven't been struck by the haute-hostess bug. Like when I became heartbroken over a dreamy coral and turquoise Hermès scarf—so much that I was inspired to call on my fellow Mermaid, and interior designer, Sarah Tallman to create one of her famous floor pillows for an Oceana-inspired cocktail hour where guests would be invited to lounge on an Hermes-inspired floor-pillow "Lido deck" and indulge in delicious Coral-adas, along with a decadent seafood tower of "Turq-Ice" oysters.

Never underestimate the utility of old clothing. A box of mixed scarves thrown on a shelf at a vintage store for $20 could make for an endless supply of brightly colored table runners, tray covers, or even used to adorn branches on the trees in your backyard for a fashionable deck party. By the way, speaking of old clothing, celebrating fashion faux-pas can be fun, too. I've always thought about hosting a "throwback" party where everyone must wear a piece of clothing they still have in their closet from a previous decade. The invitations would read, *"1982 called and wants its ____ back. You fill in the blank and wear it next Saturday to my house. Get ready to enjoy lots of endive hors d'ouevres, and don't forget your leg warmers."* And, speaking of throwbacks, even the smallest

Oceana-Inspired Cocktail Party

How to Make a Coral-ada: Pour one shot of vodka over ice. Place fresh watermelon (after removing seeds) into a blender and puree it. Add watermelon puree, to taste, to the vodka and stir. Garnish with a piece of red coral (you can some find online) and enjoy!

Tips for Creating a Seafood Plateau:
STEP 1: Invest in the right kind of serving tray. You will spend a lot of money on high-quality shellfish, so you want the presentation to be perfect. The best serving tray will be three-tiered and they are typically aluminum. You can find these at most kitchen supply stores or online.

STEP 2: Hunt for a variety of fresh shellfish. You want to have a nice mixture of seafood, lobster, clams, oysters, and shrimp. Ask the fishmonger to shuck your clams and oysters for you. And, have your fishmonger set aside lots of seafood to garnish the finished plateau.

STEP 3: Lay beds of ice on all three tiers and then arrange your shellfish in an attractive way on each tier. Don't worry too much about the arrangement being perfect, just as long as the seafood looks fresh and abundant!

STEP 4: Garnish your tiers with lemons and the extra seaweed.

STEP 5: Serve with cocktail sauce and a mignonette sauce.

Mignonette Sauce
Serves four
    1 cup red wine vinegar
    1/4 cup finely chopped shallots
    1 T cracked pepper
    1 T parsley

Place all ingredients in a bowl and mix together. Pour mignonette sauce into individual ramekins for guests to dip into or serve from one larger bowl.

Rule-of-Fin-No-More! It used to be said that you shouldn't eat oysters in months that end in a "R." I'm happy to say this is outdated! You can find great oysters year round, so, enjoy!

***fin*Tastic Idea: Don't want to purchase a three-tiered tray? You can make one with three different-sized trays stacked on two vases.**

details can inspire your next party. There is a scene in the iconic film *The Graduate* where Anne Bancroft is holding this amazing deco 1960s cigarette lighter as she coolly stares down Dustin Hoffman's character. That cigarette lighter inspired me to want to host a party themed, *"The Graduate—A Pool Party."* I'm still scouring flea markets to find a lighter like hers . . . and I don't even smoke!

RULE OF FIN:

If you go to a flea market at the end of the day—right before the stalls are packing up—sellers will be much more willing to barter and unload their merchandise, and you'll walk away with some deals and steals. Don't feel like you'll miss all the good stuff if you get there late. Remember, if it's meant to be, that piece will find you any time of the day.

Party Prepping Your Space

Every venue or home has one. It's that one room you plan your party around, the place where everyone loves to retire at the end of the night, a special spot where guests seem to migrate even if the event is outdoors. No matter where your party spot is, it should meet a few requirements.

Lighting

We've all heard the term "mood lighting," which simply means that wherever you host your event, the lighting should reflect the mood of the party. Romantic? Tea lights by the ton. Dreamy? String twinkle lights around windows, indoor or outdoor plants, and even wall mouldings. I went to this amazing outdoor party at Iron Chef winner Kevin Rathbun's home where he had these beautiful Lucite cubes lit with LED tea lights and white orchids floating in his pool—it created such a beautiful, balmy, and serene mood.

Consider hiring a VJ (a visual jockey) or a lighting specialist for your event. At an event I did in NYC, we hired this amazing VJ, David Aronson, to create the coolest multimedia experience that scrolled images of the guest of honor and his family on a wall to a great playlist.

Want to be *glow*bally inspired? You can change the mood of your room in a flash with colored light bulbs. There are some very beautiful shades on the market now: bold pinks, soft teals, fiery reds, and burnt oranges that will have your guests feeling like they're in the middle of an English garden, on a Caribbean island, or watching a gorgeous sunset in the American West. Head to your local hardware store or home improvement warehouse and let lighting inspiration strike!

Candles are another great lighting option and can be used in so many different ways. There are many types of candles on the market, from scented to soy. The classic styles are tapers, tea lights, votives, and pillars. Try putting small votives in mason jars for a casual look. Tea lights placed in overturned seashells on top of a sprinkle of sand or beach rocks are a beautiful way to line the walkway to the yard or pool. I love placing tapers in empty wine bottles and lining them in a row along a long dinner table. You can create a candelabra effect on a three-tiered tray in the center of your table by layering different-sized pillar candles on each level of the tray.

You need not look further than your kitchen to find creative candle holders! Pretty hand painted juice glasses or tiny liqueur cups make great environments for tea lights, as do brown or white paper lunch bags. Votives look sweet in fluted glasses or try putting a cluster at the bottom of a large glass hurricane vase. Teacup saucers hold pillar candles perfectly. Place thick pillars in square or round glass vases, and tuck those long tapers in everything from champagne bottles to emptied olive oil bottles or even colored glass water bottles with the labels soaked off.

RULE OF FIN:

"One Scent Per Event." I recommend sticking to just one scent during an event, or, at the very least just one scent per room, because you don't want multiple scents to overwhelm your guests. When hosting a dinner, only use unscented candles at the dinner table so as to not compete with the aromas of your food.

Here's a great tip: Before lighting a candle, trim the wick to about 1/4 inch from the wax. The candle will burn better and last longer. Extinguish the flame with a candle snuffer and allow the wick to cool. Then, repeat the process the next time you light up. If you are lighting a lot of votives for your party, after you have placed the votive candle in the glass jar, pour a little water in the bottom. This will save you loads of time during clean up because the votive will cleanly pop out, and you won't have to spend time trying to scrape and remove excess wax. Finally, light your candles thirty minutes prior to your guests arriving. Any sooner and they (tea lights especially) may burn out.

Really want to up the lighting ante? Hang a disco ball, and guests can watch "lightning bugs" spray around your room all night long!

Music

Your party space should connect to a great music system. Music should mesh with the theme of the party. Creating a well-conceived iTunes playlist or selecting the right Pandora channel prior to your event will ensure the party keeps pumping. For the less tech-savvy, tune your television to one of those themed music stations (80s, jazz standards, classic rock). Remember: at any party, the first few songs are always the most important. Your guests will be drawn to the "opening act" of your musical choices, and that will set the tone for the rest of your night.

Seating

When you are throwing an event that will re-quire multiple tables for a sit-down meal, a seating chart is a great way to get organized. But beware, seating charts can take on a life of their own. Navigating the politics of who knows whom can be the trickiest part of planning your party.

Consider enlisting each of your friends to be a "table host." Pick friends who you know will have no trouble greeting and engaging your guests in conversation, and assign each to a table. Table hosts should keep the conversations going, ask questions of the other people at the table, and generally keep the mood light and lovely.

Sometimes seating assignments can unintentionally make guests feel like there is a hierarchy, and this can be a party killer. But if you don't prepare some sort of seating plan, guests will sit with people they already know and won't mingle with other people. So, how do you ensure that guests don't just sit with people they already know, but also don't feel like they rank low in the guest hierarchy? Make seating a game! Place photos on your tables that go with your theme. For instance, if you are hosting an "Indian Wedding" party with six round tables, choose six different themed images (such as Henna, bindis, a Bollywood movie poster, spices, bangles, and a traditional sari, for example) and place a large framed picture of each image on each table. Then, place smaller card-size images of each theme in a bowl. Ask guests to draw a card randomly before dinner is served. Whatever image they draw will indicate at which table they will be seated. Guests will enjoy the suspense of this "game" and will get the opportunity to meet new people.

Consider also asking guests to switch seats midway through your event. At my friend Jonathan's party, we created these clever place cards that

had one guest's name on one side and another guest's name on the other side. After dinner, we asked guests to turn over their place cards and then go find their new seat. Everyone switched seats in time for the dessert course and got to enjoy new conversations with new people for the second half of the evening.

Should you opt to create a more traditional seating arrangement, there are a few rules to follow. First, seat your most outgoing guests in a prominent place (at the head or directly at the center of the table) to ensure that the

conversation will flow. Second, plan on providing each table (or your table hosts) with "conversation cards" full of fun questions and topics to talk about. You can write these topics on cards yourself or buy them. Third, always put a guest's name on both sides of the card so others can easily read the names of the people they are seated near. You can hire a calligrapher, print from the computer in a very cool font, or even scan a photo when creating your place cards. For more casual events, just a first name is fine. But for larger, more formal events, always include the first and last name. If two of your guests share the same first name, make sure to include the first initial of their last name. If, by chance, someone has the same first and last name, include the middle initial.

I love to get creative with place cards. For a large Bar Mitzvah that was music-themed, each table was a "band" and each place card held a different lyric from the band's most famous songs. For example, at the Rolling Stones table, I found compelling lyrics from Stones songs and wrote them on the place cards for that table. For my friend Ariane's birthday, I put a question about Ariane inside of each guest's place card. For example, "If Ariane were a bird, what kind would she be?" Or, "What is your favorite memory with Ariane?" Or, "How did you both meet?" These questions encouraged guests to strike up interesting conversa-

tions and learn something new about Ariane. As a guest at a party, never switch a place card. The host or hostess spent considerable time arranging seating, and you want to respect his or her preparation. Also, if you realize that your place card is missing, don't make a big deal about it. I remember a woman once throwing a fit at a magazine dinner I was hosting because she didn't have a place card. She was a new hire so her name hadn't made it to my list. I always have a few blank place cards and a couple of spare chairs and place-settings ready for a last-minute set up. In no time at all, she was seated with the other guests. Should you find yourself in this situation as a guest, quietly ask the hostess where she would like for you to sit. The host will thank you for your patience and understanding. Please *don't* respond like this woman did. When I assured her that all would be made right, she cried, "Oh, you don't understand. Stuff like this just *always* happens to me." Hmmm. I wonder why?

Your party space should have ample seating for guests. Be conscious of overflow: there should be another area close to the heart of the party where extra seats and floor pillows are available to pull out. Shut off your party rooms by closing other doors or even placing a red velvet rope (these can be purchased or rented) in front of staircases to prevent kids or party vagabonds from wandering upstairs.

Décor

Remember that a party room is more than four walls and some furniture. Study that room, because you can actually create another country, another decade, or even another world with a few simple additions! You don't have to repaint your walls or hire a construction crew to create a dance stage. Although if you have the time and cash, go for it! Just a few simple moves are necessary to create the best party room ever. For example, if a sofa or a table is the centerpiece of the room, invest in some bright, beautiful shawls or printed silk wraps and tablecloths. You might pick these up while you are traveling overseas or while you are shopping at Target. You can place these over the tables and seating areas to transform the colors and energy of the room. Another fast-and-festive mood makeover is to invest in paper "moons." You can buy these cheap-and-chic lanterns in many colors, they flatten easily for storage and then "pop" right back up to be hung from your ceiling, walls, a porch, or trees. All you need is some fishing line and some adhesive no-stick, no-damage hooks to hang these. A few years ago, the Mer-gods shined down on us with the creation of fabulous LED battery-operated paper lanterns, so you can finally put an end to stringing lights all over trees while trying to find power outlets and extension cords.

RULE OF FIN:

When inviting guests to your home, consider a trick my stylist friend, Dale Sudakoff of Dalestyle taught me. Purchase or rent a mobile coat rack to put outside the hallway for guests to leave their coats and boots. Then reuse it to keep your favorite ensembles organized.

RULE OF FIN:

Well placed splashes of color, pattern, and texture will transform an event space—instantly.

I love decorating. I have always been moved by a great aesthetic—by events and homes that have a living, breathing soul full of color and character. For any event, there should be a mood and energy that is conveyed. You can create a whole new universe with a coat of paint or simply by recovering your floor pillows. The décor at your event should add to the "theater" and those show-stopping moments for your guests.

Remember when stenciling was popular? Now, decaling is all the rage! I love decals for quick, easy, and temporary motifs. From quotes and monograms to names and images, you can create any mood or motif on a long table, countertop, doorway, wall, or even the front of your house. You can even put name decals right on the table as place cards. I have a bunch of decals that I am saving for a "Tattoo Parlor" party, where there will be tons of "tattoos" on the walls as guests receive temporary tattoos from artists.

A home or entertaining space can become a treasure map to all of the places you have been and the people you have met. I always try to bring back one thing from an event or trip, even if it's something as small as a pack of restaurant matches from a memorable dinner. I know I will love looking at these things and remembering the memories they evoke in the years to come. A few years ago, I was traveling

RULE OF FIN:

Cheap-and-chic mood makeovers to any room are simple to do before a party. Add one or two bouquets of flowers. Dim your lighting and light lots of candles. Place stacks of 2-4 "coffee table" style books around the room with an artful object on top. The nature of these books could change out to reflect the theme of your event. The best accessory to any room? Good friends. And it never hurts to have an adorable "party mascot" (your pooch!) to add a little charm.

in the south of Spain and stumbled upon this old barn that was just bursting with antiques. In the very back of the barn, covered in dust, I found this large ceramic bowl from North Africa. I was heartbroken I loved it so much! So very much, in fact, that I carried it by hand on five flights until I arrived home because it was too fragile to pack. Was it worth it? Of course. Every time I pass it in my kitchen, I think of that memorable trip.

Party Aromas

Growing up, I loved to brew potpourri on the stove with my mom. I remember doing this in all of our houses, and back then, we moved a lot! It was the sensory experience of the scent of potpourri and the sound of one of her favorite albums playing in the background that meant it was the weekend, and that we were in store for relaxation, visits with friends, and maybe a dinner party on Saturday night.

I love a house that smells great. My friend Melanie always comments, "Hil, whenever I visit you, I love that your place smells so good." I think that inviting someone in with every sense is important. Here are a few things my nose loves:

- Candles by Odin (odinnewyork.com)—not only are they the perfect housewarming gift because the scent and look is unisex, they also look beautiful in any room.

- Hand soap and hand cream by Grove New York (anthropologie.com)—their products smell so fresh, the fragrance uplifts the spirit, instantly!

- Truffle oil—try drizzling truffle oil on sliced bread and roasting them right before your guests arrive.

- Cinnamon rolls—for hosting brunches or luncheons, I buy the slice-and-bake cinnamon rolls because they are so easy to make, and in just minutes your entire home will smell delicious.

- French decanters—these look really chic and smell divine. Sabon makes a great one called a "diffuser bottle" with different liquid scents to fill up the bottle and light. My favorite is the lavender scent.

- Sage—burn a bundle of sage to get rid of negative energy in your space, and it smells wonderful.

- Rain—open a window after a rainstorm. What's fresher than that?

I've hosted many events where I have followed my nose. I remember one party very distinctly. It was a screening party of the hit movie *Hairspray*. The other hosts and I had planned

RECIPE BOX

Mulling Spices

This is my favorite recipe for mulling spices. It's so easy!

2 t whole allspice
1/4 t whole cloves
1 whole cinnamon stick
1 strip orange rind, thinly peeled

Put the above ingredients in a plastic zip-top bag and beat gently with a rolling pin. Bring two cups of water to a boil and then add a couple of tablespoons of your mulling spices. Simmer the mixture for a warm and inviting smell. Store the remaining mulling spices in an airtight container. An even easier way to achieve this is to simmer apple cider on the stove mixed with a few sticks of cinnamon.

Your Party Powder Room

Although it may be a taboo subject, when it comes to this room you can count on a lot of foot traffic, so it should meet a few requirements. Always have fresh flowers in your guest bathroom. Even if you have a tiny bathroom, one simple bud vase with a daisy will look sweet and welcoming on a windowsill.

hairstyle stations at our cocktail party where guests could get a hairstyle or up-do like a character in the film. Given the theme, our florist James decided it would be a good idea to spray the enormous flower arch at the entrance of the venue with hairspray so that when everyone entered the room, they would be greeted by a waft of fragrant flowers with a hint of hairspray! It was a hit, just like the movie.

Another bathroom essential is a hook on the back of the door. You never know what your guests are carting around. They could be wearing a very expensive silk wrap or toting their best evening bag, so it is courteous to equip your bathroom door with a hook to hang valuables. Again, this is a cheap-and-chic find at a hardware store and can easily be installed by even the least handy among us.

A wicker basket is a great place to store hand towels. If you can, invest in a small towel warmer. A warm towel for guests to use is like a shortcut to heaven! Another heavenly hand towel idea is to soak a few hand towels in citrus or rose water. Then, roll each hand towel and place them stacked in a glass bowl on the counter near the sink basin. The smell is luxurious and your guests will love this little bit of luxury.

Create a "beauty bar." It's nice to have a few essentials in your bathroom, especially if your party is large. These items can be set on a simple tray. Guests will appreciate things like tissues, a lint brush, breath mints, hairspray, safety pins, and a great hand cream.

One thing I like to do for a laugh is to write a message on my bathroom mirror in lipstick. I personalize it each time depending on the party, and sometimes I like to get a little cute—such as "Did you know it's Dave's birthday today? Go up and give him a big hug!" (Someone sure looked surprised, since his birthday was six months away!) Or sometimes I will write something inspirational, like, "You look like a dream on ice, darling!"

Finally, it's always nice to light a beautiful candle and have a lovely room spray on hand. I love Jo Malone room sprays.

When having your pre-party meeting with your hostess helpers, assign one person to check on the bathroom throughout the night to make sure it's clean and supplies are replenished. Alternatively, you could also set a little timer on your watch to remind yourself to go in and check.

*fin*Tastic Idea: Make your own rose water.

When prepping your powder room, purchase rose oil and pour just a few drops into a pretty bowl filled with water for guest hand towels. Or, you can mer-make your own rose water!

RECIPE BOX

Rose Water: This recipe will make 10 oz, enough to fill a bowl for your guests. Rose water can also make cute party favors or hostess gifts by bottling in pretty glass jars or bottles. Guests can take them home to use for hand water, or to add to a bath.

Ingredients:
 1 cup firmly packed rose petals
 2 cups boiling water

Rose Water (continued)

Preparation:

1. Place rose petals in a ceramic or glass bowl. Use only fresh petals (no leaves or stems). Pour boiling water over petals, and allow petals to steep until cool.

2. Strain off the petals and pour the scented liquid into a clean bowl or bottle.

If you are using for your powder room, save a petal or two and drop them into the bowl to float on top of the water for a pretty finish.

Your Party Look

"When a girl feels that she's perfectly groomed and dressed, she can forget that part of her. That's charm."

—**F. Scott Fitzgerald**

You know the story—you spent weeks planning the event, every detail is perfect and the day is finally here, but, a million little things have popped up at the last-minute. So, you spent your entire morning running errands, preparing the final touches on the menu, and setting up the decorations. All of a sudden you realize the party kicks off in fifteen minutes and you are still wearing yoga pants and your college t-shirt—hardly an acceptable outfit for a Mermaid to greet guests in! Not only do you deserve to look and feel your best at your own party, but with some careful planning, you can find some time to regroup and get into your Mermaid frame of mind (practice the Mantra!) before the doorbell starts to ring.

Remember all the careful attention and detail you put into planning your event? The embers of your

imagination were burning on the theme, menu, and décor weeks ago when you sent out the invites. Well, pay that same amount of attention to yourself! A few days before your party, write down what you are going to wear and include shoes, jewelry, and accessories. It may sound like overkill, but you need plenty of time to make sure that your dress still fits well and is clean or that you haven't loaned out your favorite pair of earrings. And, should you decide to treat yourself to something new, you will need time to shop.

> ### RULE OF FIN:
>
> *Dress the part, but don't overdo it. One or two statement pieces speak volumes. Any more, and you are no longer wearing an outfit; you are wearing a costume.*

As a hostess, it's fun to have a few statement pieces that work for any event. For me, it's cocktail rings. I have a great collection of them that range from costume jewelry to real stones. I also love hostess slippers. After all, when you are in your own home and will be the one doing the most running around, you want to be comfortable and chic. You can find all sorts of great hostess slippers and ballet flats: jeweled, embroidered, metallic, you name it. If you are feeling crafty, you could buy a pair of plain fabric flats and have them monogrammed or embroidered, or you could sew your own special beading on top. One of my "secret weapons" is to collect great pairs of big, clip-on earrings found at vintage stores, flea markets, and even department stores. I love nothing more than a pair of delicious, chunky gold knots or colorful emerald, coral, or rhinestone earrings that can be easily fastened to the top of plain black fabric flats or ballet slippers. *Voila*, you've got yourself a pair of spectacular-and-swish hostess slippers without going into debt! Statement pieces should be truly *you*, and they should give you the confidence to feel great about yourself all day or all night long.

Whenever possible, I love to dress the part of the event I am hosting. For example, at a recent event I hosted at a yacht club, I wore a navy and white striped jersey with a simple gold anchor necklace to much acclaim. But be careful you don't overdo it. Had I paired this ensemble with khakis and boat shoes, someone may have mistaken me for Mary Ann and asked to be my Gilligan. Consider this: a cowboy hat adds a little flair, but paired with cowboy boots, the look could easily flop. Hit the slopes in Aspen with a pair of oversized Eskimo snow boots and you look chic in the chill. But if you add a Navajo poncho, folks won't want to look at all. A *touch* of campy and living the theme is always well received, but overdo it, and someone may ask you if you'd like extra cheese with your pizza.

Sticking with classic styles is always a winner, even if those "classics" are a bit over the top, like a stunning Kimono dress or a sequined bat-sleeve top from the sixties! I asked my friend and ultimate style Mermaid, Marissa Webb (who *only* held the top job at J. Crew designing their women's clothes) to share with us her vision for celebratory looks:

Red Carpet: I always love to see something a little unexpected. On the Oscars red carpet in 2011, Cate Blanchett looked elegant and chic in her lavender Givenchy gown. It wasn't over the top flashy, or trying too hard to be sexy, but that's exactly why it stood out for me. That beautiful Cate smile added the final touch. It's all about personality and poise. Wear the dress, don't let it wear you.

Casual: The one thing I always try to keep in mind is casual doesn't mean sloppy–I personally would wear my most comfortable, but in-style jeans with an easy top. My trick for looking like I've put some thought into my look, no matter how casual it may be, is accessories. I throw on my bracelets and necklaces with everything— even a sweatshirt, and it completes the look. Another thing to keep in mind is a nice pedicure

and lipstick—it's amazing how these little things add so much. A different direction is to go with a comfortable dress. You don't need to think too hard about layering, and there is a flirty playfulness about a day-dress that works perfectly for a casual event.

Dinner Party: I personally prefer to be slightly overdressed, then underdressed. However, I try to make sure that my outfit is flexible. You never know which direction the evening will go in. Be prepared to find yourself at an after-party. I often throw on a blazer to dress up an outfit knowing that whatever I put on underneath it must also be able to stand alone. Also, since you are there to eat, make sure to wear something you can actually sit comfortably in and also finish what's on your plate. What is the fun of a dinner party if you don't enjoy trying all the food?

Brunch: This is the place to wear something "casual chic." Keep in mind the location while putting your outfit together. Often times the location will be your best guide. You want to look put together but not overdone. It *is* still morning or early afternoon. So dress accordingly.

Bridal Shower: The most important thing to remember about a bridal shower is the bride. I made the terrible mistake of wearing jeans to a bridal shower, and to this day I still remember how uncomfortable I felt. It wasn't so much the looks I was getting from the other guests, but knowing that I had slightly spoiled this special day for my dear friend. Unintentionally, I had ruined the image of this day she had in her mind since she was a little girl. Unless you have been told that the theme is casual, dress like a lady!

Bachelorette: This is where you get to hang out with your best girlfriends and propel yourself back a few years. So wear that mini-skirt, let your hair down, wear that daring lip color, and have fun. This is one of the last times you have a free ticket to be a bit crazy and loosen up, but . . . do not outshine the bride to be!

Want to really go big with your look? You are one click away from couture! A favorite online destination for Mermaids is called Rent The Runway (renttherunway.com). You can rent jewelry, bags, dresses, and shoes from world-renowned designers. They send two dress sizes (at no extra charge), just in case. You will look like a million bucks—for just a fraction of it! Most importantly, dress appropriately for an event—your outfit should not be cause for hushed whispers and scary stares. Some events speak for themselves, i.e. funerals are not the place for flashy, a baby shower doesn't beckon a bustier, and wedding guests do not wear white, unless instructed to do so by the bride. Think before you dress.

*fin*Tastic Idea! Invest in a classic LBD—little black dress, one that can be worn to a cocktail party, or dressed up with accessories and evening heels for a black tie event. Then, store this ensemble at your office! I was invited once to a black tie gala hosted by Oprah Winfrey and Ralph Lauren. I received a last minute invite, and the event began in just a few hours—so I had no time to rush home to change. You just never know when an invite may come along, so it's smart to be prepared.

> ### RULE OF FIN:
> *When you dress in classic styles for events, you will never age in photographs.*

The 80-Minute Rule
On the day of the event, give yourself a full eighty minutes before guests arrive to get ready. Why do I recommend eighty minutes? Because at least if you've showered eighty minutes before the event starts and then you realize you have to stop everything to pull something out of the oven, you can rest assured knowing your hair is drying on its own. I can easily get ready in thirty minutes, but when I'm hosting a party, I need more time, because I am always a little distracted. Besides, I want to look my best and have extra time to spend on my hair and makeup.

If you don't have eighty minutes to spare, or if you get called upon to hostess at the last-minute, as I did for the Kanye event, focus what little time you do have on the areas of your appearance where you can get the most bang for your buck. For instance, perhaps you can apply some smokey eye shadow, or draw on a bold lip in mere seconds that will create a dramatic appearance. Try pulling your hair into a quick ballerina bun and blow drying a few pieces down around your face for an elegant look, or twist your hair into a loose chignon, or a side fishtail braid. I love "dry shampoo," a product that was created many years ago and has become very popular today. You can use this powder to create a messy, "rock-star girl" look (one of my favorites). Whatever it is you have time for, remember to stay calm and repeat the Mermaid Mantra while doing it. A stress-free hostess is a beautiful hostess, no matter how put together she is.

Event Emotions

"I've had a lot of worries in my life, most of which never happened."—**Mark Twain**

> **RULE OF FIN:**
>
> *Focus on the people who showed up, not the ones who didn't. Typically, 20-30 percent of people will cancel, decline, or call at the very last-minute with an excuse.*

> **RULE OF FIN:**
>
> *As the hostess, think about the décor items and color palette of the party—whether it is your home or a venue—and reflect on how your outfit might compliment or add to the space. For example, at one event, every part of the décor was stark white with black accents. The hostess wore a stunning black and white gown and visually "popped" all night at her event.*

It's normal to have pre-party jitters! Just don't wear your fears on your sleeve, don't ruin your makeup by crying, and please, don't yell at your significant other or, even worse, make the ghastly mistake of yelling at guests. Mermaid mishaps happen. Just don't let a mishap stop you in your tracks and allow you to get stuck in an ugly moment.

I remember the very first dinner party I threw in New York City. I was overzealous because it was the first time I didn't have roommates and could really host a proper "adult" dinner party. Well, I went way overboard. The table was a major mess—it looked like a Las Vegas buffet with every food under the sun represented with no theme or unifying look. I wanted to try every recipe and new appliance I had received as housewarming gifts—and so I did, all at once! Luckily, my guests came hungry and they brought a lot of wine, which made up for the Mermaid mishap.

At the end of the day, entertaining is about the 3 F's: fun, friendship, and feeling good. They really are the most important ingredients for a good party, and no disaster, no matter how big, can ruin your mood. When all else fails, repeat the Mermaid Mantra.

Getting Out of a Party Rut

Here are a few tips to help you lose the 'tude. Believe me, I have been there again and again. Hosting an event can be really emotional—you may have put months into planning it, and then it's over in a flash.

One way to quickly elevate your mood is to take control of the playlist. Isn't it amazing how music and certain songs can bring you to a new place instantly? (I can be transported to the seventh grade—and actually feel butterflies over my first crush—when a certain song by Aerosmith comes on.) March over to the iPod, switch up the song order on your playlist, and pop on a song that will bring you back to happy.

While we are on the subject of sensory mood lifts, smells are another surefire way to lift you up. Keep a few little atomizers filled with your favorite scents. In seconds, you can spritz on a new mood.

Finally, smile! Studies have shown that just the mere act of smiling can lift your mood by 10 percent. Fake it till you make it, because soon enough, you will!

"Ten minutes of feeling sad is ten minutes wasted on not feeling happy." —Drew Barrymore

Mermaids & Mingling: "Swim the Room"

If you are hosting a party, it's gracious to spend most of the party "swimming" the room and making sure you say hello to every guest. You want to strike a balance between breezing through each person as opposed to spending all of your time in deep conversation with just one or two people. Each guest should feel as if he or she had a meaningful moment with you, one where you thanked him or her for coming to your party and pointed out a detail he or she might enjoy

(for example, a favorite food or decoration). If you can manage to make every guest feel this way, you will have successfully swum the room.

Next time you are a guest at a party, strike up a conversation with someone you don't know very well. Even if you only end up talking to one or two people throughout the night, if you didn't know those people before you walked in, that is *magnifique* mingling.

Keep cocktail party chatter meaningful, but stay away from issues that could potentially incense people, like politics and religion. Save those discussions for a dinner party or another event where the setting is more intimate and heated debate is desired.

Beware of being a party "latcher," that person who latches on to just one other person because they don't know a lot of people, or because they want to catch up with someone they haven't seen in ages. Beware, also, of becoming the host's shadow. The hosts need to make sure they are swimming the room and keeping the party flowing smoothly.

If you have trouble connecting with other guests at the party, here are a few tips:

- Listen! Listening is probably the best quality of a star conversationalist. Don't talk about yourself for hours on end—it's very boring.

RULE OF FIN:

A hostess makes introductions so that others can mingle. In mixed company, it is polite to address the female first. For instance, "Brittany, I want to introduce you to Paul and Ed. I know you love to shop at both Odin and Pas de Deux. Well, these two are the geniuses behind those stores!"

You'd be surprised how much more interesting *you* become when you are a good listener.

- Make eye contact. Don't let your eyes dance all around the room; instead, make eye contact with the person you are talking to. You will have a much easier time paying attention to what they are saying, and they will feel much more special.

- Don't check your cell phone while mingling or talking to a guest.

- Pay a compliment. Everyone has at least one thing that is especially attractive about him or her, whether it's the color of her eyes or the color of his tie. Say it out loud, and mean it.

RULE OF FIN:

Be mindful of your guests' conversations, and try to be respectful of interruptions. Even if you haven't had the chance to talk to a certain person, it's still rude to cut off a conversation he or she is engaged in with another guest.

Hostess Helpers

Whether you hire professional help or enlist family and friends, prepare those assisting you with important information in advance of your event. Give everyone involved a photocopy of your event run-of-show so they feel prepared for action once the doorbell starts ringing. A run-of-show is just another term for a schedule. When you are creating your run-of-show, make sure you include time approximations for each item on the schedule. This is critical for keeping everything running on time. Here's an example of a run-of-show:

Run-of-Show

Noon: Set table, arrange furniture, and set out decor and favors (or, do this the day before!)

2:30 PM: Check that bathroom has supplies

3:00 PM: Chill beverages

3:30 PM: Prep and plate hors d'ouevres, and refrigerate

4:00 PM: Defrost any frozen items to be prepared for the party

4:40 PM: **80-minute rule!** Hosts should begin their grooming process and shower, dress, start to put on jewelry and makeup, etc.

5:15 PM: Turn on music; preheat oven to warm any hot hors d'ouevres

5:30 PM: Light candles and snap a few photos; meet with helpers to discuss party details; place hot hors d'ouevres in the oven

5:40 PM: Set out food and ice

5:50 PM: Pour your signature cocktail, taste it, and set out a bunch on a tray to welcome guests

6:00 PM: Happily greet guests with that star in your eye and signature cocktail in hand!

When choosing your hostess helpers, be realistic about your friends' capabilities. For instance, is your friend—whom you absolutely adore but who also happens to be a tad distracted—really going to check on the bathroom for you throughout the night? Choose wisely, because attention to detail is important for both the hostess and her helper. If you have hired help, tape up your instructions someplace discreet so that you and your helpers are completely clear on everyone's responsibilities. Also, make sure your helpers know about what they are serving, including the ingredients and how to describe the dishes. Guests will certainly have questions, and you want your helpers to be prepared. You can add this to your tip sheet for staff and helpers.

Depending on the size and scale of your shindig, it's wise to go over details with your "staff" on the phone (or via an email chain you initiate) a few days before the event. Then, hold a live pre-party meeting about thirty minutes prior to guests arriving. This will be your opportunity to show everyone around your event space and update them on any last-minute changes to the plans.

Here's a simple checklist to help you make sure you've covered the bases with your help. Ask yourself:

- Is someone assigned to greet guests? It is ideal for the hosts to greet all of their guests, but as the party gets bustling, this can be quite hard to do. Ask your closest friend and/or the person most likely to know most of your guests if he/she will be the greeter. If no one is available for this job, try leaving the door slightly ajar or unlocked so guests can come in without waiting for someone to open it.

- Is someone assigned to take some pictures?

- Is someone assigned to take coats when people enter?

- Is someone assigned to take host/hostess gifts? This responsibility can be easily folded into the greeter's responsibilities.

- Is someone assigned to help guests' park their cars?

- Is someone assigned to serve drinks and pass hors d'ouevres?

- Have you booked a babysitter or assigned a few people to watch and entertain any kids who are party guests?

- Who is in charge of the iPod or music selection at the party?

- Who is in charge of making sure candles are lit and ice is refreshed?

- Who is in charge of refreshing all food and beverages?

- Is someone checking the bathrooms throughout the evening to make sure they are clean and stocked?

- Who is in charge of passing out gift bags or party favors at the end of the evening?

Can't afford to hire help? For a cheap-and-chic solution, ask around! Maybe it's a neighbor who is home from college for the holidays and would be glad to bartend for a little extra cash. Perhaps a friend's babysitter would be willing to provide inexpensive childcare. Look up a local high school or college music department and ask if any students would be willing to provide some elegant entertainment. Ask your cousin to play DJ. Your aspiring-artist niece may love the idea of hand painting the place cards. People love to be asked to share their unique gifts and will usually do so inexpensively, or even for free!

One last thing: Think about coordinating your hired staff's attire. I suggest all black, which is classic and unobtrusive, but if your theme allows, you can ask your staff to dress the part.

For example, Mermaids & Martinis planned a kid's party in New York City at a famous nightclub. The color palette for the event was black and pink, so the whole waitstaff wore black shirts and pants with hot pink bowties. The look was visually appealing, and it really enhanced the décor.

Party Barter!

You want to throw the champagne bash of the year but are working on a beer budget? It's okay! Why not barter with vendors or friends? Perhaps you could offer private Pilates sessions, home-cooked meals for a week (and throw in a cooking lesson!), or maybe you can work up a solid tax return. Why not offer these services in exchange for whatever it is you need to take your event to the next level? When Mermaids & Martinis was first taking off, the CEO of a major fashion brand hired us to plan a big event for his son. We were more than happy to accept his offer of dresses and accessories from one of our most beloved designers as part of our payment contract.

The Right Invite

These days, it seems everyone's schedule is overbooked. That's why it's more important than ever to give folks enough notice of your party. If you are throwing a casual affair or a cocktail party, plan to send invitations at least 2-4 weeks in advance. More formal events, like weddings, require more notice. Etiquette says to send out formal invitations at least six weeks in advance, and perhaps even eight weeks if many of your guests will have to travel to attend your event. Save the dates should be mailed six months in advance of a destination wedding, and 3–4 months in advance of a local wedding.

Okay, now that we have those details out of the way, let's talk about the fun stuff—the invitations! From embossed to debossed, evites to a printed invite, an invitation is the first impression of your event that your guests will have. Therefore, an invitation should *lure*, should *love*, and should *sing*.

The 5 W's

When crafting your invite, consider the following things. You will want to include these details on your invitation.

- **What**: What is the purpose of the event? What are you celebrating?

- **Where**: Where is it being held? Give the address and consider providing directions if your location is tricky to find, or too new to register on a GPS.

- **When**: Guests will need to know the time the event starts. Some folks even choose to state when the event will end, too.

- **Who**: This one covers a lot, like who is throwing the party? Who is the guest of honor? And, whom do you RSVP?

- **Wear**: What should guests wear?

To give your guests guidelines on attire, some terms I like to include on an invitation are as follows:

- Cocktail
- Black Tie
- Festive
- Formal
- Beachy Chic
- Casual
- Resort Wear
- Camp Clothes: This one is great for an outdoor party when lots of kids, dogs, and dirt will abound.

If you are going super casual and sending out a mass evite, make sure to use the BCC field because not everyone wants their email addresses shared. And remember, just like restaurants and hotels overbook reservations because they know there will always be last minute cancellations and no-shows, you too should over-invite guests to your party.

If you find yourself on the receiving end of an invitation, there are a few things to keep in mind. First, don't ask the host a million questions before you RSVP, like, "When is the latest I can let you know I am coming?" and "Who else is coming?" and "What are you serving?" It will make the host feel like they are going to be cast aside if a better invitation comes along for the same night. Also, try to RSVP to an email or evite within a few days of receiving the invitation. For invites that come with a response card or specify a reply-by date, make sure to factor in mail delivery time and aim to get your response back to the host before the deadline. If you RSVP after a deadline, you will likely inconvenience the host, who needs a final headcount to finish planning the party. Finally, if you are invited with a guest, it's nice to let the host know if you will be bringing someone and, if so, that person's name.

Rentals

If you are hosting a large party, why not alleviate some of your stress with rentals? Everything from tables and chairs to outdoor tents, serving platters, napkins, linens, flatware, glasses, and dishes can be rented. All you have to do (or ask your help to do) is send the dirty stuff away at the end of the night! No cleaning, and no worrying about quantities. Rentals are a great, easy way to take some of the pressure off hosting a party.

Rentals also enable you to transform your party space. I helped turn a yoga event hosted in the middle of Central Park, NYC, into a Zen heaven with rentals. You can even use a prop rental facility and rent furniture or accessories from retired Broadway shows or movie sets. I work with a company called Taylor Creative (taylorcreativeinc.com) in NYC, and from them I've rented everything from ghost chairs to white leather couches, light-up cubes, and more! For the premiere of *Spartacus*, we served "blood & sand" cocktails in some great cast-iron goblets that were rented. The great thing about rentals is that it really lets your creativity soar. If you can imagine it, you can probably rent it, and then you can take your party to a whole new level of fun and inspiration.

Mermaid Memory: *Mermaid Hilary*

Even back in college I was a burgeoning hostess. I went to Boston University, and I remember co-hosting a party with my roomie Cat right before graduation day. Our guests commented that they just couldn't believe we had taken the time to so artfully design sushi platters, a signature cocktail, and flowers. They may have been artfully placed next to a keg stand of beer, but they were there!

Well, unfortunately for us, we lived in an apartment building with paper-thin walls, and a neighbor (or a few neighbors) complained of noise. Soon enough, two Boston police officers showed up at the door. I opened the door and apologized profusely, informing the two police officers that we were leaving immediately to go to an event, so all noise would stop ASAP. I assured them, "This will NOT happen again." We left the apartment abruptly, and the rest of the night was wonderful.

On the very next evening, I had agreed to help two of my best Mermaids, Nicole and Stefi, co-host a party they were throwing right down the street at their place. At parties, I am like a "door fairy." There's a knock on the door or a bell rings, and no matter how loud the event is, my ears seem to hear it and "poof!" I'm there to open the door! Well, once again, this party had turned into a bit of a rager—more people just kept showing up. The neighbors must have complained. I heard knocking on the door, ran to it, and opened it to see before me the exact same two Boston cops. What did I do? I shut the door immediately! I was shocked. Then, I quickly composed myself and opened it again to see them both standing there with big smirks on their faces. Well, the only thing I could think to do was to invite them in for a beer. And since then, I can happily say I've never had another "cop crash!"

Timing is Everything

Fashionably Late

The concept of being fashionably late originated when those people who were in high demand on the social scene always showed up late to a party. And because those people were in high demand, their lateness wasn't rude; it was fashionable. Think about all of the red carpet events you've watched on TV. The most famous nominees or super-celebs tend to walk the carpet at the very end—right before the show begins.

Fashionably late does not mean that arriving at the end of someone's event just to seem cool is acceptable. No matter who you are, it's considered rude. If the party you are attending is a cocktail party, the maximum lateness that is acceptable is thirty minutes. If you are attending a wedding or a sit-down dinner, it is best to be on time or even a little early.

> **RULE OF FIN:**
>
> *Always invite your neighbors when you are hosting a party—this will eliminate any potential grudges and also provide a heads-up about any noise disruptions the evening of the party.*

> **RULE OF FIN:**
>
> *Consider renting a tent or purchasing a pop-up canopy if you are hosting a party outdoors. You can find very inexpensive ones. Then, dress them up with different fabrics and festive décor accents depending on the theme of your party.*

The Un-Funny "Knock-Knock" Joke

On the flip side, arriving at an event too early can be just as wrong. We all know the type. These folks are the "early girlies," who wouldn't think of leaving their bedroom to go to the kitchen for breakfast without a watch on.

As a host, there is nothing more distressing than hearing "knock, knock" a half an hour before the event starts. The host is trying to do everything in orchestrated synchronicity, and unless you have been invited to come a bit early to help, you are not doing the host any favors by showing up even ten minutes early. Trust me!

Just Dropping By?

So, now that you've arrived at the proper time, how long should you stay at a party? No matter the event, plan on staying at least one hour. For some occasions—like weddings—it is inappropriate to leave during the ceremony or immediately after the bride has arrived at the reception. If you have a previous engagement before or after an event and therefore can only drop by for a short while, make sure to let the hosts know in advance. They will appreciate your courtesy. And if you are having the time of your life at a party? Well, contrary to belief, it's more than okay to be the first to arrive at a party, and the last to leave.

RSVP "With Regrets"

Sometimes you just can't make the party. No matter whether the invitation calls for an RSVP or regrets only, it's nice to give the host advance notice. And, if you can, why not be there in spirit? I invited a bunch of friends to a beach weekend in East Hampton, and when we pulled up to the house, there was a huge box waiting for us on the front steps. Our friend Liz, who wasn't able to attend that weekend, had sent us a BBQ box filled with different rubs and sauces that we put to use all weekend long. At another event, a friend who couldn't attend sent gorgeous flowers that reminded me of him every time I looked at them during the evening.

The Bar

"Let me fix you a drink . . ." is music to a guest's ears and one of the first things a good host will say. Whether it's a mocktail or a cocktail, there are some Rules of Fin for building your bar! Don't be overwhelmed. With just a few items, you will have a complete party-ready bar.

Must-Haves

- Cocktail shaker: A Boston shaker set is a classic way to start building your bar.

- Hawthorne strainer (named after the maker of the tool): the coil ensures a fit with a wide range of glass sizes.

- Julep strainer: This is used for cocktails that require the crushing of herbs and fruit.

- Jiggers: You'll want to purchase at least two.

RULE OF FIN:

If you don't want to use jiggers, then use this old trick for a proper pour, count "One Mississippi, two Mississippi, three Mississippi, four" as you tip the bottle. At "four," stop pouring.

Nice-to-Haves

- Double strainer: For drinks that require a lot of mint or herbs, this nifty gadget will help you strain more efficiently.

- Muddler: This is great for muddling blueberries, mint leaves, sugar, and anything else the recipe might call for.

- Long bar spoon: This is handy when you are going to stir up drinks with a lot of garnish, like a mojito.

Bar Rules

Here are a few rules that every Mermaid should follow when it comes to setting up a bar:

- Plan on 2-4 drinks per guest at an average party. We usually estimate one drink per person for every hour of the party.

- Use these party parameters to estimate how much beer and liquor you will need to buy for your party: (PS: All rules on how much wine to buy found later in the book!)

  - For a **twenty-person party** with a full bar (wine, beer, liquor), you need about two cases of beer and one bottle each of gin, rum, tequila, vodka, and whiskey (or scotch or bourbon).

  - For a **fifty-person party** with a full bar (wine, beer, liquor), you need about five cases of beer, at least one bottle each of gin, rum, and tequila, and two bottles each of vodka and whiskey (or scotch or bourbon).

  - For a **hundred-person party** with a full bar (wine, beer, liquor), you need about ten cases of beer, at least two bottles each of gin, rum, and tequila, and four bottles each of vodka and whiskey (or scotch or bourbon).

- Never shake a Manhattan; only stir it.

- Vodka should be stored in the freezer.

- For brunches or big affairs, it's nice to create pitchers of beverages, like bloody marys, mimosas, or punches. Pre-packaged bloody mary mixers are wonderful and can save you a lot of time. I love the one that Williams-Sonoma sells. If you use a pre-packaged mix, add fresh cracked pepper and fresh celery stalks to dress it up.

- Use fresh-squeezed lemon and lime juices when flavoring your drinks. Never use the bottled kind.

- A hint of bitterness will add complexity to a cocktail. Vermouth, flavored bitters, and Aperol will balance sweetness. Most people won't mind a sweeter cocktail when it's balanced.

- My dad will often make pitchers of cosmopolitans (my mom's favorite) and then freeze them in plastic air-tight containers to take out in a pinch for when their friends drop by. He also likes to freeze grapes and throw those in drinks or serve in a bowl as a quick and delicious snack.

- It's better to be *overstocked* on ice and drinks than understocked! Have a few phone numbers for places that will rush deliver just in case you run out.

- Create a signature cocktail before the party, and create cocktail cards that accompany the cocktails on trays or set a few on the bar.

Simple Syrup

Here's a *fin*Tastic idea: Flavor your simple syrup! Simple syrup is easy to make and you can flavor it with anything from mint leaves, thyme sprigs, sage leaves, cinnamon sticks, cloves, peppercorns, lemon zest, and orange zest to add complexity so that the drinks aren't just sugary sweet, but also have herbal notes and/or a bit of spice.

> **RECIPE BOX**
>
> **Simple Syrup**
> 1 cup white sugar
> 1 cup water
>
> In a medium saucepan, combine sugar and water. Bring to a boil, stirring, until sugar has dissolved. Add your flavor(s), and allow the syrup to cool for one hour. Strain through a mesh strainer to remove your flavor additives, and enjoy!

Ice

I consider myself a bit of an ice connoisseur. Cubed, circular, rectangular, big ice, small ice—I just love ice. The sounds it makes clinking in a glass, the way it cools down a drink, and the way it melts beautifully.

These days, there are some really great flex ice trays that come in all different shapes and sizes. You can probably find an ice-cube tray to match almost any theme and shape you can think of! Here's a great tip for keeping your ice fresh and free from that stale freezer taste. Before pouring the water into a tray, boil it. Then, let it come down to room temperature before you freeze it. You will get a cleaner, crisper cube. If you've already frozen your cubes and are concerned about the taste, place them in a glass and pour tap water over them. Quickly drain the water, this helps wash away any odors or unfortunate flavors.

As much as I love festively shaped ice cubes, I also love crushed ice. And it's a must for certain drinks. If you don't have a crusher on your fridge, you can put your ice into a cloth kitchen towel and use a meat tenderizer to beat it. As a bonus, you alleviate any built-up party stress!

Want to really wow your guests? Consider creating ice with a twist! This is one of my favorite things to do for a party. Here's how: place things like mint, rosemary, blueberries, elder flowers, and other colorful accents into ice trays. Depending on the size of your trays, you can even fit small cinnamon sticks or baby acorns. Fill with water and freeze. The resulting ice cubes will make absolutely unforgettable accents to your cocktails, they will look beautiful as the ice melts into the cocktail *and* continue to flavor the drinks.

RULE OF FIN:

When making your "Ice with a Twist," make sure to prep well in advance of your party. Ice seems to have a mind of it's own, and I suggest prepping this twenty-four hours ahead of time to make sure the creations are thoroughly frozen.

Glassware

Fun glassware will always liven up a party. At one time I thought all glasses should match. I also lived by the rule that you should always buy things in sets of twelve. While that rule is good if you tend to break things, I've learned that it's more fun to mix and match and shake things up. If you are a curator of glassware, how fun is it to give each guest a wonderfully unique glass to use during your party? I used to buy a lot of glasses from this enchanting shop in Chelsea called Mr. Pinks. My mom has the ultimate glass collection, so I would find some great gifts for her there. She really lives on the edge when it comes to glassware (much to my dad's embarrassment) because when she and my dad *fin*Tastic idea: One Christmas, I wanted to honor my best Mermaids, so I held a White Elephant gift swap at my place. I had a great old bar cart on wheels that I had just found, and I was eager to put it to good use. I created a drink menu inspired by all of my girlfriends. One of the most Mermaid-y elements of the evening was how I served the cocktails. I took milk cartons, emptied and washed them out, and cut off the tops and placed bottles of vodka and other spirits inside. I poured water around the bottles to the top of the cartons and added sliced lemons, whole cherries, limes, rosemary, and sprigs of mint. I froze the whole creation, and then I simply peeled off the milk cartons and placed the ice sculptures on pretty trays. This idea really lived up to our Mermaid motto: *"It's the small things that make life big!"*

eat out together, if she likes her glass, she will actually ask to speak to the restaurant owner aboutpurchasing a set. And she does not take "no" for an answer! Whether you are a bold collector like my mom or simply like to peruse flea markets and antique shops, always keep an eye out for great glassware. You never know, it might become the star of your next party!

A pretty way to display glasses on a bar is to create a "pyramid" which I do at many events. Arrange the glasses in the shape of a triangle on top of the table or bar (picture a pool triangle laid flat on a pool table and that is the shape to mimic). Start with the longest row facing the bartender, and then remove a glass or two per each row until you reach the tip of the table with one single glass, creating the top of the triangle. The bartender can replenish the glasses as guests help themselves. Lastly, don't forget to set out your signature drink cards and garnishes!

For those Mermaids entertaining in smaller spaces to a smaller crowd, you can create a bar from an existing countertop, a smaller table, or even with a simple tray that you place near guests on a side table or ottoman. Just adding simple acroutrements to the tray like small bowls of mixed nuts, olives, cocktail onions, lemon peels or cherries, and you've created a miniature bar.

Parties in a Pinch

We all get busy and can pulled in a million directions every week. Sometimes it can be hard just to go to the grocery store. But if you make sure you always have these basics in your pantry, you will be ready to accept surprise visitors or invite anyone over at the last minute for dinner and a cocktail.

Key Condiments: Olive oil, salt, pepper, vinegar (red and white wine), and dried and fresh herbs.

Drinks: Bottled water (both still and sparkling), soft drinks, beer, wine, coffee, and tea.

Food: Boxes of pasta, jars of tomato sauce, canned black and garbanzo beans (for hummus and quesadillas), tortillas (frozen is fine), tortilla chips, cheese (mozzarella and cheddar), salsa, frozen pizzas, canned cinnamon buns (for

RULE OF FIN:

When setting up a bar at home, start with a 6 or 8 foot table. Then, drape a white tablecloth or linen of your choice over the top. If you are renting glassware for your event, one simple style glass is perfectly fine— a standard stemmed glass can be used for wine, beer, soft drinks and water. I recommend renting 3-4 glasses per person. I say this because people will not always reuse their same glass throughout the night and you don't want to run out!

breakfast and for party aromas), a pint of ice cream, cheese straws, top-quality crackers, olives, and mixed nuts.

Food for kids: Sometimes people will stop by with their kids, and you want to make sure that you have things on hand for them, like popcorn, pretzels, raisins, applesauce, and candy.

With the above items in stock, you can create an endless number of parties in a pinch. Of course, it's always fine to order out when you are hosting an impromptu get-together. Just make sure to present the delivery pizza or carry-out Chinese in a *fin*Tastic way. Use matching plates, bowls, and glasses, and even consider cloth napkins. Light some candles, check your Mermaid treasure chest for any last minute add-ons, and you are set.

*fin*Tastic Idea! Infuse your own olive oil with herbs at home. Try rosemary, cilantro, sage, basil or thyme. You can infuse with just one of these herbs or a combination! Just buy a glass bottle with a tight cover or cork to keep the flavor fresh. Dried herbs work well but if you have a

RULE OF FIN:

When hosting a party in a pinch, you can dress up carry-out with your own Mermaid twist— ask your favorite Italian restaurant to include some extra bread in the delivery. Slice it, drizzle homemade infused olive or truffle oil on top and pop in the oven along with a bulb of garlic to roast as a quick and delicious spread for guests. Dress up Mexican take-out by cutting up some limes and using them as pretty garnishes along a great serving platter to compliment the food. With any type of food delivery, include a mixed green salad in the order, you can whip up a fresh, homemade salad dressing to display on the side in no time.

When planning a party, there are many ways to stay organized. One such way is the online grocer, which, in many cities and towns, will deliver. Not only will this save you the time it takes to make a trip to the store, but it will help you with future parties, too. Just remember to save your party grocery list on the grocer's website in the archives section. Next time you throw a shindig, you can pull up your list in one click. Your list should include the basics, like paper towels, mixers, charcoal, olive oil, sodas, garbage bags, dish soap, and mixed nuts. Even if you don't use a delivery service, there are still ways to take advantage of this timesaver. Create a "template," or a saved grocery list in your drafts inbox on email, on your mobile PDA, as a hard copy in your handbag, or tape it someplace in your kitchen as a reminder and you will be ready to buy party supplies wherever you are.

garden or fresh herbs, even better! Wash and dry them well. Then, put the herbs into your olive oil (you can cut herb leaves or leave them whole). You can also use garlic cloves, lemon or lime peels, red peppers or any other flavor you fancy. Let these infuse for one week in the bottle. A week is a good time frame to allow the flavors to be fully absorbed. These also make a great hostess gift or party favors for guests!

"Sure I made dinner, when I made the reservation!"
—A Mermaid who prefers to remain anonymous

The Food

As I mentioned before, when serving a crowd, too many choices are never a good thing. Just like my unintentional Las Vegas buffet—most people prefer being told what they are eating. Let's talk about some things to keep in mind when planning your party's menu.

You have to try to cater to a multitude of palettes when hosting an event, but always aim to have a unifying theme for your food. I try to prepare at least one vegetarian dish, one savory dish, and one sweet dish, no matter what the size of the party. Keep the menu consistent, and think about what kinds of foods work well with each other.

Consider using natural garnishes on your food platters. For an outdoor party, flowers and vegetables from your garden used as garnishes on serving trays look naturally beautiful. How about using a ginger root as a garnish for a sushi platter, or tying a pair of chopsticks with gold ribbon and an exotic orchid bud to adorn a white platter of Chinese food?

Whatever type of party you are throwing, whether an outdoor BBQ or an indoor fireside gathering, remember that the food you are serving should be the appropriate temperature for guests to enjoy for hours. For example, when I recently did a garden party, I made sure that the foods I served could sit safely outdoors for four hours and still retain their flavor. This can be a little tricky if you are serving hot food on a cold day, but you can rent or purchase warming plates to alleviate any problems you might have keeping your food hot.

Shopping for your food is an important part of your party prep. My friend and talented chef David Lapham is a master at creating the most delicious and healthy meals. Together, we have toured farmer's markets to create amazing party platters, fish markets to put together a raw bar for seafood soirees, and markets in Chinatown and Little India for a wide variety of spices.

Chef David and I always recommend going fresh and local whenever you can. With that in mind, here are some of Chef David's suggestions for hunting and gathering the best food for your next party:

- Find the location of your closest farmer's market. Spend time going through the market and meeting the various purveyors, and establish relationships with the ones you like. Always plan your menu around what is in season. Let the food do the talking. This is great because it will simplify your food choices. For example, when tomatoes are in season, serve gazpacho. When butternut squash is in season, butternut squash soup is the way to go. Eat by the seasons, and cooking won't seem very complicated.

- **Fruit**: Ripe fruit should be heavy. When ripe and ready to eat, fruit like watermelons, cantaloupes, honeydews, and peaches will smell beautifully fragrant.

- **Herbs**: As a general rule, fresh herbs are better than dried. The one exception to this rule is oregano. Of course, dried herbs are a great staple for your pantry for a party in a pinch.

- **Garlic**: Garlic is a king in the kitchen. It should never have green sprouts coming out of the top of the bulb. This means it's gone bad.

- **Fish**: Fish should have bright eyes and should smell like the ocean, not like, well, fish. The gills should be bright red, and the flesh should spring back to the touch.

- **Poultry**: Chickens and turkeys should smell like nothing. They also should never have any type of film on them.

- **Meats**: Be as diligent choosing your meats as you would your other groceries. Pay attention to where it came from and how it was raised. With all of the environmental and ethical concerns about meat, finding a reputable source is more important than ever.

- **Spices**: Some key spices to have in your pantry are curry powder, cayenne pepper, paprika, and cumin. You can build your spice collection slowly, because spices can be expensive.

RULE OF FIN:

The fresher the food, the better it's going to taste, and the more you are going to look like a "Top Chef" in the kitchen.

The Cheese Platter. For a basic cheese platter, plan to use an odd number of cheeses. Three or five varieties are usually adequate. You will want to offer different types of cheese, including soft, hard, semi-soft, and goat cheese. The most important thing to remember about your cheese platter is to serve cheese at room temperature so that guests can enjoy the full flavor. Garnish your platter with crostinis, crackers, grapes, apple slices, nuts, and honey.

The Charcuterie Platter. Generally, this type of platter consists of cured meats, vegetables such as artichoke hearts, radishes, and olives, and a variety of cheeses. A charcuterie platter can be a very festive way to entertain during a cocktail party or while watching a big event like the Super Bowl or the Academy Awards. Good meat choices for a charcuterie are prosciutto, bresaloa, salami, serrano ham, pepperoni, and capicola. Serve on a wooden cutting board or slate stone, and give each meat its own special treatment. For instance, you might roll up the salami into long, thin rolls and spear with toothpicks, and you might cut the pepperoni into discs and lay out in rows.

Buffet Basics

Planning to have a buffet at your party? Follow these tips, and the buffet service will go off without a hitch.

- Place plates at the beginning of the buffet and silverware and glasses at the end of the buffet. This way guests will have as little to carry as possible while they are filling their plates and will help overall flow.

- If possible, have a helper on hand to describe the foods and ingredients. If not, place meaningful menu cards in front of each dish. You can be clever and use descriptions like, "Dennis's Favorite Dish: Coq Au Vin" or "Grandma's Famous Mashed Potatoes."

- Stagger your platters and plates of food at different heights along the buffet table to add depth and beauty to the overall presentation.

- Chargers and silver services are great, but they are not essential.

- Consider investing in some buffet basics, like a couple of classic white serving platters, a large salad bowl and set of tongs, a couple of beverage pitchers, a neutral table runner or tablecloth, and a great bread basket.

RULE OF FIN:

Typically, food looks much better when served on white plates and platters. If you are incorporating lots of color or prints into your party theme via your serving accessories, then this rule does not apply.

Just like a night at the theater, a well designed dinner party will have acts and scenes that flow from one mood to the next seamlessly. Traditional party "acts" will be, in order, cocktails and hors d'ouerves, dinner, dessert, and nightcaps. If you have the space, consider hosting each act in a different room. So, cocktails may take place on your deck, dinner may take place in the formal dining room, and dessert may take place in the great room followed by nightcaps on the porch under the stars. If your venue isn't large enough for each act to have it's own room, you can designate different areas of one large room for each act. This should be done so that guests flow through the party space organically and always have enough room to enjoy the food and the company.

Spotless Table Top

No matter the number of courses you are serving, your table should be easy to navigate, well organized, and visually appealing. Here are a few tricks to keep you on top!

- If using silver service, remember to polish.

- Check your glassware, flatware, and candle holders for spots.

- Confirm that the correct number of glasses, utensils, serving spoons, and place settings are laid out on the table.

- Clean and press all linens, napkins, and tablecloths.

- Make sure your table essentials, like salt and pepper shakers, condiments, and water pitchers are present and accounted for.

Dinner Party Do's and Don'ts

If you are hosting or attending a formal sit-down dinner, there are some rules of etiquette you should keep in mind.

- Always serve food from the left and clear plates from the right.

- Never, ever, ever place a purse or a PDA on the table. The call can wait!

- Lipstick should only be re-applied in the powder room.

- Don't dramatically push your plate away and say things like, "I'm so full. I can't believe I ate so much. I am so stuffed, I feel awful." It's discourteous to your host and annoying to the other guests.

- Wait until everyone is seated and plated before you dive into your dish.

- When you have finished your meal, place your silverware at the 5 o'clock position on your plate to indicate to the server that your plate may be cleared.

- Place your napkin on your lap until the end of the dessert course. Only then is it appropriate to place the napkin back on the table.

- To avoid awkward silences at the beginning of a dinner party, have pre-set items on the table, like glasses of champagne or platters of antipasto. It gives guests something to do, drink and eat while the party chatter is getting started.

Mermaids don't have to graduate from Miss Porter's to know how to set a table properly. And, these days, it's pretty easy because we usually aren't hosting dinner parties that require multiple utensils. An easy way to remember what goes where is this acronym:

FFPKSG: "Food, Fun, People—Keep Smiling, Goodnight!"

Each letter in the acronym represents a utensil or plate. From left to right, they are salad fork (F), dinner fork (F), plate (P), knife (K), spoon (S), and glass (G). Another way to remember this order is that the silverware your guests will use first (salad fork comes before dinner fork) goes on the outside and the silverware they use last (dinner fork) goes on the inside near the plate, so that guests work their way towards the plate as they eat each course.

Noteworthy Napkins:
You can be very creative about how you fold and place napkins at your place settings. You can fold napkins into different shapes, or you can slip guest place cards inside the fold. You could also place accents such as a fresh flower or a twig into the fold of a napkin, or even trinkets or meaningful items that tie into your theme for pretty, noteworthy napkins.

Meaningful Menus:
The menu for your dinner party is an important part of the décor. Here are some fun ways to display your menu:

- House your menus in picture frames and prop them in front of each place setting. You could use the same picture frame for each spot or use a variety of frames. I love to mix frames of different colors and textures, like silver with gold, or a bunch of leather frames that are a combination of crocodile, patent, or traditional leather.

- Feature your menu right on the table! Lay down your brown or white craft paper as a tablecloth and write the menu in the middle of the paper. This doubles as a cheap-and-chic centerpiece, too! You can also do individual hand-written menus with a colored marker on the craft paper right in front of each place setting.

- Go bistro-style and lean a large blackboard in a prominent place with the menu for the event written in chalk. Or, find mini blackboards for personalized menus at each place setting.

- Customize your menu to the theme! For one bride we created a menu for her bridal shower that featured items like "Tie-the-Knot Tuna Tartare" and a "You Say Tomato" caprese salad.

Be as traditional or creative as you feel. It's always nice to prepare guests for what they will be eating, and doing it in a fun way will make them anticipate the meal with that much more excitement.

A Few Reminders
Remember when there were no cell phones? You couldn't just call your husband while he was at the store to remind him that you forgot to put eggs or milk on the grocery list. Because of that, you probably took a little more time to write your list, which is a habit we should all get back into. Take time to go through your list while you walk around your house and do an inventory of your cupboards and refrigerator. You will be surprised at how much time and money you can save simply by being thorough on the front end.

The day before your party, do a walk-through of your house. In the event industry, we do an initial site visit a few weeks or months prior to the event and then at least one more walk-through a few days before the event. In your home, very typical oversights, such as forgetting to put fresh hand towels in the bathroom or noticing you don't have enough flatware or spare umbrellas to hand out to forgetful guests in case of torrential rain or snow can be avoided by doing a thorough walk-through the day before. In addition to a walk-through, here are some things I love to do the day before an event:

- I love to set my table. This way all I have to do on party day is put out food and ice and light the candles.

- I love to listen to the playlist on my computer or iPod. This way I can make sure there are no bumps in the tracks and I haven't forgotten any great songs.

- I love to do a taste test with a friend or boyfriend. I only pick the people who I know will be honest with me. When I hear, "Babe, that drink was a little too spicy. No, really, my nose is running." I think, *Well, better him than the guests!* This way I can make menu adjustments without stress on the day of the event.

- I love to write names on place cards, and tie or wrap my party favors and set them out.

- I love to freeze my ice cubes with a "twist" to allow the ice twenty-four hours to work its magic.

- I love to create my flower arrangements and centerpieces. Or, if I am having them delivered for the event, I like to have them delivered the day before. Flowers almost always look better on the second day you have them, don't they?

- I love to get "dolled up" if I can—i.e. a manicure and pedicure the day before. Even getting your hair blown-out the day before an event can save a bundle of time. Why not multitask your makeover! Consider doing an at-home hair or facial masque the day before—you can prep for the party at home while luxuriating your skin and hair at the same time.

- I love to set out my outfit and accessories and go to bed early so that I am well rested the next day.

for guests
that forget—
we won't let
you get wet!

Party Photos

Sometimes your party photos are not picture perfect. Blurry, out-of-focus shots of the birthday girl blowing out the candles don't really hold much esteem in the afterglow of an event! I asked my favorite photographers to share their best tips on taking a great photo.

By photographer Daniel Movitz:

Light, perspective, and a steady hand are all crucial when capturing the infamous blowing out of the birthday candles. Traditionally, ambient lights are turned off, so get close to the action! Try positioning the camera in front of the cake so the candles are in the foreground. This will allow more light to enter the lens, which quickens the shutter speed, reducing the amount of blur. However, if the timing just wasn't right, simply request a reenactment once the lights have been turned back on. In any case, challenge yourself to explore untraditional angles in order to capture that unforgettable moment.

By photographer Brian Friedman:

Shooting parties is something I do often and love. But it can be a real challenge getting unique photos that are sharp when there isn't much light, which makes it harder to preserve and record the atmosphere of the party itself without blowing it out with a flash. Fortunately, today's DSLR (Digital Single-Lens Reflex) cameras have the ability to take beautiful and meaningful photos right out of the box. Here are a few tips and tricks that will help you think and shoot like a pro in almost any party situation.

- **Open up.** Put your camera in A mode (aperture priority) and "open up," allowing light to get into the camera more quickly. At it's widest, most lenses get down to f/3.5 or f/4. This will raise your shutter speed and allow you to freeze action a little more easily.

- **Be a little more sensitive.** Most cameras today still get amazing results at higher ISO settings. Change your ISO setting to 800 or even 1600, making the sensor in the camera more sensitive to light. You'll be able to freeze action more easily by raising the ISO setting as the camera will raise its shutter speed accordingly. This works best combined with "opening up" described above. Expect to see a little "grain" in your photo, but it's better to have a sharp, grainy photo, than any kind of blurry one!

- **Bounce your light.** If you own a flash other than what's attached to your camera, try pointing the flash straight up or even off to the side. This works ideally when the ceiling and walls are white, but it can be done in almost any situation. You'll be very surprised by how beautiful the light will be when it's bounced off another surface. More often than not, that's how the pros are shooting.

- **Get down, and not just on the dance floor**. To make unique photos, start by changing your perspective, especially with kids or table arrangements. It will make for a more unique photo if you crouch down or even sit on the ground and take photos.

- **Windows are (sort of) your friends**. Don't shoot "into" the light coming from a window. Shoot in the direction the light is traveling in. In other words, if you are indoors and there is strong light coming in from a window, turn your back toward that window and use the light coming in to light your subject.

- **Try a 50, not a 40.** Both Canon and Nikon make an affordable 50 f/1.8 lens. Pick one up, put your camera in A mode, and shoot the entire party at f/1.8 with your ISO setting at 1600. You'll be amazed at the results with just this setup. You'll be able to get the kinds of photos where the subject is sharp and everything else is "blurred out." Try it!

- **Burst**. Change the shooting mode from "single" to "continuous" and fire off a series of shots, not just one. Then pick the best out of what you just shot, and delete the rest. Most professional photographers delete way more photos than they actually deliver to their clients, so don't be afraid to do the same!

By photographer Clark Mitchell:

- If your party is in the evening and outside, try shooting people with the sun in front of you instead of behind you. This will give you a dreamy, golden light in the photo.

- Don't forget detail shots—they make for a good mix. For a narrow depth of field, use f stop 5.6 or less and do a tight focus on one thing, whether it's a hand holding a drink, a place card, or a plate of food. Everything but the item you're focusing on will appear blurred out.

- Use a slow shutter speed (and a steady hand or tripod) to capture movement in a photo.

- Experiment with old film cameras if you want to get a vintage look. Polaroids, for example, are fun at a party and give you instant gratification as well as a timeless image.

Planning Worksheets

Throughout the book are a few worksheets and planning tools that Mermaids have developed and used over the years. You can download these templates at mermaidsandmartinis.com when preparing for your next event. We Mermaids are virtual and want to help you every step of the way.

Mermaids, now that we've talked about all of the details that lead up to making any party a memory, let's talk about the really fun stuff—the party! The rest of this book is dedicated to inspiring you to host a myriad of parties, from traditional birthday bashes to fabulous holiday and themed parties. You can read through these sections all at once, or you can pull out those mini sticky notes from your treasure chest and use them to tag the book as a reference guide when you are planning a specific type of party. Either way, stay true to your inner Mermaid, and you will be the best hostess the world has ever seen.

Note: I frequently refer to ideas or parties as either "spectacular-and-swish" or "cheap-and-chic." I use these phrases to indicate whether an idea is best suited for a big budget or a small budget. No matter how much money you have to spend on a party, remember that Mermaids believe that meaning is the new money . . . and it doesn't hurt that we make the most of every dime!

RULE OF FIN:

Less can be more! Throughout the book, there are a lot of ideas tied to each theme. This is meant to inspire you, not to overwhelm you. Choose one or two elements for your party or use them all if you like. But Mermaids know that less can be more, especially when done with meaning.

Amanda Middlebrooks was born a Mermaid. Beautiful, smart, and full of charm that most can only dream of, she has the esteemed position of "hostess with the mostest" at the exclusive private-members club and hotel Soho House in New York City.

Q: What's the best supplement to a party?
A: I think the best supplement to a party is a calm and happy host. Everyone is feeding off the energy of the host, and if she is relaxed and happy, then everyone else will be. If the host is unhappy, well, I think people feel that, too.

Q: Who are some of your favorite guests or types of guests?
A: For me, it is always important to have a wide variety of guests at an event, especially if it is a dinner party. I always find it better if the guests work in different fields or are from different walks of life. Then the conversation is always interesting. The one thing that all guests must have in common is the desire to have a good time.

Q: What is your favorite thing to do when preparing for an event?
A: I work best under pressure, so I actually love to run around at the last-minute and make sure everything is in place. I don't do as well when I have too much time on my hands! So, while I would love to say I am calmly listening to music, I am usually running around. Good, comfortable heels always help.

Q: What has been your favorite event to attend or host, and why?
A: Oh, this is hard. I always love the event that I have most recently hosted because it is freshest in my mind. We just had a performance by Theophilus London, and he was such an amazing performer. He jumped on top of a couch and was absolutely electric. The crowd was dancing and the mood was perfect.

Q: What makes a party a memory for you?
A: First and foremost, good friends. But it always comes down to the details. Make sure to have more than enough food that will cater to a variety of tastes, and more than enough drinks. Also, it is always important to get the music right, and make sure everyone dances!

Q: What's your Rule of Fin?
A: Keep calm and carry on. Or, expect the unexpected and be okay with a couple of surprises. Sometimes the most exciting moments at an event can come from surprises.

Q: What is your secret to unwinding when the party is over? A: A glass of wine.

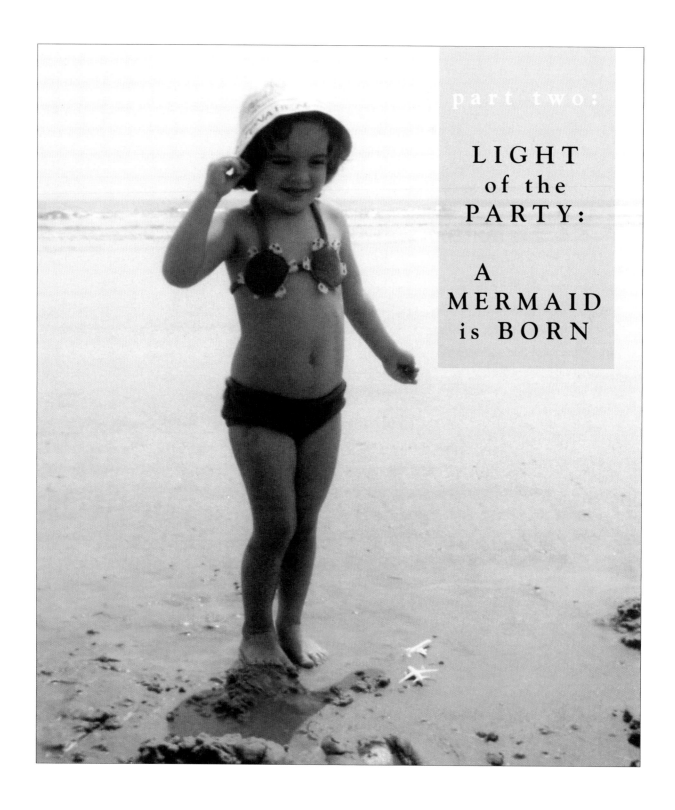

part two:

LIGHT
of the
PARTY:

A
MERMAID
is BORN

chapter two

Beautiful Birthdays

"The man who views the world at fifty the same as he did at twenty has wasted thirty years of his life."
—**Muhammad Ali**

I LOVE CELEBRATING my birthday and friends' birthdays, but there can come a time when birthday celebrations get a little (excuse the pun) *old*. You turn a certain age and suddenly the magic—the fun and frivolity of the day—seems to be gone. But this doesn't have to be the case, Mermaids! Using some of the inspirational bits and personalization tips in this chapter will surely chase away the birthday blues and have you practically looking forward to welcoming a new year as the older and wiser (and therefore, more beautiful) version of you.

Personalization is the most important thing to remember when planning a birthday party. After all, the celebration is about a very specific someone. Here are some great examples of personalized birthday parties for that special someone.

Whether hosting a birthday party in your honor or in honor of someone else, do NOT, under any circumstances, invest in any napkin, card, or plastic cup that has the words "over the hill" on it! No one wants to feel closer to death. Instead, breathe life into a party! Mermaids keep a youthful mindset no matter what age they are. *Age is only a number to a Mermaid.*

Dad loves bird watching? Search through the bird section of your favorite bookstore or library and buy or photocopy images of all his favorite feathered pals. Hang them from a clothesline across the party space or use them as place cards at the table during his birthday dinner. Match each bird to each guest's personality, and I'm sure you will get a few laughs.

Mom has an obsession with golf? Order a big batch of white golf balls (search the Internet for discounts on recycled golf balls) and use them to fill large, clear glass hurricane vases. You also might consider personalizing the golf balls with a birthday message or her initials (you can do this with permanent markers or pre-order at some online stores). Use these vases as table centerpieces in lieu of flower arrangements. Mom can keep the vases as décor for her house, and she can use the balls the next time she tees up! Speaking of golf tees, they make cute hors d'oeuvre picks for those yummy appetizers you are serving. Don't forget to decorate your serving platters and trays of food with fresh-cut grass from your lawn or garden or long sprigs of dill, which will also provide a delicious smell.

Your sister is really into running right now?

> **It's not the years in your life that count. It's the life in your years!**
> (Abe Lincoln)

Send invitations that are marathon race numbers overlaid with the party details. Ask guests to bring their invite/number to the party to be entered in a raffle to win a special gift at the end of the night. Create an actual "race course map" to hand out to guests that they can follow around your house and your yard with a few different activities hosted at each stop on the map. A faux gold medal can be placed in the center of her birthday cake, or you can create one with frosting or fondant. Place pairs of running shoes or sneakers on the steps or pathway leading up to your house— inside of them, place shallow vases or low glass bowls filled with flower arrangements.

Little brother is the next Martin Scorsese? For his birthday, consider setting up a projector to play a movie on the side of the house or on a blank interior wall. You can run some of his favorite films on mute or even have a movie viewing complete with popcorn, movie candy, and fountain sodas in "branded" paper cups. Simply buy white paper or styrofoam cups with lids and straws and then grab a permanent marker or print stickers to personalize them. For an intimate gathering, the invitation could be a DVD of his favorite movie with a clever caption. For instance, *"Come and celebrate the birthday of our favorite film fan Brandon in a galaxy far, far away."*

For larger gatherings, consider creating an invitation that looks like a movie ticket, and replace the show date and time with the party date and time.

Your best friend is hardly ever home because she is always jet-setting, and she never has time to do the "normal" things in life, like grocery shop or even just go to the movies. So, for her party, set up a movie projector and host an "Airplane Movie Night" at home. Serve little packs of peanuts and a selection of mini-sized bottles of spirits. Show a movie you know she will love, and pass out blue "airline" blankets and pairs of blue socks for guests. The perfect favor? Sleep masks.

The birthday guy has a serious love of classic rock and roll? Why not resurrect his favorite bands and ask everyone to come in character . . . fully made up, complete with leather and chains? Hire a DJ to play all the classics, and to dress the part, too. Clear your space to make room for a rockin' dance floor and host Guitar Hero or Rock Band stations in a couple of different rooms. For a spec-and-swish idea, you could rent a private recording booth, which I did for an event recently . Guests will love recording their own song and taking their renditions home on a CD. Order or bake a cake in the shape of an electric guitar. Send guests home with wireless microphones as party favors—they have great, inexpensive ones that you can plug into any

at-home Karaoke system to keep the concert tour alive well past the party.

The birthday lady who loves to cook and entertain? Hire a personal chef and spend the night working in teams to create a five-course, five-star meal. Guests will love being a part of the action, learn-ing a few tricks of the trade, and of course, enjoying the great food and wine! The perfect party favor? Personalized chef hats for the guys, and monogrammed aprons for the ladies. You can tweak this for the baker by host-ing a "Food Network

Challenge" party, which is exactly what I would do for my friend Tracie Turinese. (She actually won a Food Network Challenge! Check out this photo of one of her famous birthday cakes.)

These are just a few examples of ways you can creatively tailor a party for the birthday lady or gent. You don't have to follow the traditional birthday party rules, nor do you have to spend lots of money to personalize a birthday celebration. A few creative ideas are all it takes to make the birthday boy or girl feel like the world stopped just for them that day. So host your next birthday like a true Mermaid would by casting your net a bit wider, personalizing the event, and discovering what new thoughts come in with the tide.

> *"Sometimes I would rather have people take away years of my life than take away a moment."*—**Pearl Bailey**

Occasions are gifts in themselves, right? If Mermaids have a choice between a material possession or an experience, we choose the experience! Doesn't it seem like these give back so much more? You will always learn something via an experience (good or bad) and come back from it a bit changed. As my cousin Ashley once said, "Experience is what it is . . . if it's good or if it's bad—it's still growth."

Birthday gifts are a great opportunity to personalize. Consider giving the birthday boy or gal a memory-making experience rather than another handbag or DVD. After all, the memories from the experience will last longer and have more meaning than any gift ever could. If the birthday girl is a casual acquaintance, perhaps you could take her to the new hot lunch spot in town. Spa days or mani/pedi's make for a great bonding time with a sister or close friend. And for your significant other, consider a weekend away, even if it's just to a fabulous hotel right in town. I had a fantastic friend who used to work in the hotel industry in New York City, and he and I would pick different hotels to try out for lunch, dinner, or spa treatments. I would stow away (in my memory—not my suitcase) all the best parts of what made the hotel come alive and reuse the ideas for my next party.

My friend Cat is definitely a choose-the-experience-over-the-gift kind of Mermaid. So, over the years we have given her some fun, experiential birthday gifts, like a massage that was done in only chocolate (her favorite), a donation to her favorite charity, a salsa lesson, a golf session with a pro, a night at a trendy hotel with her beau, and sailing classes on the Hudson River. A cheap-and-chic way to make someone feel *fin*Tastic on his or her birthday is to write out fifty-two things (memories, jokes) about the birthday boy or girl on tiny little pieces of paper. Place these notes in a keepsake box and ask the

Mermaid Memory: *Mermaid Hilary*

Before they were married, my dear friend, and fellow Mermaid, Vanessa wanted to throw a birthday party for her uber-hip, t-shirt-loving boyfriend Asad, who could make even the corniest t-shirts look cool. Vanessa met Asad in high school near Manila, Philippines, where they grew up, and reconnected with him in NYC years later. Vanessa wanted to do something really special for Asad, so we had a meeting of the Mer-minds to brainstorm. We took our cues from Asad's love of t-shirts, and we decided that the theme would start with the invitations, which would say, "Asad is turning 28. Come celebrate with us! If you have an old t-shirt with a cool or crazy saying or logo, please wear it to the party on January 18th." Vanessa also wanted to honor where Asad spent his high school years and how they met. So, we planned to purchase adobo, which is a Filipino spice available at most stores, empty the spice boxes, wash them and refill with wildflowers, and make beautiful centerpieces. We also planned to purchase a bunch of funky and vintage t-shirts at rummage sales and thrift stores, and these would be hung from a twine clothesline strung across the ceiling. At the end of the night, each guest would take home a t-shirt as a party favor.

I've been lucky to travel to the Philippines twice, and the people are so loving and warm. They are very fond of giving each other fun nicknames, like, "Lollipop," "Toto," or "Baby." So, of course, our place cards were Filipino names that we thought would best match each guest. And our specialty cocktail, the "Thrilla From Manila!"

Well guess what? Asad was called to an extended business trip overseas, so we never got to throw him this party! But, I did reuse most of the ideas for Vanessa's birthday party the following year. Just because one party falls through doesn't mean you can't save that vision board you created, or file away your ideas for a future event.

receiver to open one each week of the year. If you are feeling ambitious, go for 365 reasons. You'd be surprised how easy this is when you really love someone! Talk about the gift that keeps on giving. By the way, this idea can be reversed, as well.

One birthday a few of my best friends took me to dinner to celebrate. I wanted to thank them in advance for their thoughtfulness, so I made each friend a list based on how old I was: *"Melissa, 30 reasons you make my day."* I presented my friends with their special lists during dinner so they could see just how much they meant to me. Another great way to liven up a birthday dinner is to pass around the famous astrology book *The Secret Language of Birthdays* by Gary Goldschneider so everyone can read a little bit about their star sign.

When Mermaids Nicole and Alvina decided to celebrate a milestone birthday together, their friends and I wanted to do something really spectacular-and-swish for both of them! We designed an invitation that read: *"Chase the Sun. Chase the Moon."* On a beautiful sunny Saturday morning, we gathered our best group of gals, and spent a day in the lap of luxury at the Peninsula Hotel and Spa in New York City. We enjoyed a poolside lunch on the hotel's beautiful roof deck before indulging in massages, facials, mani/pedi's, and blow-outs. The poolside pampering was followed by an intimate girls-only cocktail hour at my apartment, which we decorated with tons of silver and blue balloons and tea lights to mirror the NYC city skyline. Finally, we made personalized, framed lithographs based on signature cocktails we served. Each guest was handed a gift bag that fit the indulgent theme of the day. Filled with mini bottles of champagne, hotel travel candles, and "foot petals" for running around town in our heels, we immediately put the goodies to use as we carried our celebrations into Manhattan to chase the moon all night long!

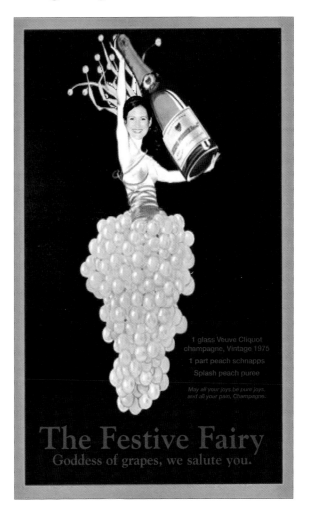

RULE OF FIN:
Don't forget whom the birthday celebration is for!

As you can see from these ideas, making a memory is sometimes the best way to celebrate a loved one's birthday, especially when that memory is tailored to the person's own passions and pursuits.

Here are four easy ways to personalize a birthday celebration:

Invitation Idea. Scan a special childhood photo and print it in black and white. On the back, write something clever about a unique quality of the birthday person. Don't forget to include the salient party details!

Signature Cocktail. Create a cocktail inspired by the birthday person. You can simply rename the traditional favorites (think, a Brit-tini or a Meg-arita), or you could dig in a little more and create a cocktail that pays homage to the personality of the person. For instance, if the birthday girl is full of moxie and fire, serve something fizzy or bubbly like strawberry champagne cocktails or a classic gin fizz. If the birthday guy is super mellow and chill, consider a smooth, simple drink like scotch on the rocks or his favorite beer. Two of my favorite and funny cocktails to serve are the

RECIPE BOX

Birthday Cake
2 oz CUPCAKE vanilla vodka
5 oz pineapple juice
1/2 oz Chambord
1/2 oz Liquer 43

Shake together all ingredients with ice in a shaker, and pour into a martini glass. Garnish by tying mini colored balloons to the stem of the glass

"Birthday Suit" and a sweet "Birthday Cake," which truly tastes like birthday cake. Consider creating custom-designed cocktail napkins by either stamping their initials at home or ordering napkins from sites like ForYourParty.com. Another great birthday idea is to write conversation starters on coasters and cocktail napkins. Guests will love reading and talking about your questions for inspired conversation!

Delightful Décor. The look and feel of the event should always represent something meaningful about the birthday person. Remember Asad and his t-shirts? Hone in on the one thing that the birthday boy or girl really loves, and use it as the decorating theme. Is Mike the comedian of the group? Consider writing little jokes on coasters and placing them throughout the venue. One-liners

We Mermaids love to personalize. One great way to do this for a party is by infusing our own vodka at home. This is super easy.

First, decide if you'd like to infuse with fruit, berries or herbs, and, to give your vodka a more spicy flair, you could use peppers. There are so many types of infusions out there, but my favorites are blueberry, mint, apple, lemon, cherry, and melon.

What you need: A simple glass jar with a tight fitting lid will work. If you can get a proper infusion jar with a spigot at the bottom, even better! Plan for the glass container to hold up to a liter of vodka.

Once you have decided on your flavor, it's time to prepare it! The following are good guidelines for working with approximately 1 liter of vodka.

- If infusing vodka with fruit, how many to use will depend on the size of the fruit. For apples, plums, and oranges you will want to use three to four. For a large fruit like a melon or a grapefruit, you should only need one.

- If infusing vodka with herbs, use 1-2 handfuls of the herb. If using dry herbs and spices, you can cut this measurement in half.

- If infusing berries, use 3-5 fists filled with the berries.

- If infusing peppers, use as many as you want. The more you use and the longer you infuse, the spicier the end product will be.

Remember, just like buying food, the fresher the ingredients, the more vibrant the flavor of the vodka will be!

Infusing Process:
1.) Wash all fresh ingredients. Slice fruits finely and remove any pits, seeds, or stems. Leave berries whole, but gently squeeze them to help release more flavor before infusion. Crush herbs gently, as it will help to release flavors.
2.) When using fruits, cut up finely and fill up the glass jar. Fill it but don't jam-pack them, you need to leave room for the vodka. Your goal is to completely cover all the fruits in the container with the vodka.
3.) Store the bottle in a cool dark place or the refrigerator. A good timeframe is approximately 3 days for citrus and about a week for the other items. Taste test every few days to your desired potency.
4.) When infused and ready, strain out any pulps and enjoy your infused vodka with friends or give as a gift!

RECIPE BOX

The Birthday Suit
  1 1/2 oz vodka
  3/4 oz dry vermouth

This one speaks for itself. Make a straight-up, clear, and "naked" shot by shaking the vodka and vermouth together with several ice cubes in a shaker. Strain the liquid into a snifter glass and serve with an olive. For the garnish, tie a tuxedo bowtie the glass stem.

Here's a *fin*Tastic idea: For classic style martinis and drinks, garnishes are key. Stuff olives with blue cheese, cream cheese, garlic, peppers, or even lemon zest. Use an icing piper to stuff your olives in an easy and quick way.

RECIPE BOX

Thrilla From Manila
  1 cup vodka
  1/2 cup lemon juice
  2 cups pineapple juice
  2 mangos
  1 T superfine sugar

Place all ingredients into a blender and blend until it's nice and smooth. Pour into cocktail glasses with ice, and garnish with a lemon wedge or mango slice.

that can also inspire "conversation starters" scribbled on mini Post-Its and stuck to the bottom of wine glasses make great conversation pieces, and help guests remember which glass belongs to them.

Fun Favors. The perfect way to end the night is to send guests home with something to remember the event by. Consider having Polaroid cameras placed on each table so guests can snap pictures throughout the party. Edible party favors can be easy and fun, too. Does the birthday gal love cupcakes? How about sending everyone home with a two-pack?

No matter how hard you try, you can't stop the calendar from turning over every year. Mermaids know that this doesn't have to be a bad thing. With just a few clever ideas, you can make someone's birthday the best day of the year. Just remember the most important rule: *personalize*!

"The more you know who you are and what you want, the less you let things upset you."

—**"Bob Harris,"** *Lost in Translation*
(Bill Murray's character)

Peg Samuel is an author and founder of Social Diva (socialdiva.com). She has hosted hundreds of memorable events around the country and the world, and here she shares some of her favorite ways to celebrate.

Q: What's the best supplement to a party?
A: The atmosphere of a party is very important, so we won't host a party at a place that hasn't been pre-tested and pre-approved. For music, we're incredibly into house music—we even have our own albums ("Strictly Social Diva"). But, of course, the most important part of any party is the guest list!

Q: Who are some of your favorite guests or types of guests?
A: Interesting people who are smart, funny, and like-minded. The perfect guest mix is like the perfect combination of accessories: if they don't contribute something to the evening, then they shouldn't be there.

Q: What is your favorite thing to do when preparing for an event?
A: Hair and makeup—hello!

Q: What has been your favorite event to attend or host, and why?
A: One of my all-time favorites was an event we held at the Hotel on Rivington. With a spectacular penthouse view of NYC, the backdrop was set. We provided our own muse for the music—our "Strictly Social Diva" playlist. The staff was amazing, and the divas were haute. The whole night I kept envisioning the penthouse as my apartment, and that the party was mine— private and with staff, of course. It put me in the best frame of mind, and the event was just . . . flawless.

Q: What makes a party a memory for you?
A: You can't go wrong with a stellar venue, but nothing makes a party more memorable than a great conversation or serendipitous meetings.

Q: What is your secret to unwinding when the party is over?
A: I do something nice for myself to unwind. Sometimes I indulge in a pedicure at the 24-hour salon on my block. And sleeping in the next morning is always part of the plan.

chapter three

Yes! Engagement Parties

> *"If I'm honest, I have to tell you I still read fairytales and I like them best of all."*—**Audrey Hepburn**

THERE MAY COME a time in a Mermaid's life when she finds her soul Mer-mate. Love is in the air, sparks are flying, and all of a sudden she finds herself saying "YES!" and accepting the invitation to a new, exciting, and challenging adventure—marriage.

For Mermaids, the events leading up to the actual wedding can be just as special and meaningful as the big day itself. One of these events is the engagement party, which is becoming a more and more popular staple in the pre-wedding-day festivities. Regardless of the budget, a Mermaid can make an engagement party an unforgettable event for the bride-to-be, groom-to-be, and all of their friends and families.

Where birthday parties are all about the birthday boy or girl, engagement parties are all about the pair. Start by finding inspiration in the couple themselves. Do they share a love for a particular hobby or activity? If so, weave that hobby into the party's details. Did they fall in love while traveling in a foreign country? Create a dinner menu based on that ethnic cuisine. Even the mundane can be a source of inspiration. Perhaps the couple fell in love while working in the same law firm. Law books stacked in the center of tables and topped with bud vases and tea lights make great centerpieces. The more you can celebrate what makes the couple unique, the better your celebration will be.

When a friend, and fellow Mermaid, got engaged one summer, we hosted a "Midsummer Night's Dream" themed engagement party. This theme had the double bonus of fitting the season and celebrating a shared love of the couple's: "Shakespeare in the Park." The invitations had passages from the Shakespeare classic, inviting guests into a picturesque midsummer night's dream in a beautiful garden. I had recently purchased whimsical fairy wings for chair backs, and tiaras, crowns and magic wands as table centerpieces for another party I hosted, so I really wanted to put them to great use again! For a dreamy look, place white candles in small white paper bags to line the path from the parking area into the party. Guests dined on light, fresh, summery fare that was served at room temperature, since the evening was hosted outdoors. The whole atmosphere was dreamy and romantic—just perfect for my newly engaged friends. For this kind of event, consider hiring live musicians and even local actors to do a few Shakespeare readings throughout the party.

While this party was spectacular-and-swish, Mermaids can accomplish magical moments and still be cheap-and-chic. If you don't have a big budget for invitations, consider using a photo of the couple from when they first met, or create a faux newspaper announcement on your computer and include the details of their background and union. You could find a great illustrator to hand draw a picture of an oak tree with the couple's names such as "Robin Loves Kevin" inscribed on the tree trunk. Feel free to be as clever or as sappy as you like. Buy some specialty ice cube trays shaped like diamonds and jewels to create some bling for your drinks. Instead of serving a meal, offer some heavy hors d'oeuvres. And, to be cheap-and-chic, just a few white candles and wildflowers can create a romantic atmosphere on a dime.

Engagement parties are usually hosted by a family member or close friends of the couple. A gift for those hosts might be a package of nice stationery (so they can spread the word about the engagement!) or an oyster serving set paired with a fancy oyster sauce, jar of caper berries, and other accoutrements to wish *them* a lifelong aphrodisiac for lasting love.

RULE OF FIN:

An engagement party should reflect the couple. Focus on what makes them the perfect pair.

Here's a *fin*Tastic idea: Be sneaky and get a spare set of keys to the couple's apartment or house. Grab a friend, and while the engagement party is still going, disappear for an hour and make up their bedroom like a five-star honeymoon resort would. Place flower petals in the shape of their monogram on the bed, have champagne chilling, and accompany the

champagne with chocolate-covered strawberries—all the sappy stuff! Sappy can be great when it comes to love.

Here are four ways you can personalize an engagement party to make a big impression.

Invitation Idea. Engagement events are the kind of party that celebrate all of the sparkle and excitement ahead for the couple: from the sparkle in their eyes to the sparkle on her finger. For the invites, consider using silver or iridescent paper to emphasize the bling.

Signature Cocktail. Gussy up your guest's libations with flirty names like the "Perfect Pear" or "Rock Candy Cosmos."

Delightful Décor. For a fairytale fete, prior to the event invite guests to write a short fairytale about the duo on colorful paper and ask them to bring the fairytales with them to the bash. These can be "based" on true-life funny tales. As guests arrive, hang each story throughout the venue. Accompany the stories with fun pictures of the couple in sparkly frames. Guests and the couple of honor will enjoy reading these fairytales throughout the evening. Cute ideas for a meaningful menu for this type of event include Hansel-and-Gretel breadcrumbs and dip, Rapunzel linguini, and Cinderella pumpkin ravioli paired with Sleeping-Beauty-and-the-Prince

The Perfect Pear Martini

1.5 oz puree of fresh green pear

2 oz pear-flavored vodka or your own pear-infused vodka

1/2 oz fresh-squeezed lemon

A pear slice cut as a heart with a cookie cutter for garnish.

Take the pears, peel and core them. Heat them up in boiling water, until they start to get a little soft and then blend them in blender. Combine all of the ingredients into a shaker with two or three ice cubes. Shake for thirty seconds or until thoroughly chilled. Strain into a glass and serve immediately. Garnish.

Rock Candy Cosmo

Rim your martini glasses with lemon juice. Then, smash a package of pop rock candy into even smaller granules. Dip the glass rims into the rock candy, and fill with a classic cosmopolitan.

Fun Favors. It's all about the love, so send guests home with something romantic. Classic tales of epic love stories from the greats like Shakespeare, a collection of love poems by Pablo Neruda, or even a stack of drugstore romance novels make for a fun and cheeky favor. For those with a sweet tooth, send guests home with Ring Pops. If you themed your cocktails around "The Perfect Pear" you could send guests home with mini wooden crates filled with exotic Asian pears or a pear-flavored liquor. Also consider having a "Candy to my Soul" candy bar—where guests can prepare candy favors for themselves in plastic bags.

potions (i.e. cocktails!). At the end of the event, collect all of the fairytales and printed menu cards to put together a "storybook" to give to the couple for a very happy ending.

chapter four

Bridal Showers

> *"I'd like to add his initial to my monogram."*
>
> —**Song lyric by Cole Porter**

A BRIDAL SHOWER is the perfect time for girlfriends to celebrate their friend as she transitions from being a "me" to a "we." Traditionally, the bridal shower is an opportunity for friends and family to gift the bride and groom with items they need to set up their home together after the wedding. But in recent years, bridal showers have morphed from a thing of necessity (think pots and pans and dishes) to a thing of fancy (think, whimsical holiday ornaments, lingerie, or even honeymoon gifts).

WATCH OUT for registry blunders. I once saw a ghastly registry where the groom and bride registered for honeymoon hotel dollars. Mermaids everywhere cringed. Although a meaningful gift such as a spa treatment or a bottle of champagne sent to the hotel room is great, registering for money is a big tacky. Instead, send something that you know they will use on their honeymoon, and make sure to include a note with your well wishes.

There are so many fabulous and fun ways to shower a bride before her wedding, it would be impossible to describe them all here. Instead, we will focus on the basics of all great bridal showers. A good way to start planning a shower is to ask the bride if there's anything she and her future husband really need. If the answer is yes, honor tradition and plan a shower that will help the bride and groom get settled after the wedding. If the answer is no, then whole vistas of creative opportunities are open to you. Do the bride and groom celebrate Christmas? If so, how about a Christmas-themed shower where guests bring Christmas decorations or ornaments as gifts? Thanks to the Internet, it's easy to find this stuff year round. Do the bride and groom love a particular sport? Plan a shower with the sport as a theme and ask guests to bring gear, tickets to sporting events in which the couples' favorite team is playing, or even movies about that sport as gifts. Speaking of movies, another fabulous shower idea is to host a movie-themed shower and ask guests to help the bride and groom build their movie collection. The bridal party can chip in for a great flatscreen TV and guests can bring everything from DVDs to a cute set of popcorn bowls.

I've been to stock-the-bar showers, build-the-kitchen showers, and outdoor rain-or-shine showers (where guests purchased things to outfit the bride and groom's new deck or patio and their garden). No matter what the theme, the key is to keep it personal. With a little creativity, you can create a bridal shower that will give the bride and groom things they never even knew they needed!

When *Mermaid Jamie* was getting married, her friends and I wanted her to "live it up" lavishly. Jamie loves all things luxury, so a queen-for-the-day shower was right up her alley. Her spectacular-and-swish champagne bridal brunch also included some cheap-and-chic factors that were personalized for her and her fiancé, Josh. Utilizing empty champagne

Mermaid Memory

Mermaid Jamie

MY BRIDAL SHOWER was one of the best afternoons of my life. From the pictures of our engagement placed all over the room to the sparkling "diamond" ring at my place setting, it was perfect. Though these were just little things, they were just for me! I felt special and loved all day long.

You will hear me talk about Mermaid Jamie a lot in this book. She gives us lots of reasons to celebrate and is an incredible party planner with a background of doing events at some of the most prestigious hotels in New York City.

RULE OF FIN:

There is nothing worse than sending guests home with another trinket to be stuffed in a junk drawer. Instead, think about making a donation in everyone's honor to an organization that is meaningful to the bride and groom.

Here are four ways to throw a fabulous bridal shower.

Invitation Idea. Just as the couple's relationship continues to grow, invite guests to the bridal shower with little packets of flower seeds attached to the invitation. Crafty Mermaids can even design their own package and customize with the details of the event and a few personal notes about the couple.

Signature Cocktail. Champagne, the timeless celebratory drink of choice, is always a great place to start when designing a bridal shower cocktail. One of my favorites is the Blossoming Bellini, which is fruity, fun, and delicious.

bottles as vases, we decorated the venue with her favorite flowers. We used the champagne corks as place card holders and strung up black and white photos of the happy couple around the room. Guests left with champagne bubble bath bottles. On Jamie's plate we set a big, sparkling faux diamond ring. Jamie's shower made her feel loved, lavished, and totally relaxed before her journey to the altar.

Blossoming Bellini

2 oz peach juice or peach puree
(Cipriani makes a great canned version)
4 oz champagne

Pour the peach juice or peach puree into a champagne flute. Slowly add the champagne. Garnish with an edible flower.

Here's a *fin*Tastic idea: You can make Bellinis with any and all kinds of fruit purees. Consider setting up a "Bellini Bar" at your next party with a variety of pureed fruits and berries placed in pretty bowls and let guests mix and match to their taste preferences.

Delightful Décor. In keeping with the floral motif, consider decorating mini terracotta pots and filling them with multicolored flowers. Any hardware or home improvement store will sell them. You can mark them with colored chalk and write love quotes. Or, you can use them as place settings with guests names written on them. One of the brides I worked with wanted to create a memory by wrapping each of her bridesmaid's bouquets in sheet music, so she asked all of her bridesmaids to choose their favorite love song, and she purchased sheet music for it. The black and white song lyrics looked just beautiful wrapped around bouquets of red roses. For her bridal shower, I asked each bridesmaid to tell me what that bride would be if *she* were a song. They sent me songs or lyrics that reminded them of her, or had some special or funny meaning. I placed copies of these songs around the venue and also burned them to a CD, which played in the background. Then, when the shower was over, the bride took home a book with all of the printed songs inside as a keepsake of the day.

Fun Favors. Depending on the theme of the shower, you can send guests away with something to remember it by. So, for example, if it was a lingerie shower, send guests home with a great lingerie satchel for travel. Or, if it was a stock-the-kitchen shower, how about glass or crystal pineapples (the traditional sign for "welcome" and inviting friends into your home). Every bridesmaid will appreciate a small gift set that includes all of the things they will need on the wedding day—lip gloss, a mini sewing kit with pins, a pack of tissues, small compact mirror, throat drops (nothing is worse than coughing at the altar with nothing to reach for), and a small pack of facial blotting papers.

Leanne Shear is a writer for *The New York Times* and co-author of *Cocktail Therapy* and *The Perfect Manhattan*. She is also the founder of Rogue Female Fitness. Gosh, she keeps busy! Here she shares with us some of her thoughts on entertaining.

Q: What's the best supplement to a party?
A: Music is key. In my opinion, the host of the party should never play his or her favorites; he or she should create playlists that are crowd pleasers! Putting together a great mix of oldies, classic rock, pop, and hip hop will get every guest in the mood for a party.

Q: Who are some of your favorite guests or types of guests?
A: I always love the "Budweiser Player of the Game" guest. You know, the random person who comes out of the woodwork and is the life of the party. I love people who are the life of the party. Wallflowers scare me!

Q: What is your favorite thing to do when preparing for an event?
A: Drink wine and eat half of the appetizers I am preparing for guests!

Q: What has been your favorite event to attend or host, and why?
A: I attend or host so many events it's hard to pinpoint exactly which one is my all-time favorite. But I recently hosted a little event at my apartment for my partners and employees in the fitness company I started. We all worked out together and were in our gym clothes. We were going to have a quick glass of wine and some snacks. Well, a glass of wine turned into eight bottles, which turned into a bottle of tequila, which turned into a bottle of rum . . . it culminated into this hilarious dance party, not to mention a bonding experience for those of us who had just started working together. It was an awesome night!

Q: What makes a party a memory for you?
A: How many boys I kissed!

Q: What's your Rule of Fin?
A: Have a smile on my face at all times, which translates into openness to meeting new people.

Q: What is your secret to unwinding when the party is over?
A: Going to bed; then, the next morning, going for a run followed by a Bloody Mary!

chapter five

Bachelorette Parties

"Go girl, seek happy nights to happy days."

—William Shakespeare

WHERE A BRIDAL SHOWER is a more formal affair, the bachelorette party should be anything but! A growing trend in celebrating the bride's final days as a bachelorette is to plan a girls-only trip to some fabulous destination. But even if your budget doesn't allow for a weekend getaway, there are plenty of ways to plan a fabulous celebration. The key ingredients are the 3 F's: friends, fun, and food. Exactly what each of those things looks like all depends on the bride and her group of friends. Perhaps the bride loves to go out on the town. Friends, fun, and food might mean everyone dressed to the nines for dinner at a trendy restaurant, drinks at an even trendier bar, and then late night dancing at the trendiest club. If your bride is more of a laid-back, stay-at-home kind of gal, plan a fabulous night in. Order some of her favorite carryout, rent some great movies, stock up on sweets, and indulge in some quality time at someone's house. Whatever you plan, as long as it incorporates friends, fun, and food, the bride is sure to be sent off into wedded bliss in style.

> **RULE OF FIN:**
> *Should you want to dine in, an inexpensive way is to hire a private chef by calling your local culinary school. Students are always looking for an opportunity to practice their craft, and usually will do so at a greatly discounted rate.*

Calling all Cats! When it came time to honor a bride-to-be's former days on the prowl, my Mermaids and I planned a fantastic feline-inspired fete for our friend. For this bachelorette party we rented a large, beautiful home near the beach. We started the night off with a fresh farm-table dinner. For fun, we adorned the table with cheap-and-chic fishbowl centerpieces filled with goldfish, and we served Swedish Fish cocktails—the theme of the night for the single ladies being *"there are plenty of fish in the sea!"* Guests were encouraged to wear cat ears as we danced the night away at a local hotspot. Food, fun, and friends—everything we needed for a perfect bachelorette party.

Games always make for a fun time at a bachelorette party. One of my favorites is the "How Well Do You Know Your Fiancé?" game. This game takes a little preparation, so plan to call or email the fiancé before the party and ask him a series of questions. Then, ask those same questions of the bride, and for every answer she gets correct, she wins a prize. If you live near the couple, it's even more fun to schedule a time with the groom-to-be and use your mobile device or video camera to tape him answering the questions. You could even host a live "Skype" session at the party to include the groom in this part.

Here are some of my favorite questions:

- *What is your favorite food?*
- *Who are you named after?*
- *When did you know it was love and she was "the one"?*
- *What is your shoe size?*
- *What is your favorite song?*
- *If you were a cartoon character, who would you be?*
- *What is your least favorite food?*
- *What is your family nickname?*
- *What do you think the bride-to-be's most annoying habit is?*

- *What was the name of your first pet?*
- *If the bride-to-be were a tattoo on your body, what would be the symbol/icon?*
- *If she were a theme song (or, had a theme song) what would it be?*
- *What is your favorite movie?*
- *What is your favorite outfit she wears?*
- *On which date did you first kiss?*
- *What is your favorite part of her body?*
- *What is your dream job?*
- *What is your nightmare job?*
- *Where would you go for a dream vacation?*
- *If you could have dinner with anyone, dead or alive, who would it be?*
- *If you were a car, which car would you be?*
- *If you could jump into a movie and play a character, who would it be?*
- *What celebrity does she remind you of?*
- *Who was your best friend growing up?*
- *Who is your celebrity crush?*
- *What sports did you play in high school?*
- *Where would you take the bride-to-be for her perfect night on the town?*

> **RULE OF FIN:**
> *The bride-to-be shouldn't spend a dime at her bachelorette party, or feel any pressure to do something she might regret the next day.*

Here are four ways to throw a fabulous bachelorette party:

Invitation Idea. Formal invitations aren't necessary for a bachelorette party. Because the attendees will all be good friends, a thematic evite is all it takes to announce the bachelorette weekend. For our feline-themed event, we sent a custom evite featuring a vintage illustration from the cartoon "Josie & the Pussycats" with the bride's headshot edited into the picture.

Signature Cocktail. It all depends on the evening's theme. Champagne, or a good prosecco is a great place to start for a dressy evening. A night on the town will surely include some cocktails. But for a night in? Maybe some blended drinks, like daiquiris and pina coladas. For our "Calling all Cats" celebration we poured prosecco into flutes with a speared red Swedish Fish garnish. We named the drink the "On the Prowl" Prosecco.

On-The-Prowl Prosecco! Because there are Plenty of Fish in the Sea!

RECIPE BOX

I like to call the guests of a bachelorette weekend or party the "Bettes." In honor of the Bettes, this signature cocktail is custom created for a weekend of fun. Cheers!

The Bette:
1 1/2 oz vodka
3/4 oz triple sec
3/4 oz pomegranate juice
1 oz fresh lime juice

Pour the vodka, triple sec, pomegranate juice, and lime juice into a cocktail shaker half-filled with ice cubes. Shake well, strain into a cocktail glass, and serve. Drop a few pomegranate seeds into the glass, and further compliment the cocktail by serving a bowl of the seeds as bar snacks.

Delightful Décor. Go beyond the boa! Since most of the festivities will likely take place in ever-changing venues (restaurants, bars, clubs, hotels), props are fun for a bachelorette party! In the case of our feline-inspired fete, we got a little silly and wore cat ears, but it did add an air of whimsy to the night. Here are some other fun ideas:

- Temporary tattoos—get really fun and creative on where to tattoo the bride-to-be and her Bettes!
- Fun lipstick pens—these make great gifts for guests, and are a great way to keep track of a list of "challenges" during the night that you may assign to the bride-to-be.
- Turban—create a turban for the bride-to-be out of tissue paper. Grab some leftover tissue (from her gift bags) and pierce with a jeweled broach or piece of costume jewelry, a flower, peacock feather, or shell, depending on where you are celebrating! She will look so cute rocking her hand-made turban all night.
- Rings—oh, how I love a good costume ring. You can find inexpensive rings even at stores like Target. And all of the ladies will look great sparkling around town.

Fun Favors. Props make for great favors. It's usually something fun and silly that will always evoke a happy memory. If you decide to stay away from props, consider giving the attendees

The Bride With Too Many Friends

Not everyone always knows each other at bachelorette parties. Some brides will invite every friend from kindergarten to her work colleagues. Starting the night off at someone's home sets a relaxing tone and allows guests to get to know each other. Here are a few fun games to break the ice: oracle cards (where each guest randomly pulls one card from the deck to read aloud a personal message "meant" for them) or tarot cards. My friend Chiera King created Kismet Cards, which are DIY tarot cards that I love bringing to parties.

something girly that can be put to good use, like cheap-and-chic colorful pashmina wraps that the girls can wear while running around to different locations all night. Once, I found these beautiful resin rings carved in the shape of black roses. We were automatically

transformed into "Bond Girls" because the tops of these rings flipped open to secretly reveal a pot of lip gloss. That night, we looked beautiful and acted fearless!

The Big Day!

> *"The most precious gift one can receive is the heart of another."*
>
> —**Mermaid Brittany**

Well, that's our next book! All kidding aside, the Mermaids are already working on a new book dedicated just to weddings, because this kind of event truly requires an entire book unto itself. But, we thought we would share just a few ideas that we have learned from being guests, bridesmaids, brides, and wedding planners at quite a few spectacular-and-swish *and* cheap-and-chic weddings.

It goes without saying that a wedding day should be unforgettable. Even with all of the planning and anticipation, this day will come and go in a flash. Nothing is more intimate and personal than a wedding. Therefore, the more personalized the day is, the more memorable it becomes for the bride, groom, and guests. Regardless of the theme or traditions to be included, remember that this day is about celebrating the love that the couple shares for each other.

I have attended (and helped plan) many fantastic weddings all over the world, from South Boston to the South of France! From all of the different cultures, traditions, and themes, here are a few I simply can't forget:

- A West Hampton Beach Club bash featured the most incredibly curated and delicious raw bar display I'd ever seen—and the fact that we were overlooking the ocean didn't hurt. The shellfish must have jumped from the ocean right onto our plates that day, they tasted so good!

- A Newport, Rhode Island, wedding boasted a fancy buffet with a toned-down twist—the groom had a serious love of onion rings, and the bride loved mac & cheese, so there was an entire buffet featuring different varieties of just those items.

- One of the most magical weddings I've been a part of was hosted in Ireland at Dromoland, an old-world castle with a history that stretches back to the 5th century. This grand gathering was held on St. Patrick's Day, complete with a display of fireworks over a rain-misted lake to honor the groom's mom, who had passed. The evening was finished with a live Guinness sing-along, of course, at four o'clock in the morning.

- One bride, with Mexican roots, was married inside an actual bull-fighting ring in Mexico. When the weather didn't cooperate, this bride did not let a little rain ruin her evening. Instead, she had a beautiful clear tent hoisted right over the ring so guests could enjoy a luxurious dinner, and dancing all night long.

- I was the maid of honor at a wedding hosted in a centuries-old abbey in Fontainebleau, France, which boasted a four-hour wine and cheese reception—and that was BEFORE dinner! All the ladies who attended wore fantastic hats and feathers in their hair— which added to the whimsical decadence. As for the celebrated couple, they had traveled all over Europe, so they labeled each table's centerpiece with a country they had traveled to. Included in the centerpieces were photos and memorabilia from that particular country. The party continued into the early morning hours, and guests were bid adieu with mini vats of French onion soup and bottles of Kronenbourg beer.

- A lovely Vermont wedding hosted in the antique barn of a farmhouse strung up with twinkle lights, featured a casual buffet that was sweet and perfect. The bride wore flowers in her hair and a quietly beautiful dress—just like her.

- A wedding hosted in the midst of rolling hills and hundreds of oak trees (the original *Robin Hood* was filmed there!) was dramatic and bold. The bridesmaids all wore elegant black dresses fitted to their own taste, size, and style, and they held bright red rose bouquets. The traditional chuppah was adorned with red bougainvilleas, and there were hand-written notes from guests that were collected for months before the event strewn into the canopy of the structure. It was very meaningful because the bride and groom stood under this beautiful creation and read their handwritten vows beneath notes from all the people they loved most. The bride has Argentinean roots—so she and her groom surprised all of us by starting the evening with a first dance that was a rehearsed tango.

- At the wedding of some friends who love music, the couple decided to get creative with how individual tables were called to join the buffet line. Instead of having the DJ call each table one by one, each table was assigned a song. When that song played, guests knew it was their turn to boogey up to the food.

- My friend Katy had a traditional Indian wedding in Chicago. I was moved by the traditions, the artistic henna designs on Katy, the Indian food, lively music, and the fact that her sister Alvina brought me back a traditional sari from India that I wore that day. The event was pure mood magic!

- Friends were married in Charleston, South Carolina, in true Southern style. I loved that the bride hired a live gospel group to perform during the cocktail hour and sent guests home with authentic sweetgrass baskets.

- For a beach wedding in the Bahamas, all of the guests were asked to wear white. The bride changed it up and walked down the aisle in a beautiful blush pink dress! Not only did this take a lot of pressure off the guests (no worrying about what to wear), but it also showed a very confident bride.

- A laid-back professional wake boarder and his fun-loving bride really wanted their wedding to be an all-out party. They served yummy comfort food, including a brick-oven pizza bar, and s'mores made on an open fire pit. A trunk of dress-up items was placed near a gorgeous backdrop of floating orchids, and Polaroid cameras were left around for guests to snap away! The bride changed into a white sweat suit and flip flops for dancing, which set the mood for a massive dance party.

- Mermaid Jamie's friends, Erin and David, made their big move together in Mexico. Who doesn't love a reason to go on vacation? The rehearsal dinner was held on a great lawn overlooking the resort, but what really set this celebration apart was the DJ. A very talented friend played the most amazing dance music. Every single guest danced and no one wanted to leave when the music stopped. So, the party was extended by two hours!

- A California couple wed at a historic venue in Malibu overlooking the ocean. The mother-of-the-bride decided to hire docents who gave guests tours around this beautiful property, that was rich in history, and told stories during the cocktail hour.

- A wedding that Mermaids & Martinis recently planned featured a beautiful couple with mixed backgrounds and religions, so, to honor their different faiths, we placed little "blessing bouquets" on each table that had messages like beauty, bliss, courage, and hope.

- And, I will never forget the wedding I attended in New England during the month of February. The heat stopped working halfway through the event, so we all danced with our winter coats on!

Customization makes a big day even bigger. Here are four ways to bring the WOW to your wedding.

Invitation Idea. No matter what theme or style your wedding will take, the invitation is the first thing a guest will see. It should, above all, reflect the couple's personality. Anything goes, as long as it sets the tone for the entire event. Ordinary stationery need not apply!

Signature Cocktail. His-and-her drinks are a must, as well as whimsical signatures such as "The Something Blue" and "Cranberry Kiss."

RULE OF FIN:
Weddings go by in a heartbeat. Take time to let it all in. Breathe, smile, and be grateful for all that love in the room.

The Maid of Honor (i.e., the "MOH")

So the bride asked you to be a maid of honor, matron of honor, or a co-maid-of-honor? Any way you say it, you've got some responsibilities ahead! Make like a cruise director on the Love Boat and take charge of the bridesmaids. Make sure they've all ordered their dresses, show up on time for the wedding activities, know what they are doing on the big day, and where to go. Most MOH's get the honor of acting as a witness when the couple signs their marriage license.

MOH's are also meant to spearhead the task of planning the bridal shower and bachelorette party. Although family members and bridesmaids will surely help out, it's up to you to take the lead by initiating an email or phone conversation about the events. You might also be asked to give a toast on the big day. More on great toasts later in the book.

RECIPE

The MOH

A splash of St-Germain
Elderflower Liqueur
5 oz champagne
edible gold

Pour ingredients into a chilled, fluted glass, and stir lightly. Garnish with some edible gold glitter on the rim of the glass (because, after all, the MOH is the glue that holds the wedding party together). Trace a lemon slice around the rim to provide stickiness for the edible gold and then drop the lemon slice right into the drink—the flavor will add a nice kick!

The Bridesmaid

Typically, a bridesmaid is chosen because she is a trusted friend of the bride and someone who the bride considers to be special in her life—so special that she has asked her to stand up with her on her wedding day. "Duties" are to be emotionally supportive, make the bride laugh if she appears to be on the verge of a meltdown (or at least distract her with a story not related to the wedding), and also help plan (and pay for) both the bridal shower and the bachelorette party.

On the big day, offer to help the bride and groom with any last minute errands they may have to run, and plan to be "on call." At the reception it's part of your job to get the party started (by hitting the dance floor and encouraging others to join) and keep it running smoothly. Check in with the bride and groom often, as they may not have the chance to eat, drink, or even get to the powder room!

To make this drink, pour a fluted glass full of rose champagne and garnish with a petite rose petal. This is a beautiful drink with a sweet, hand-picked garnish, just like your best girls.

RECIPE

My Ty

I had this idea for one of my best Mermaids, Annie, when she married the love of her life, Ty. I thought it would be cute to have a specialty cocktail called "My Ty" using the original Mai Tai recipe. If you don't have a Ty of your own, you can change the name of the drink to the "My Tie," for your own special guy.

    1 oz light rum
    1 oz gold rum
    1/2 oz crème de almond
    1 oz triple sec
    8 oz pineapple juice
    1/2 oz dark rum

(My Ty continued)

This drink should be served in a 14 oz Hurricane glass since it's a biggie with a lot of ingredients. Pour light rum, gold rum, crème de almond and triple sec in that order into a hurricane glass with ice. Fill the glass almost to the top with pineapple juice. Add dark rum, a maraschino cherry garnish and a large straw. Serve unstirred.

RECIPE

The Something Blue

An easy way to add something blue to your ensemble is to adorn the bottom of your shoes with blue crystals in the letters of the couple. I've also know brides to wear blue undergarments or blue satin evening heels. And, of course, this cocktail will do the trick, too!

2 oz white rum
1 oz blue Curacao
4 oz grapefruit juice
Soda water

Stir the first three ingredients together, and pour over ice into a highball glass. Top with soda water.

RECIPE

Cranberry Kiss

When our Mermaid friend Katy married her love, she kept things simple and elegant. Her specialty cocktail was the "Cranberry Kiss," and we love it!

Fill a fluted glass with champagne. Drop a few cranberries in the glass. Enjoy the perfect kiss to new beginnings!

Delightful Décor. From spectacular-and-swish to cheap-and-chic, a wedding only needs to make the new couple feel special in order to be a success. Flowers, greenery, candles, fabric—anything goes, as long as it reflects the couple. Consider using natural elements found in the outdoors to make a beautiful wedding also eco-chic. For example, consider filling a bird bath with ice and using that as your "bar," or use an old stone wall for the buffet table during a lovely outdoor cocktail hour…whatever elements you can work with at your venue.

One bride and groom "reserved" seats for loved ones who had passed. It was a meaningful tribute during the ceremony. I helped another bride create a "Memory Bar" over the actual bar of her party. She and her groom were already married at City Hall, so we displayed photos from the ceremony for all the guests at their wedding celebration to enjoy.

Fun Favors. With help from the wedding DJ, guests will be able to dance every night away, long after the wedding, with a pre-programmed iPod Shuffle with their name engraved on the back. A special bride and groom send-off? Remind them of their sparkling evening and send them off using actual sparklers. (Bonus: this is a lot cleaner than rice, bird seed, or flower petals!)

Eating should be fun! That's what chef David Lapham tries to share with all his clients. As a personal chef in New York City, he's cooked for a wide range of people, each with distinct culinary preferences. If asked what his favorite foods to prepare are, he'd say themed hors d'oeuvres: "It's the best way to show off one's creativity and a sense of what the event is all about."

Q: What's the best supplement to a party?
A: Great food.

Q: What makes a party a memory for you?
A: What else? The food.

Q: Who are some of your favorite guests or types of guests?
A: I like a group of people who want to have a great time getting to know each other while enjoying the food, music, and ambiance.

Q: What is your favorite thing to do when preparing for an event?
A: I love to make a music mix on my iPod.

Q: What has been your favorite event to attend or host, and why?
A: A Mermaids & Martinis Halloween party. It had all of the right components: themed décor, great food, scary music and personalized activities for all ages.

Q: What is your secret to unwinding when the party is over?
A: A glass of vintage port.

Q: What's your Rule of Fin?
A: Don't take entertaining too seriously. Remember, it's about having fun.

part four:
MERMAIDS & MILK AND COOKIES

chapter seven

Baby Showers

> *"Babies are such a nice way to start people."*
>
> —Don Herold

THERE IS NO GREATER JOY for a Mermaid than finding out that either she or a fellow friend is going to become a Mer-mama. As with every great life moment, a celebration is in order.

Timing is *everything* (I can't emphasize this enough) for baby showers. You don't want to plan the shower too early, before the mama-to-be is showing, or has had an opportunity to find out the baby's gender, if she plans to do so. But you also don't want to wait too long—babies are unpredictable and often come earlier than planned. Plus, you want your pregnant friend to still be comfortable enough to enjoy the shower. Ideally, a baby shower would happen during the seventh or eighth month of pregnancy. And because these showers really do serve a practical purpose (unlike brides, first-time moms rarely have the gear they need to settle into their new lifestyle), make sure the parents-to-be have had an opportunity to register.

Once the registry is in place and the date is set, it's time to start planning a theme!

Gender-based themes are always classic and easy to plan. Our friend Megan was expecting twin baby girls who decided to come into the world really early—at six months. We knew this would be a very emotional and challenging time, but if anyone could handle it with grace and success, it would be Megan! We themed her baby shower "Pink with a Silver Lining." Though the babies were still in the hospital, we celebrated by placing pink balloons tied with silver strings everywhere. Mermaid Jamie found two block letters in "N" (the first initial of both baby girls' names). She stripped them down and painted one silver and one pink. The party favors were bottles of pink nail polish called "Ballerina Slippers" and "Pink Lemonade." Beverages included pink cans of Sofia Coppola champagne paired with pink straws (offer a sparkling mocktail alternative for mamas-to-be), and pink lemonade. For this very girly affair, we used shimmery silver candles and served lots of sweet treats dusted with pink sanding sugar, which sparkles. You can even sprinkle extra sugar on serving trays for more shimmer! Finally, pink and white flowers accompanied by greenery created the perfect centerpiece for this sparkling soiree. Our gift to Megan, since she was so busy traveling back and forth to the hospital each day, was to decorate the twins' nursery to welcome them home. After hours of hunting and gathering, we transformed the twins' room into a whimsical pink garden of fairies and magic owls, for under $500! Mermaid Jamie even found a beautiful hourglass filled with sand, that looked like pink sugar crystals, as a perfect finish to the nursery.

As much fun as it is to create a girly or boyish shower, themes don't have to be based on gender. Fresh and unexpected themes can reflect a particular love of the parents or can be a play on the baby's name. For example, if this mommy Mermaid loves to be spectacular-and-swish, consider a *"Ga Ga for GOLD!"* theme where the invite is done in gold calligraphy: *"We don't think Stefi's baby should grow up with a silver spoon in its mouth. We think the spoon should be GOLD! Go ga ga for gold with us on September 12th and celebrate her bump with a blinged-out bash!"* Serve the food and drinks on brushed gold trays and sprinkle edible gold dust on the cake or desserts. A gift for this Mama is a gold piggy bank where guests can place notes for the baby. As a bonus, this makes a cute and chic accent to any nursery. My friend Stefi actually did incorporate jewels into one of her showers: We all made bracelets and necklaces that were the perfect party favors. Want to go really spec-and-swish? Invite a jeweler whom you love to come with her goods and let the guests choose something to take home. A great game to play is "Celebrity Baby," where you hang celebrity baby photos on the wall and have guests guess which baby matches the celebrity.

When you don't know the baby's gender, a fun theme is "Pickles & Ice Cream." Centerpieces can be glass jars lined with dill pickles that serve as vases for beautiful pink, yellow and blue flowers and greenery. You can also take large waffle cones and use those as containers for flowers or creative centerpieces. The place card holders can be small wafer ice cream cones with name cards inserted into the top of the cones, and, of course, dessert should be an ice cream bar where guests can personalize their own frozen treat. Place pickles into a large jar and ask guests to guess how many pickles are in the jar to win a prize. Sweet *and* salty snacks, such as chocolate-covered pretzels, caramel-covered popcorn, and peanut brittle go well with this theme. Send guests home with a set of silver ice cream scoops, which will serve to remind guests of the party long after it's over.

Another great gender-neutral party theme is "Moons and Stars," which we created for Mermaid Jamie. We thought it would be great to bring in constellation light lamps and put them on the floor where they would sprinkle a beautiful light constellation on the ceiling of the room. We hired an astrologer to give readings to the guests, and the specialty cocktails were Little Stars and the Goodnight Moon— a flute of champagne with "blueberry moons" dropped inside. I ordered cocktail napkins and had them customized with different sayings from nursery rhymes and even pop songs, like Madonna's "Lucky Star." It was a charming, wonderful event. We know Jamie's new baby Charlie loves his giraffe, which came with Charlie's own star (that we actually registered in the solar system) hung around the giraffe's neck.

Remember, not every baby shower has to break the piggy bank. There are many wonderful ways to create an inexpensive and meaningful baby shower. One cheap-and-chic option is to create a sentimental soiree by asking guests to email you a baby picture of themselves prior to the event. Print these out and use them as place cards. Every guest will know *exactly* where he or she is sitting (we hope!). At each seat, place a white onesie or a bib and a fabric marker. Guests can personalize each onesie or bib with well wishes, advice, or a favorite quote. The new baby will be living in love for weeks to come! If onesies and bibs are too expensive, purchase a pack of diapers instead. The new mom will actually look forward to changing her baby's diaper if she gets to read sentiments from her friends every time!

Another cheap-and-chic idea is to host a potluck dinner shower where guests are asked to provide their favorite dish along with the recipe on a recipe card. In the end, the Mer-Mama will have an entire recipe book filled with dishes that are personal to her and her friends. Decorations can consist of baby bottle centerpieces filled with flowers and surrounded by inexpensive baby gear (think baby books, rattles, and little silver baby spoons). For dessert, serve cupcakes adorned with pacifiers on the tops. Once the party is over, mom can reuse the bottles and pacifiers. Who doesn't love décor that is eco-friendly and thematic?

Here are four ways to create a fabulous and meaningful baby shower:

Invitation Idea. Send each guest a personalized invitation with their birthday and zodiac sign's meaning. Include a game to guess what the baby's birthday and time of birth will be and ask guests to bring it to the shower. Display the answers at the shower, and email the winner's name to everyone once the baby is born!

Signature Cocktail. Because you don't want the mama to miss out on all the fun, bright and fruity martinis and mimosas can instantly be turned into Mom-osas and Mom-tini mocktails by replacing alcohol with sparkling water.

Delightful Décor. Make it mini! My friend Samantha served "baby" food at her party. From baby shrimp on skewers, shot glasses of gazpacho, to mini personal pizzas, mini quesadillas, mini sliders, mini mac & cheeses in tiny white ramekins, and bite-sized cupcakes, everything was miniature and just adorable. It really added to the theme of her baby shower, which was held in a 19th century, red brick schoolhouse where miniature blackboards served as guests' place cards, and the flower arrangements were mini bud vases with miniature roses. She sent guests away with gourmet red candy apples.

Fun Favors. Go with your theme! If it was

> ### RULE OF FIN:
> *Make sure the Mer-mama has a comfortable chair close by and a mocktail in her hand at all times. Also, assign a couple of Mermaids to help her unwrap gifts and get around the room to say hello to everyone. It could be her last social outing for a while!*

Go Ga Ga for Gold
    champagne or prosecco
    (for a "golden" glow!)
    blueberries
    semi-sweet chocolate morsels
    edible gold dust

Melt the chocolate in the microwave or in a double boiler. Roll blueberries (you'll want to have three or four for each drink) in the chocolate and then roll them in the edible gold dust. Place the chocolate and gold covered blueberries on a cookie sheet to chill in the refrigerator for thirty minutes. Rim the champagne glass with edible gold. Pour champagne in fluted glasses and drop a few gold blueberries into each glass.

Pickles & Ice Cream
(Makes one pitcher, serves 4-6)
    1/2 cup Irish cream liqueur
    1/4 cup chocolate vodka
    1 pint coffee ice cream
    1 banana, sliced and frozen
    2 T chocolate syrup
    chocolate chips

Add all of the ingredients (except the chocolate chips) to a blender and blend on high until smooth, about 2-3 minutes. Pour into glasses. Garnish by sprinkling 2-4 minature chocolate chips on the top of drink.

The Little Star
    passion fruit juice
    sparkling water
    star fruit

Pour sparkling water into a martini glass. Top with passion fruit juice. Stir. Garnish with a star fruit.

"Pickles & Ice Cream," send guests away with a cute ice cream scoop or a jar of gourmet sundae toppings. Or, go back to the tried-and-true idea that a favor should not be something you stick in a junk drawer—consider sending guests away with a bottle of great wine or a package of artisanal snacks, especially if it's a "Jack & Jill" shower—one that hosts the mommy-to-be *and* daddy-to-be's friends.

Nashville-based event planner and founder of Reveal Event Style, Jennifer Edwards Milam tells us what turns a party to a memory for her!

Q: What's the best supplement to a party?
A: The elements of surprise and delight! As an event designer, I note the one detail that is of most importance to the client and knock that out grandly. Everything else should be designed to direct our focus back to the feature element.

Q: Who are some of your favorite guests or types of guests?
A: Well, there are the funny guests, the pouty guests, the bossy guests, the "hit the bar first" guests, the "dance with all the old women" guests, the "dance with all the young girls" guests, the long-winded toasters, the inquisitive guests, the guests who want to "help," the guests who dance on everything but the dance floor, the guests who want to sing with the band, the critical guests, the guests you just cannot please, the guests who come to entertain and be entertained, and the first guests on the dance floor who have to be sent away screaming, "Do we have to leave??!!" How do you not love them all? They make the party!

Q: What is your favorite thing to do when preparing for an event?
A: I get a thrill writing the event story. It's a mini script for the event that describes in cinematic-poetic detail the feelings, the visual treats, and experience that the hosts and their guests will enjoy.

Q: What has been your favorite event to attend or host, and why?
A: My favorite event that I have attended? My wedding.

Q: What makes a party a memory for you?
A: When I don't want to be anywhere but in the moment at this party. Everyone is dancing, the lighting is gorgeous, the music is elevating, we are all celebrating life, and I'm smiling so much my face hurts!

Q: What's your Rule of Fin?
A: Make them feel like stars tonight!

Q: What is your secret to unwinding when the party is over?
A: It's no secret. Wine.

chapter eight

Celebrate Your Littles

WHEN A LITTLE MER-BABY enters the world all bright and beautiful it is indeed a cause for celebration; from traditional christenings and baby dedications to a fifth birthday bash, Mermaids always want to capture these priceless moments. For your little guest of honor, the party should be as much about him or her as the other littles in attendance. How great would it be if the party could not only be the birthday little's best childhood memory, but also one of the little guest's too?

There are many ways to celebrate our littles. From their first day of school to their first lost tooth—there is always something to celebrate. Here are a few ways to really celebrate your littles.

Invitation Idea. Send customized, oversized wooden clothespins "holding" invites to anything related to a baby. For a little kid's party, send out a copy of a fairytale book

RULE OF FIN:

Remember, each time a child is born the world lights up with new possibilites. Think of this as you brainstorm ways to celebrate this new little person's entry into the world.

cover with your little one's picture on the cover, or create customized books that feature your little and their friends as main characters in the story and write the invitation party details on the inside cover. Another invitation idea is to send out Whirly Pops and use edible food markers to write the party details on the back of the lollipops.

Blessing of the Baby

This is an event where parents host a gathering to perform a non-religious but spiritual and personal ceremony after the birth of their baby. This isn't a baby shower per se, but just a great way to encapsulate everyone's well wishes, while still maintaining the parents' traditions. Think of it as a little welcome party that friends and family can share. Consider hosting one, and ask guests to frame their personalized blessing (including translations if needed!) from their own backgrounds, heritages, and traditions. This kind of event is less about the formal and all about spending a day together to greet the new baby and share in the love.

RECIPE BOX

Chocolate Milk
   2 oz vodka
   1 oz Godiva chocolate liqueur
   light cream
Pour the vodka and coffee liqueur over ice cubes in an old-fashioned glass. Top with light cream, and serve with a warm chocolate chip cookie.

Kiddie Version: Mix Hershey's syrup in milk and serve in chilled glasses with chocolate chip cookies for dipping.

Signature Cocktail. Shirley Temples (some made with vodka and some without) and Bailey's "Chocolate Milk" (with a side of warm chocolate chip cookies as a dipping option!) make enjoyable libations for both grown-ups and kids.

Delightful Décor. Place different types of brightly colored candies in large jars and vases and use these as centerpieces. Guests will find themselves nibbling away on centerpieces that are tasty to both the eye *and* palette!

Fun Favors. Choose favors that reflect the nature of the event or your little's personal

Mermaid Memory
Mermaid Jamie

My favorite book for a very long time was *Teddy Bear Picnic*. Because I was so obsessed with it, the obvious thing for my mom to do was theme my next birthday party around the book. She laid out a huge blanket in our living room, asked all of my friends to bring their favorite stuffed animal, and had a picnic for all of us, including all of the stuffed animals she could find in the house! There were the usual birthday games, but I remember this being my best birthday party ever. And all because of a simple teddy bear.

style. For instance, if your little loves the story "Alice in Wonderland," consider sending guests home with small teapots and hand-made tea bag tags with personalized messages written on each one. You can find inexpensive favors at stores like Target, or you can browse sites like Etsy to find beautiful, handmade items.

chapter nine

Kid-Hosted Parties

"When adult parties start to get old, hang with the younger set for a day—they really know how to party!"

—Mermaid Jamie

MERMAIDS ARE A WHIMSICAL and youthful bunch, and we relate well to children because kids *really* know how to party. Kids are creative, uninhibited, and without cynicism, and it doesn't take much for them to get their fun on! Kids arrive at a get-together and, like honing devices, they seem to automatically know what the most fun thing to do is. It may not be the things you think they would be drawn to, either. You've heard of the parents who spend hundreds of dollars on a custom tent for their backyard, hire two clowns, three ponies, and a juggler, and all the kids want to do is play with the sprinkler and lawn hose. Go ahead and swim along with it! Have a stack of dry towels ready, and remember, this is *their* party.

Allowing Mer-kids to host their own parties is a great way to teach kids how to socially interact, learn about the likes and dislikes of others, share, and use their imagination. It allows kids to have responsibility in a fun and exciting way—the party will be something that kids can take ownership of and feel good about, and, with a little luck, parents can enjoy it, too.

I asked some of my favorite littles what their dream party would be if they could have anything they wanted! And, here is what they said:

Valentina, age 6: "Um, there would be dancing, singing, karaoke, and a band at a pool. There would be juice boxes and root beer, and everyone would arrive in a limo. And, the best part would be hanging out with my friends."

Blake, age 4: "There would be lots of balloons, pizza, cupcakes, and lots of more presents."

Hannah, age 7: "I would like to have an animal party. And, parties are very fun because there are lots of children that we know there."

Madison, age 7: "I'd like to have a party pretending we were in India. Parties can be very loud and sometimes they hurt my ears but I still have fun because I am a kid. I like all of the games and music."

Victor, age 6: "I would like a giant Captain Jack Sparrow LEGO on top of my cake."

Zander, age 3: "Cupcakes."

Sienna, age 8: "I'd want a Justin Beiber party! My favorite thing at a party is to break open the piñata. And, eating cake!"

Faye, age 4: "My dream party is to invite all of the Disney princesses. And, my favorite part of a party is eating the cake."

Michaela, age 3: "I would like to have a tea party. And I would love dressing up in Mommy's pretty clothes."

Jason, age 6: "It would be a sports-themed party with many different sports stations playing on televisions during the party. The sports would be the best part for sure."

To start co-planning a kid-hosted party with your little, ask your child what his or her favorite thing to do with friends is. You might be surprised at how simple your child's answer is.

Mermaid Memory
Mermaid Hilary

I remember being about six or seven years old when my teachers told my parents during a parent-teacher meeting that I had completely taken over recess on the playground by recreating episodes from reruns I had seen of the television show *Happy Days*. I went to an all-girls school at the time, so there were some interesting casting choices (although I do recall inviting pals into my "office" which doubled as the see-saw), but our imaginations were so big and beautiful then, and we were allowed to be free. Do you remember a time when you were uninhibited and free? Channel the creativity of that time whenever you can.

You don't need a spectacular-and-swish budget to help your kids throw a fabulous party. Just focus on what things your kid and his or her friends enjoy, and build your party around those ideas. Along the way you can throw in cheap-and-chic or spectacular-and-swish ideas. For example, one kid-hosted party that would be a big hit for the Wii set is a Wednesday night "Wii and Waffles" party. Your little

Mermaid or Merman could invite his or her friends over for a do-it-yourself Belgian waffle bar and a night full of active Wii games. Keep it simple or swish it up by organizing Wii tournaments and offering prizes of different Wii games to the winners.

A great party for a true girly girl is a tea-and-tiara day, where she can gather with her friends for some tea and cookies. Place tiaras at each place setting and watch as your daughter and her friends transform into princesses. Want to add a spectacular-and-swish touch? Purchase expandable kiddie costume cocktail rings as napkin rings (a great party favor, too!) and feature a beautiful multicolored macaron tower in the middle of the table.

I love the idea of a "Tortoise and the Hare" party. Stock up on chocolate bunnies at Easter and freeze them so that you can host this party any time of year. Get little guests hopping with rabbit ears and toy bunny noses. Someone can read the fable of the "Tortoise and the Hare" at the beginning of the event. To dress your table—use tortoise shell dishes and flatware, put little faux white "rabbit fur" stoles (that you can get on eBay) on the back of the little girls' chairs (and don't forget to tell them they are fake!) Then host games for "turtles" and "rabbits," like relay races and fast-paced games for "rabbits," and arts & crafts or a laid back movie for the "turtles."

When my little friend Valentina was celebrating a birthday, she knew exactly how she wanted to host her party! She asked her mom if she could rent a limousine for the night and pick up eight of her best girlfriends to go for a ride together. Valentina then asked her little girl-friends what their favorite song was, which led to the best part of this event. Each time the limousine stopped at one of the houses, the driver rolled out a pink carpet to greet each one and blared their favorite song on the radio as they walked down the carpet to the limo. The girls loved rolling "celebrity-style" to the local park for cake and ice cream and taking home CD's with all of their favorite songs. During the event, Valentina's family really got into the theme—her mom wore a VIP-style badge that said "Val's Momager," her aunt's badge read "Val's Aunt-ourage," and her dad was on photography duty all day, so his read "Papa-razzi."

*fin*Tastic Idea: This idea is inspired by a restaurant near Paris, France. Want to create a table topper that is a visual feast for the eyes and also makes for a fun party favor? Cover a table with a white tablecloth and then place white saucer-sized or salad plates flush with one another all over. Fill each plate with a different type of candy. The more variety in shape and color you have, the prettier the display. Think Hershey's Kisses, Lemon Drops, Red Hots, caramels, etc. Keep some paper bags nearby. Children will flock to the candy table and be thrilled to learn that they get to create their own candy assortment as a party favor.

Kid-hosted parties are even more fun when they incorporate a family tradition, or mark a big event. A friend of mine loved appetizers growing up, so much that his mom made every Tuesday night "Appetizer Tuesday" at their home where a selection of appetizers were served instead of dinner. A cute tradition like this could inspire any kid to want to host an appetizer party for their friends. Another friend told me that every year on her birthday, her mom would come into her bedroom with a birthday cake for breakfast. Traditions are fun for families, and when incorporated into a party, it gives kids consistency mixed with a little creative whimsy.

Creative themes can also help to transform the ordinary into something extraordinary. Invite a local petting zoo to your home, ask guests to dress in khaki pants and white shirts, pass out straw hats when guests arrive, and watch as your backyard is transformed into a "Swanky Safari." Your littles will love sipping "bug juice" boxes while inspecting the animals with plastic binoculars.

To host a "Summer Camp" themed overnight party, set up your yard by building teepees decorated with different fabrics and stocked with flashlights, snacks and sleeping bags. Set up an archery station and host an arts and crafts table. As the sun goes down, play "Catch the Lightning Bugs," a game I loved to play with my cousins growing up. Pass out emptied coffee cans to the kids (to catch the bugs) and have pre-poked holes on the plastic lid covers. As the night goes on, build a campfire for storytelling and pass out "Sky Maps" to help the kids navigate the Big Dipper, Little Bear, and other constellations. Place lots of LED lanterns around your yard overnight so you can keep an eye on the action (once in a while!) from the house.

Build Your Own Teepee

Teepees are one of the oldest Native American traditions, and they're also a cool addition to any yard, party, or even a room! Learning how to fashion a homemade teepee may not be as difficult as you think. You just need the right materials and a little time . . . and don't forget to add your own Mermaid twist—use fun, printed fabrics that you love, or old vintage sheets or tablecloths.

A quick and easy way to make a teepee is to look no further than your yard and your linen closet. Start with eight poles each about eight feet long. Bamboo or wooden poles work great, or if you live where you can easily collect strong branches, eight branches will work great, too. Ask your kids to help tie them together in a bundle at one end with thick twine or rope. Make sure to tie this very tight, as this will support the top of the teepee.

Pull out the ends of the poles that are not bound together to resemble "spider legs" spread out. Push the poles into the dirt to anchor them to the ground. Once the frame is built and anchored, toss a sheet (or sheets), fabric, or a tablecloth over the poles or branches to form the walls of the teepee. Secure the top of the sheet(s) to the frame with some string. Next, stake down the base of the sheet(s) to keep it secure. Wooden clothespins make convenient stakes when you cut small slits into the bottom of the fabric. Cut a large garbage bag and lay this down to make the floor of the teepee. Then, place a nice blanket or quilt on top of the garbage bag. Add some cushioned floor pillows, a stack of flashlights and snacks and you have a great addition to your party.

Now, it's teepee time!

Whatever the event may be, and whether it is spectacular-and-swish or cheap-and-chic, with a little imagination and help from you, your child will be hosting a fabulous party for his or her friends. Just remember to let your kid take the lead on creating the party ideas. This is, after all, their party!

The Truck Stops Here

One thing that is always a surefire hit at any kid party (and at most grown-up parties, too) is the rental of a vendor's "themed" truck. I once attended a wonderful benefit at the Central Park Boathouse in NYC. The party featured a big band and martini bar. But, best of all, at the end of this idyllic summer evening, guests indulged their sweet tooth at the Krispy Kreme truck parked in front of the Boathouse. Guests loved eating those sweet treats while on an open-air trolley that was hired to drive us out of the park and onto Fifth Avenue. And what a sight for the taxis waiting on Fifth Avenue to suddenly witness one hundred New Yorkers waving for a cab as they tumbled into the street in formal attire and carrying donuts! Some Mermaid friends attended an event overlooking the Bristol, Rhode Island Harbor, where the party only got tastier once the "Spike Specialty Hot Dogs" truck arrived.

Kids love the idea of a "surprise special guest" like this at their event. From ice cream trucks to classic New York pretzels, roasted nuts to

RULE OF FIN:
Give your littles guidelines to follow, but let them be creative and free to plan the party of the year!

taco trucks, Middle Eastern gyros to Chicago-style pizza, healthy smoothies to a sweets truck, there are many options out there to make each event extraordinary. I even recently saw a traveling truck serving lunch-time lobster specials!

Here are four ways you can help your kid create a fabulous event for his or her friends:

Invitation Idea. To make this an event your child can take ownership of, start with the invitation. Ask your little to come up with a theme, and, using arts and crafts, have them create and personalize the invitations for each of their friends. Other ideas include mocking up movie or concert tickets on the computer for a simple and fun way to invite the gang over for a karaoke-inspired shindig or movie night. Guitar picks can easily be personalized through online websites, send them out with the details for a Guitar Hero bash.

Signature Cocktail. Create a milkshake bar where kids can customize their own classic frothy drink. Offer a selection of ice creams and toppings, including fruit, whipped cream, nuts, and chocolate. Or, create fruity, frozen mocktails with extravagant garnishes and mini umbrellas for instant cool.

Delightful Décor. Sometimes the simplest ideas can make the biggest impact. Stimulate the imagination with just a few key ingredients for your theme. For instance, if you're searching for the perfect decorations to turn your backyard into an art studio—head to the hardware store for drop cloths, gallons of paint, and paint brushes; then, set up a long canvas and mini stools (or overturned paint buckets) for the kids to sit on while they paint their masterpieces.

Fun Favors. Purchase some inexpensive disposable cameras and let each guest play "paparazzi" for the night. If you want to be a little more spectacular-and-swish, rent a red carpet, a velvet rope and photo booth, then pick up some great "dress-up" props for the kids to use while they have their photos taken.

finTastic Idea:
Mermaids & Martinis planned an event at a well-known nightclub in NYC. We had a step & repeat customized with a "Z" logo created for the celebrated guest whose first name was Zev. The kids and adults loved having their photos taken in front posing on a red carpet just like a Hollywood premiere.

Aisling McDonagh works at Buzz Media and can be found buzzing around town to parties each week. Entertaining clients has been her livelihood for years, but she loves gathering with friends and family. Here she shares some of her tips for throwing a great party.

Q: What's the best supplement to a party?
A: Depends on the party. If I'm having people over for a cocktail party, a fully stocked bar and great music are musts. If they're coming for a dinner party, then it's food and beverage. I pull out all the stops and prep for two days! I don't kill myself over décor, but I do make an effort to get fresh flowers and break out my entertaining ware (vases, platters, etc).

Q: Who are some of your favorite guests or types of guests? A: I like a good mix of people at my parties, and fortunately my friends tend to reflect various parts of my personality: funny, quiet, jocks, yogis, bankers, artists, from the US, and from abroad. This eclectic mix of people makes for great conversations!

Q: What is your favorite thing to do when preparing for an event? A: Oh dear, WHAT AM I GOING TO WEAR?! Sounds silly, but it is true. The one thing I get excited about for an event is my outfit. Oh, and the playlist! You need a solid mix of good tunes.

chapter ten

New Year Celebrations

"Cheers to a new year and another chance for us to get it right."—**Oprah Winfrey**

REMEMBER THE MILLENNIUM? The fear of Y2K, and the possibility that the world was about to end? The end of any year is a time of reflection and letting go, and also of welcoming the new.

For me, the turn of the millennium year from 1999 to 2000 seemed like doomsday in more ways than one: I was just out of college and new to the big city life, recovering from a break-up, in the middle of changing jobs, and the world was scheduled to come to an end at the stroke of midnight? Well, with the way I was feeling, good riddance! So, after a night of cocktails, and only a little convincing from my Mermaid friends, the next thing I knew I was flying across the world to the Philippines to attend a New Year's Eve gala and travel with friends. And of course, just as the world kept going after the stroke of midnight, so did I. Mermaids love to embrace change and challenges, and what better time to toast the journey of the past and embrace challenge and change than at the dawn of a new year?

New Year's Eve

A New Year's Eve party is your opportunity to send off the previous year with a bang. Host a get-together with friends by transforming your home into a faraway landscape, or travel through time to a different era. Remember, regardless of the theme, it's about surrounding yourself with close friends and family. Offer guests a mixed selection of foods and drinks that represent different countries, then ring in the New Year multiple times throughout the night by celebrating each time the clock strikes midnight around the world. New Year's Eve is a night when even the most conservative female may wear a dress that's a few inches shorter, a lipstick a few shades brighter, and her hair done up in a red-carpet formal up-do.

Here are a few ways to create an unforgettable New Year's Eve:

Invitation Idea. Invite and entice guests using metallic, silvery stationary asking, *"Who will you kiss at midnight?"* Want to go cheap-and-chic? Buy simple stationary and invest in a fire-engine red lipstick. Kiss each invite on the bottom before you seal and send.

Signature Cocktail. Serve "Countdown Cocktails" by buying a bunch of cheap-and-chic plastic stopwatches, setting the alarms for midnight, and strapping them around the stems of your guests' glasses. You can dress up some of the stopwatches by glueing jewels or beads on them, whatever you like! Countdown Cocktails look great next to "Pop-the-Cork" placecard holders at a sit-down dinner. You can make these place card holders by slicing an incision into the top of a champagne cork and inserting the place card in the incision. Another idea is to serve a different signature cocktail at the start of each hour during your NYE party—all night long.

Delightful Décor. A hostess could put out "Resolutions Boards"—chalkboards and color-ful chalk so that guests can jot down "What I will kiss goodbye" and "What I can't wait to greet with a kiss!" I also love using branches as décor. You can buy these at flower shops, or, if

you live near a lot of trees, you can collect your own. Spray-paint them gold, red, silver, or any color you want! Go to a fabric or craft store

and buy a bunch of colored glass beads and crystals. Use ribbons to hang these beads from the branches. One last idea for festive décor (and this one doubles as a game of sorts) is inspired by Mermaid Jamie. For one party we hosted recently, Mermaid Jamie found unpainted ceramic piggy banks, and we decorated them with jewels. We called them our "Prosperity Pigs" and sprinkled them around the party venue so that guests could drop little notes, well wishes, or even cash inside. At the end of the night, these make great raffle prizes!

Fun Favors: Pack gift bags for guests that include a beautifully bound journal and a great writing pen. This will encourage guests to write down their resolutions. Also, consider sending guests home with Joss paper, which is paper that burns really easily. Tell guests to use the paper to do a "release" ceremony at home by writing down that which they want to release in the new year, and then burn the paper. After all, before you can welcome the new, you have to release the old!

New Year's Day

Nothing starts a new year off right like a little rest and relaxation. Why not invite your best friends over to celebrate New Year's Day with a spa brunch? You can go spectacular-and-swish and treat your friends to some pampering at their favorite spa, or be cheap-and-chic and do it yourself at home! Assign guests to bring at least one product and one food item. As the lovely Kym Douglas and Cindy Pearlman write in their book, *The Beauty Cookbook*, forget about break-the-bank treatments at your local spa. You can achieve the same results in your

own home by just looking in your pantry, fridge, and your medicine cabinet. Set up a buffet of these products and let guests get creative. At-home recipes for spa concoctions from the cupboards are a fabulous and in-expensive way to really pamper yourself. You can find recipes online or in books like Kym's. If you want, send your guests home with a little party favor, purchase small tubs or containers and let each guest pack up some of the con-coctions to use at home.

> **RULE OF FIN:**
> *Kick off the new year surrounded only by people who lift you up, not those who bring you down. It's the perfect time of year to commit to a new philosophy: "Out with the old and in with the new."*

Here are some other fun New Year's Day party ideas:

Recharge after the Revel. The holidays were crazy, right? If you weren't hosting, you were reveling. Take a day to recharge with friends. Invite a masseuse and a manicurist to come to your house and give guests foot and neck mas-sages, and pedicures and manicures. Set your iPod to a great playlist of calming "spa" music and enjoy the beauty of not doing much.

Unpack-the-Pounds Party. All of those holiday parties were a blast, but they may have tipped the scale in the wrong direction! If you live where the weather is warm, host an exercise class on your lawn or deck, and serve up spa cuisine and smoothies. If it's cold in your part of the world on January 1st, host a yoga, Pilates, or other indoor exercise class. Serve healthy mocktails, hire a nutritionist (or ask a nutri-tionist friend) to do a session with the group on healthy grocery shopping and cooking, and send guests home with a yoga mat or a healthy cookbook.

Meditation Station. Invite friends over to experience something new and healing on New Year's Day by hosting a meditation party. Light a lot of candles, and have comfy blankets or meditation pillows on hand for guests to sit and lay down. Play soothing music and serve a variety of hot teas and sparkling waters. You could even hire an energy healer, acupunctur-ist, or meditation guide to come and lead a session. At the end of the party, set a group intention (which is always more successful than an individual intention) to start the new year off with a bang, together.

Movie Marathon Get-Together. After a long night of partying, inviting friends over in their comfiest clothes to lay about and watch a marathon of light, rom-com movies is the perfect way to relax. Prepare my truffle salt popcorn (simply sprinkle truffle salt and a drizzle of truffle oil over fresh popped corn and shake the paper bag until kernels are seasoned well—dee-lish!) or visit the "Parties in a Pinch" section to create a snack tray or a meal. With this party, less is more. You deserve to be on the couch!

I asked my friend Gabby Bernstein, author of *Add More ~Ing to your Life* and *Spirit Junkies* to share her tips on welcoming your best year yet. Here are her three tips to bringing in a happier and healthier New Year:

Step One: Take Inventory. Become conscious of the fear-based behaviors you have held onto in the past. Make a commitment to release these behaviors in the new year. You can begin this commitment with thirty days of prayer. Pray daily: "I am willing to release my fears, and I am ready to see things differently." This intention will prepare you energetically and help you stay committed to change. By acknowledging this desire daily, you sign a contract with the Universe that you *are* ready for change.

Step Two: Gratitude is the Attitude. Practicing gratitude unleashes the loving presence within you. Rather than beginning a new year with feelings of doubt, choose to focus on the good stuff! Make a gratitude list and read it every night for a week. Paying attention to what you're grateful for takes the focus off of what you don't have and refocuses you onto what is real.

Step Three: Practice the F Word. I'm not talking about that F word. This new year, practice forgiveness. Make a list of those people you have been unwilling to forgive. Become clear about how you have been contributing to the negativity, and then make the commitment to release it. Write in your journal, "I am willing to forgive this person and I welcome the guidance to do so." Then sit back and witness the miracles.

This new year, toast your very own unique journey. I used to beat myself up every eve of every new year about all the things I could have or should have done differently, but as I got into my Mermaid frame of mind, I learned to take some time to really reflect.

RECIPE BOX

The Countdown Cocktail
    2 oz Citron vodka
    2 oz triple sec
    1 oz lemon or lime juice (fresh)
    top with cranberry juice

Shake all four ingredients together and pour into a martini glasss. Tie a mini stop-watch, with the alarm set to midnight, around the base of each glass.

Rejuvenation-Tini
    1/2 oz Grand Marnier
    2 oz lemon flavored vodka
    (or infuse your own vodka with lemon)
    5 oz chilled green tea
Combine ingredients in a martini shaker

with ice, and shake until chilled. Pour into a martini glass. Rim the glass with lime juice and crushed ginger. Garnish with a gingered lime slice.

A Champagne Bar: Invest in some great bottles of bubbly in a wide variety of sparkle: Rosé, French, California Sparkling, and Italian Prosecco. Also include some bubbly garnishes, like little dishes of blueberries, cranberries, raspberries, strawberries, dark chocolate pieces, and more! You can also buy great "essences" like violet and rose, and add a splash into a glass of champagne for great effect and taste.

And when I did, I realized I had accomplished quite a bit. We all have. We deserve to take a breath and acknowledge the strides of the year, so why not get together with a few close friends and host a party to celebrate all the good that came to you this year?

Honor the place that is exactly where you are.

Mermaid Sarah Tallman is the founder and owner of Sarah Tallman Design, an interior- and floral-design firm. Sarah loves to design, create, and develop in all of the areas she loves—homes, parties, flowers, and fragrance. She has worked on multiple *Mermaids & Martinis* events, and she always gets rave reviews! Here she shares some of her thoughts on entertaining:

Q: What's the best supplement to a party?
A: Beautiful bouquets of fragrant flowers to set the stage.

Q: Who are some of your favorite guests or types of guests?
A: I love having a broad spectrum—the intellectuals, the characters, the reserved, the witty. I think it's important to have a good mix of personalities . . . it's all about the depth. And if it's a sit-down dinner, you will want to seat them accordingly.

Q: What is your favorite thing to do when preparing for an event?
A: I am a flower girl, so of course I love to arrange flowers. My favorite time is when I get to put the arrangements together in the actual event space—this helps because then you're able to work with the other elements of the party.

Q: What has been your favorite event to attend or host, and why?
A: I loved an intimate wedding I attended on an estate in Westchester. The ceremony was held under a tree in a clear tent so you could see the stars. The tables were long and filled with herbed topiaries, olive oil bottles, bread baskets, and plates of antipasto. The feeling was magical.

Q: What makes a party a memory for you?
A: A specific feeling I get as I walk in and out of the door. It's all about the atmosphere—directing my senses. I want to enjoy myself and be able to let my guard down, but I also want to be taken on a journey from start to finish.

Q: What is your secret to unwinding when the party is over?
A: I like to grab a quick bite with a friend to unwind. Then, sleep!

Q: What's your Rule of Fin?
A: Formal is great. Stuffy, not so great.

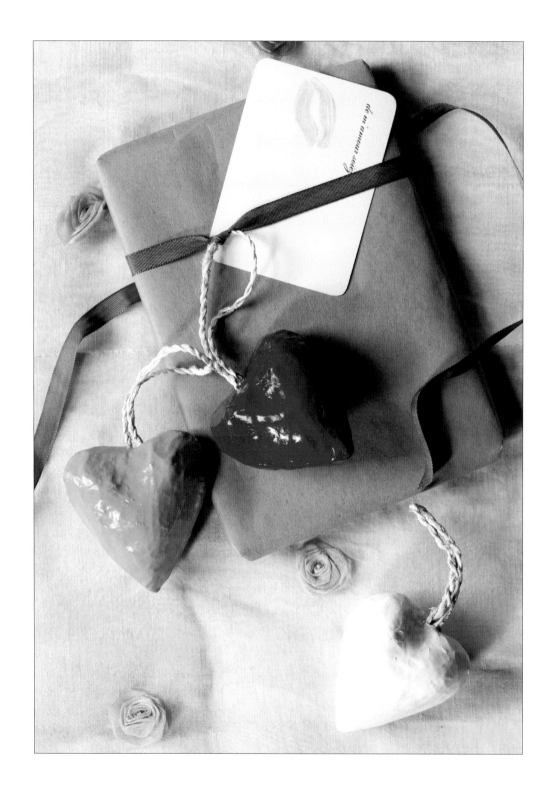

chapter eleven

Valentine's Day

> *"Love yourself, first, and everything else falls in line. You really have to love yourself to get anything done in this world."*
>
> **—Lucille Ball**

LOVE. OH, THE BEAUTY OF IT. And oh, the heartbreak of it! Mermaids have the ability to rise to the surface even in love's stormy waters, but sometimes we need the help of our "rocks" (family and friends) to keep us steady in the turbulent waves. That's why a holiday like Valentine's Day should be celebrated not only by romantically involved couples but also by singles who want to celebrate the people they love. It's an annual opportunity to say, "I love you. Thank you for loving me back."

My friend Kirsten knows all about this. One year before Valentine's Day, she went through a rough patch after a rocky relationship. She decided to "swim up" from her low place and throw a party. It was themed "Out of the Rabbit Hole." Her cake

---

Mermaid Memory
Mermaid Michele, Hilary's Mom

When Hilary was two years old, I took her shopping at a department store in Connecticut. Desi Arnaz just happened to be doing a promotional appearance that day. Distraught, Hilary walked right up to Desi and asked "But, where is Lucy?"

---

was baked in the shape a large rabbit face and her friends wore bunny ears throughout the night. It was her way of thanking all of her friends for sticking by her during a hard time.

If you and your Mermaids are single, invite everyone to a "Cupid (on) Strike Party." You might think Cupid's on strike, but you never know when (or where) he will strike! My friends and I once celebrated Valentine's Day at a dinner party in Paris and the table was a mix of couples and singles. We mixed up the seating chart (the Rule of Fin is to break apart couples and alternate men and women) and placed little place cards that said "I Heart Scott," "I Heart Jen," etc., at everyone's seat. We drank bottles of Rosé champagne in honor of the day and enjoyed a long meal full of laughter and telling old stories. My friend Alethea, who is a professional opera singer, capped off that dinner with a private concert for us!

Another fun way to celebrate Valentine's Day is to host an Elizabeth Taylor, themed cocktail party. I love the idea of this one because the beautiful Liz always had the remarkable ability to bounce back from adversity, and she knew how to reinvent herself after a heartbreak. She always moved on—married eight times to seven husbands! Ok, so that is a little extreme, and I personally don't believe in the "Tarzan School of Love" when it comes to romantic relationships—i.e., *grabbing onto the next vine before you've let go of the one you're holding!* (Overlapping is for guppies, right?) But, who can't applaud Liz for her amazing ability to bounce back—the idea being that if you fall down, don't stay there too long; swim right back up and think about what's next. It can be exciting to reinvent yourself after a heartbreak. For the "Elizabeth Taylor" party, invite female guests to wear their flashiest jewels and dresses, and invite guys to emulate their favorite iconic leading man. (For inspiration, just think of Liz's husbands. And, Richard Burton was the one she married twice.) You could even extend this party theme to all of Hollywood and ask guests to arrive dressed as their most beloved and iconic leading lady, leading man, or leading couple—Marilyn Monroe, Ginger and Fred, Lauren and Bogie, Angelina and Brad, Elvis Presley, the possibilities are endless. Hang vintage photos from Hollywood love stories around the venue to set the mood. Pick a room in your home to try and recreate Elvis's infamous "Jungle Room" and who knows what could happen!

If you are blessed by Cupid on this day, love every minute of it! For a romantic rendezvous with your mate, create a night to remember. You can go spectacular-and-swish by having a dinner for two catered at home. Or, impress your mate and stay cheap-and-chic by looking up recipes from your favorite chefs and preparing dinner yourself. Anything goes! For dessert, consider a candle in a chocolate cupcake. For Valentine's Day, simple is better. You want to focus on each other and nothing else.

> **RULE OF FIN:**
> *Entertain with love. Whether you are part of a couple or are single, remind yourself that there are only three things that last: faith, hope and love. And LOVE is the most important.*

Here are four ways to make your next Valentine's Day celebration memorable.

Invitation Idea. Send an old fashioned, handmade Valentine to your sweetheart. Some red construction paper and a lace doily are all you need to create this look. Partying with your friends? Evite.com and Paperlesspost.com are great sites for electronic invitations. For the singles, try sending an invite with this wording: "Woody Allen once said, 'Ninety percent of luck in life is just showing up!' You never know who you might meet so RSVP, YES!"

Signature Cocktail. For your romantic rendezvous, consider a great bottle of wine. Want to create your very own "wine cellar" in a cheap-and-chic way? My friend Tracy works for *Food & Wine* magazine, and she turned me on to their "Wine of the Month" club. It truly is affordable, and every season I look forward to my box with six amazing bottles of wine. You could open your inaugural bottle on Valentine's Day. Then, every time you drink another bottle, you and your sweetie will remember this special day. For a party with your friends, consider serving "Love Potions," which are what you can call any fun cocktail that's red or pink. Use wild hibiscus garnishes to enhance these great cocktails, and consider making bow-and-arrow swizzle sticks for your friends. This can easily be made with colored cocktail swords; pierce them through small gummy hearts. Finally, bowls of conversation hearts always look cute on a tabletop.

RECIPE BOX

Love Potion
2 oz white tequila
2 oz PAMA liqueur
or pomegranate juice
1 oz triple sec
1 1/2 oz simple syrup
lemon juice
wild hibiscus garnish

Pour all ingredients into a shaker and shake well with ice. Strain into a chilled martini glass. Garnish with a wild hibiscus flower.

Cupid's Cocktail: This one is dreamy and will lull you into a lovely state of mind. Mix equal parts gin, St. Germain Elderflower liqueur, lemon juice. Add muddled wild cherries—yum!

Delightful Décor. Table for two! Create a personalized restaurant-style menu filled with all of your favorite homemade dishes, or, if you can, recreate your first date menu. Write the menu bistro-style on your chalkboard or print out a lovely menu on parchment-style paper. Get a bunch of throw pillows and eat dinner on the floor for a cozy picnic. Or, dress your table to the hilt with flowers, candles, fine china, silver, and crystal, and recreate the five-star restaurant look.

"A bit of fragrance always clings to the hand that gives roses." **—Chinese Proverb**

Fun Favors. For a Valentine's Day party with your friends, great, cheap-and-chic favors are conversation heart candies. For your love, create a memory box. Take a traditional Valentine's Day chocolate box (emptied of chocolates) and fill it with all the little things you love about your Valentine—mementos, "inside" jokes, a meaningful letter, and photos. The best gift of all for friends or your love? Time spent together.

If you want to create an inimitable home-cooked meal for your honey, consider steak. After all, don't they say the key to a man's heart is through his stomach? A good red wine and dessert probably won't hurt either. I asked chef David Lapham to help me prepare a Valentine's Day dinner, and here it is. Ladies, be careful. This one is lethal when it comes to love!

Steak for Two
    2 top-quality beef tenderloins
      or New York strips
    1/2 lb. gorgonzola or blue cheese
    1/2 cup heavy cream
    1/2 cup chopped chives
    squeeze of lemon juice

Preheat the oven to 375°. Season the steaks (both sides) with salt and pepper. In a medium-sized skillet, heat the canola oil until it is smoking. Place the steaks in the hot oil, and don't move them for three minutes per side because you want to sear in the flavor. Once you have seared each side, place the skillet in the oven to finish the cooking. This should take twenty-five minutes for well done, fifteen minutes for medium rare, and ten minutes for rare. Remove the steaks and cover with foil. Let the steaks rest for at least ten minutes before cutting into them.

The Sauce
Put cheese and heavy cream in a saucepan and heat until cheese is melted and cream is fully mixed in. After the cheese and cream are well blended, let the skillet simmer on low heat for ten minutes or until the sauce thickens. Add chives and a squeeze of lemon juice. Serve over the steaks.

Chocolate Pot De Crèmes

    2 cups whipping cream
    1/2 cup whole milk
    5 oz semisweet
        chocolate, chopped
    6 large egg yolks
    1/3 cup sugar

Preheat the oven to 325°. Bring the cream and milk just to simmer in a heavy medium-sized saucepan over medium heat. Remove from heat. Add the chocolate; whisk until melted and smooth. Whisk the egg yolks and sugar in a large bowl to blend. Gradually whisk in the hot chocolate mixture. Strain this mixture into another bowl. Cool for ten minutes, skimming any foam from the surface.

Divide the custard mixture among six 3/4 cup custard cups or soufflé dishes.

Cover each with foil. Place the cups in a large baking pan. Add enough hot water to the pan so that the water comes halfway up sides of the cups. Bake until the custards are set but the centers still move slightly when gently shaken, about fifty-five minutes. Remove the cups from the water. Remove the foil. Chill custards until cold, about three hours. Serve and enjoy.

Note: This dish can be made two days ahead.

Alvina Patel is a fashionista Mermaid-about-town. You can usually find her sparkling in fabulous jewelry since she dresses celebrities on the red carpet for the exclusive house of Van Cleef & Arpels. Below she shares her thoughts on an event that will shine.

Q: What's the best supplement to a party?
A: A mix of the right people, and an activity to get people talking.

Q: Who are some of your favorite guests or types of guests?
A: My favorite guests are those who enjoy lively conversations about enjoyable and intellectual topics. These are people who come from different places in the world but are open to finding things in common with others.

Q: What is your favorite thing to do when preparing for an event?
A: I really enjoy planning the menu. I love food!

Q: What has been your favorite event to attend or host, and why?
A: I love to host any event that celebrates a close friend, whether it's a birthday party or a baby shower. Making any occasion in someone's life a true celebration is such a pleasure for me. I also enjoy attending events that involve my personal interests. One of my favorite New York City events is the New York Academy of Art's "Take Home a Nude," where every guest has an opportunity to take home a piece of art while benefiting the Academy.

Q: What makes a party a memory for you?
A: Meeting someone I would never have crossed paths with in my everyday life and making a lasting connection thereafter.

Q: What is your secret to unwinding when the party is over?
A: Having one last glass of wine or champagne with a good friend to recap the highlights of the evening.

Q: What's your Rule of Fin?
A: Relax and enjoy the party! Don't make your guests feel as if hosting them is stopping you from having a good time!

chapter twelve

St. Patrick's Day

"May your pockets be heavy and your heart be light. May good luck pursue you each morning and night." —**Irish Blessing**

IN AMERICA, we have a real fascination with our family's origins. Perhaps it's because this country is a melting pot of people who emigrated here from so many other countries. Whatever the reason, most folks I know are keenly aware of their heritage, and that's a great thing! Mermaids love to celebrate, and heritage often provides one more opportunity to throw a party.

My last name is Pereira, and people often ask me if I'm Spanish or Italian, but I'm actually one half Portuguese (with a dash of Brazilian) and the other half Irish. My mother's maiden name is McLoughlin. She is a spirited redhead with beautiful blue eyes and adorable freckles (or "beauty spots," as she likes to call them). I had always wanted to climb up my family tree and see my heritage on both sides of our family, so I traveled to Portugal and Ireland with friends and family. While in Ireland for the first time, I remember feeling the congeniality of the people there; everyone was so welcoming, and so gracious. So welcoming were they, in fact, that I felt compelled to fully participate in a Guinness sing-along in a traditional pub. Close friends will not be surprised by this admission! For me, every St. Patrick's Day is a great way to revisit the homeland, even if only in spirit.

The luck of the Irish can be contagious. To celebrate, host your own party. Fabulous décor includes anything green. Think of grass centerpieces, clover in bud vases, bells of Ireland, and other flowers surrounded by lots of greenery. At each place setting, spread a few chocolate gold coins. If there's one central area for the party, consider filling a large copper pot with a selection of "lucky charms," from candy to collectibles. Whoever dresses the most festive gets to take home the pot of gold as a prize!

Traditional Irish fare like corned beef and cabbage can get a little dull, so try a modern twist. Invite guests to enjoy an "Irish Mashed Potato bar". Include an assortment of mashed potatoes, such as wasabi-mash, sweet potato, and truffled, and offer a variety of toppings, like veggies, cheeses, and bacon. Throw in some traditional soda bread and a shepherd's pie, and no guest will go hungry. For dessert, consider serving Irish coffees. And, of course, no well-stocked bar on St. Patrick's Day is without Guinness and a host of Irish whiskeys.

While guests are enjoying this feast of food and beverage, rock out to a compilation of your favorite U2 hits. Send guests home with green to-go gift bags with all the leftovers. (Bonus: Makes for easy clean up!)

RULE OF FIN:

If you are lucky enough to be Irish, ask your parents or grandparents how your family has traditionally celebrated this holiday and incorporate some of those ideas into your next party. Do the same for whatever your heritage and see how easy it is to top your next party with tradition.

Here are four fabulous ways to make your next St. Patrick's Day unforgettable.

Invitation Idea. Want to be cheap-and-chic? Guests will know that they're invited to a great party when they receive a message in a bottle, a Guinness beer bottle preferably! Write the details in calligraphy on old-fashioned parchment paper, roll it up, place it in the empty glass bottle, and hand deliver or ship carefully to your friends. For another idea, look up the origin and meaning of each guest's name and create a "crest" on your computer to include on invitations you print at home. For instance, the name McLoughlin means "expert sailor," so you could put an image or clip art of a sailor on the top of your invitation to the McLoughlin's, along with a rendering of their name in an old-fashioned font. The website zelo.com will help you discover the meaning of many names. Want to be spec-and-swish? Send guests traditional Irish linen napkins that are monogrammed, and insert your invite inside.

Signature Cocktail. With your guests sipping on "Whistling Whiskeys," everyone will feel Irish, at least for the day. A clover leaf garnish is a sweet and simple touch.

Delightful Décor. Create a rainbow with balloons by buying a multitude of colored balloons,

---

Mermaid Memory
Mermaid Hilary

One year I went to Ireland with some friends. We rented a cute little green "bug" of a car and decided to go camping on our first night of the trip. It was so freezing-cold that night that we awoke before the sun came up and proceeded to take a long drive (in our warm car!) through the beautiful Connemara Valley. In one of my travel books I had read that if you saw a wild pony running in this valley it is considered good luck. The ponies are very hard to spot and often stay away from the roads and people. Well, I was relegated to the back seat for this part of the journey, and just as the sun was rising, I saw a flash of gray out of the corner of my window. When I turned around to look out the back window of the car, I realized that what I saw was a flash of the gray mane of a pony. I watched this gorgoeus gray pony run up a hill and then disappear into the rocks of the valley. Just like magic. (Or maybe it was just the luck of the Irish.)

RECIPE BOX

Whistling Whiskeys: Fill a highball glass with ice. Pour an Irish whiskey like Jameson into the glass using the "One Mississippi, two Mississippi" rule as your guide. Top with ginger ale, and garnish with a four-leaf clover.

---

inflating them, and then tying them together with string in the shape of an arch. Sprinkle gold coin candy on the ground leading to a big steel bucket (found at the trusty hardware store) filled with ice and a slew of Irish beers like McSorley's and Caffrey's, a variety of wines, sparkling waters, sodas, and a sprinkle of extra gold coins around the ice. For spectacular-and-swish music, ask a talented musician to play Irish music on a fiddle or hire an Irish group or band that will engage the crowd in traditional dances. To keep it cheap-and-chic, a great CD makes a nice alternative to live music. The group Celtic Women is a great option for festive background music, and they even have a Pandora channel. Bring the outdoors in by buying lots of shamrock pots and flowers. Guests can take them home at the end of the party and search for a four-leaf clover. Set your table with Irish linens. This is the day to take out your best Waterford Crystal for lucky toasts.

Fun Favors. Give guests a cute pouch filled with a wish or a "lucky note" and include a lottery ticket. Add miniature leprechaun figurines to the pouches for fun. Other ideas may be a rabbit's foot or "lucky stones." These can be stones from your own yard, but you can actually buy these rocks in Ireland—supposedly from the magical Connemara Valley. Include a note to make a wish while rubbing the stone! For a spec-and-swish favor, consider a small piece of Waterford Crystal.

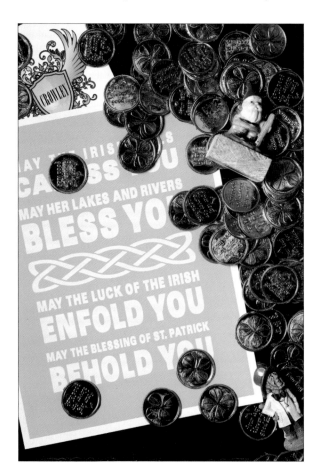

So how do you make those cute shapes (hearts, shamrocks) in the foam of your Guinness?

First, practice drawing the shamrock on paper to get a feel for the movement. Once you have perfected your pen-and-ink shamrock, swap the pen and paper for a knife and a foamy glass of Guinness. Using the tip of the knife, slowly and without lifting the knife from the foam until you have finished, "draw" the shamrock in the foam. The imprint won't last long, but it makes a lovely first impression. You can also try using a cookie cutter. Insert and remove in one smooth motion to avoid stirring the foam.

Dominique Love is the CEO and co-founder of the Atlanta Food & Wine Festival. A Colorado girl with deep Mississippi roots, Dominique delights in entertaining friends and family with memorable dinners, trying to perfect bacon caramel corn and mint julep ice cream, and teaching her three-and-a-half year old son how to cook.

Q: What's the best supplement to a party?
A: Food and booze! If your guests are taking the time to be with you, then make sure you reciprocate with good food and drink. If your guests have good food and drink, they won't notice if you're missing a flower arrangement or if you skimped on the band. They'll be too happy and full to care.

Q: Who are some of your favorite guests or types of guests?
A: My favorite quote from an unknown source is, "Bring to the room what you want to find in the room." I like fun, interesting, and engaging people. I make it my goal to bring those traits to the party and, when I do, I always find them there, too.

Q: What is your favorite thing to do when preparing for an event?
A: I like planning the menu. I can spend days flipping through cookbooks and perusing recipes online to plan the perfect menu for my guests.

Q: What has been your favorite event to attend or host, and why?
A: I love intimate gatherings where guests can actually interact and have good discussions. I spend my days running from client to client and employee to employee, so I crave the calm of a dinner party or an evening where I can actually have a meaningful conversation with someone.

Q: What makes a party a memory for you?
A: I tend to remember the unexpected elements of a party—a surprising dish, a special cocktail, a small detail that you know the hostess put a lot of energy into, or a funny moment.

Q: What's your Rule of Fin?
A: Be a true hostess. Go the extra mile, add a personal touch, greet your guests at the door with a cocktail, and make everyone feel welcome and relaxed.

Q: What is your secret to unwinding when the party is over?
A: Cleaning up and going to bed!

chapter thirteen

Easter

"Spring is nature's way of saying 'Let's party!'"
—Robin Williams

THIS HOLIDAY is truly a beautiful day for people to gather and celebrate friendship, family, and the little bunnies in your life! Many families may host an after-church gathering at their home or a restaurant to celebrate over a lovely brunch or dinner. If you are hosting at home, one way to bring your table to life is to make an "eggs-in-a-nest" cake. Bake any layer cake you like and ice the top and sides. Use a squeeze bottle filled with melted caramel to pipe a nest on top. Place colorful Cadbury Mini Eggs or jelly beans in the nest for a fresh, fun cake that kids will love! Note: You could also try what my grandmother used to do; set hard-boiled eggs, dyed in pastels, on top of the cake for a beautiful effect.

Easter does not have to be just about the kiddos. The White House hosts an annual Easter Egg Roll that you could recreate for your family and friends. This holiday tradition dates back to 1878 when President Hayes officially opened the White House grounds to local children for egg rolling on Easter Monday. Create an adult Easter egg hunt for your friends and family by hiding plastic Easter eggs around your yard filled with a mixture of treats and pieces of paper with numbers on them. The numbers correspond with a list of challenges, like, walk ten yards holding an egg on a spoon. After the hunt is over, guests open their eggs to reveal their numbers, and those who have the same number must compete against each other to complete the challenge and win a prize. Everyone will have so much fun, and your Easter Egg Roll will become an annual tradition.

RULE OF FIN:

When hard-boiling eggs for decorating, make sure not to overcook them. Overcooked eggs are more likely to crack. Wait until the eggs are completely dry before decorating with colored dyes, glitter, stencils, or even fabrics.

Nearly as indispensible as the Easter egg is the Easter Bunny. Hares and rabbits have long been symbols of fertility. The inclusion of the hare into Easter customs appears to have originated in Germany, where tales were told of an "Easter hare" who laid eggs for children to find. Cakes were baked for Easter in the shape of hares, and many practiced making chocolate bunnies and eggs. This tradition was brought to America (probably by a Mermaid!) and spread to the wide public today!

It is said that in Medieval Europe, the eating of eggs was forbidden during Lent. Eggs laid during that time were often boiled, or otherwise preserved, and thus became a mainstay of Easter meals, and a prized Easter gift for children. Whether you dye them, color them, hide them, roll them, buy them in plastic, or just eat them, the humble egg is undeniably the star of any Easter celebration. Plan on stocking up!

Spring Showers Bring May Flowers!

Beautiful flowers in bloom include cherry blossoms, tulips, ranunculus, Gerber daisies, roses, hyacinth, forsythia, lilacs, hydrangeas, daffodils, iris, anemones, freesia, grape hyacinths, Calla lilies, Gerberas, lily of the valley, peonies, and sweet peas. Consider using these lovely flowers when constructing spring centerpieces.

Here are four fabulous ways to make your next Easter celebration unforgettable:

Invitation Idea. Be cheap-and-chic by sending a cute note with a cotton ball glued to the front (to look like bunny tail) and a festive message. For a spec-and-swish option, stuff an invitation inside a papier mâché Easter egg and send it to guests in a small brown box filled with fake grass or brown raffia made to look like a nest.

Signature Cocktail. The "Spring Tulip" is a huge hit with adults.

Delightful Décor. Scatter chocolate eggs wrapped in colorful foil on the table. Set white eggs in ceramic egg cup holders and write guests names on them in pastel colors as place cards. You can also create different floral centerpieces that incorporate many beautiful spring flowers. Consider making smaller arrangements in Mason jars to use at each place setting. Guests can take home their flowers after the party. The great thing about Easter is that spring provides such a natural and beautiful backdrop for a party. Everything is colorful, fresh, and lovely. Take advantage of what's already available in nature as you decorate.

Fun Favors. Little guests can go home with Easter baskets or bonnets filled with chocolate eggs and candy. Or, create family Easter baskets that everyone can enjoy. You can find inexpensive baskets at craft stores or dollar stores. Fillers can include chocolates, candy, candles, and even a DVD for the whole family to watch together.

RECIPE BOX

The Spring Tulip (Serves 4-6)
1 (12 oz) can frozen pink lemonade concentrate, thawed
3/4 cup vodka, chilled
lemon, sliced
granulated sugar

Stir together the pink lemonade and vodka, and serve over ice in tulip glasses. Garnish glass rims with a lemon slice dipped in pink sugar.

COME LIGHT THE NIGHT WITH US!

90 BRICK LANE • JULY 4TH, 4PM

FIREWORKS BEGIN 8PM

chapter fourteen

Fourth of July

"From every mountain-side, let freedom ring."

—Samuel F. Smith

THE FOURTH OF JULY is not only a celebration that signifies independence and pride for this amazing country we live in, but it's also a fun and spirited way to get together with friends and enjoy the spirit of summer.

One of my favorite Independence Day celebrations was one I spent with my friend Nicole and her family. We went to her brother Paul's beautiful roof deck on top of his apartment in New York City and watched the Macy's 4th of July Fireworks. We prepared and enjoyed the classic flag cake (pound cake with whipped cream on top, adorned with strawberries and blueberries to create the stars and stripes) and sipped good American brews and California wines. It was a beautiful way to spend a sizzling summer evening. This is definitely one of my favorite New York memories, ever!

Look what we did with "Mellie" the Watermelon for a fruit salad at one summer soiree. This is a festive and easy way to create a great Fourth of July edible centerpiece. Another great way to use a watermelon? The night before your party, cut a small hole into the watermelon, pour in a bottle

Summer Blooms

Fourth of July is a celebration of summer. For this holiday and other summer celebrations, consider using a few of these seasonal blooms for centerpieces: sunflowers, dahlias, tropicals, roses, lotus flowers, Casablanca lilies, gloriosa lilies, Lily of the Nile, stephanotis, delphiniums, hypericums, phlox, and lisianthus.

of your favorite vodka, and seal. By the next day, the fruit will make delicious "shooters" that you can cut and serve for spiked fruit salad.

For festive fare, serve a selection of appetizers that match the theme of red, white, and blue; skewers of cherry tomatoes, mozzarella balls, and blueberries; blue tortilla chips paired with red salsa and white cheddar cheese; and, of course, the flag cake will finish off a festive table.

> **RULE OF FIN:**
> *No matter where a Mermaid's birth-place is, she doesn't pass up a chance to celebrate a fun tradition. I love asking friends or people I meet in my travels to share their patriotic pastimes. I almost always get new ideas for celebrations!*

COME LIGHT THE NIGHT WITH US!

90 BRICK LANE • JULY 4TH, 4PM

FIREWORKS BEGIN 8PM

ATTIRE: POOLSIDE CASUAL • RSVP: GEORGEGREEN@REDWHITE.BLUE

Here are four ways to create a patriotic Fourth of July celebration.

Invitation Idea. For a spectacular-and-swish event, send your guests a little box of sparklers with a note that says: *"Come light the night with us on the 4th of July!"* If you want to keep it cheap-and-chic, take a white string with a rope-like texture (easy enough to get from the hardware store) and burn the ends with a lighter. Then, tie it through a hole-punched card that is inscribed with the details of the event to send as your invitation.

Signature Cocktail. Organic microbrews made in the USA are always refreshing on a steamy night, and are a cheap-and-chic way to celebrate the birth of America. If you want to spec-and-swish it up, make a signature martini like the "Red, White, & Blue" martini: spear a white cocktail onion alongside a blue cheese stuffed olive and a red cherry tomato onto a mini-flag toothpick garnish and add to a classic martini. Or, for a large group, prepare pitchers of "Shining Star Sangria" and "Berry Breezes" for the kids. And of course, it's also always fun to serve your watermelon coolers at an outdoor party.

Delightful Décor. Paper lanterns never fail for an outdoor party. Keep in mind that if you are serving festive food in reds, whites, and blues, you need less décor. Dress up your table with a blue and white striped tablecloth, and feature mini American flags in Mason jars, which can also double as cute hors d'ouvres picks. Place alternating bowls of colorful farmstand blueberries and strawberries on your table. Sunflowers are in season and will compliment all of the red, white, and blue.

Fun Favors. If you don't use sparklers for the invitation, consider sending your guests home with some. Or, you could use the small flags and tie them to a small bouquet of white and red roses and blue hydrangeas. Watching the fireworks by the water will make these red, white, and blue cupcakes the perfect parting gift for any guest.

RECIPE BOX

Shining Star Sangria (serves 4)
   1 bottle white wine (your preference)
   1 cup blueberries
   1 cup strawberries or raspberries
     (frozen are fine)
   1/3 cup sugar
     (or use agave or stevia for a healthier option)
   2 cups ginger ale

Pour wine into a pitcher. Toss in the fruit, and add the sugar. Carefully stir until well blended. Chill overnight. Add ginger ale and ice just before serving.

Berry Breezes (For the Kids)
   1 cup ice cubes
   1/2 cup strawberries
   1/2 cup frozen concentrate limeade
   1/2 cup water

Place the ice cubes in a blender or food processor and pulse until they are crushed. Add the strawberries, concentrate limeade, and water. Puree the mixture until smooth and thick. Pour into tall glasses with flexi straws.

Tracey Toomey McQuade is an actress, on-air personality, and the co-author of *Cocktail Therapy* and *The Perfect Manhattan*. She shares her thoughts on parties below.

Q: What's the best supplement to a party?
A: The guests make the party. If you can assemble a good group of fun-loving, interactive people, it's going to be a great party. Once that is in place, music is the next most important ingredient. A killer playlist that mixes classic "crowd-pleaser" songs with some newer and more eclectic selections always takes a party to the next level.

Q: Who are some of your favorite guests or types of guests? A: I love guests who aren't afraid to leave their date or their friends and mingle! Nothing is worse than a party where everyone is keeping to their safe little cluster of people. When planning a guest list, try to make sure you have a few "fun-starters"—people who aren't afraid to interact with others and get the party started!

Q: What is your favorite thing to do when preparing for an event? A: Definitely make a playlist with the people who are coming in mind. I threw my sister's bridal shower last year and it was so fun coming up with a playlist of songs from our youth (old-school Madonna) and new songs that I know my sister loves. It's a great way to personalize a party for the guest of honor.

Q: What has been your favorite event to attend or host, and why? A: My friend Heather Buchanan throws the most amazing dinner parties, and I love going to them. She assembles a really diverse, interesting group of people, so the conversations are always amazing. She's also an amazing cook and baker—she always uses local, seasonal ingredients, and she always serves a signature cocktail before dinner.

Q: What makes a party a memory for you?
A: Again, it's the people. If I have met some great people and really felt like I was able to make a connection, I will definitely remember the party.

Q: What's your Rule of Fin?
A: When hosting a party, it's important to prepare as much as you can *before* the event so that you can have fun with your guests. The host sets the tone of the party, and if she is stressed, the guests will feel it. Plus, who wants to assemble a group of their most favorite people and then spend the evening in the kitchen prepping and cooking ?!

Q: What is your secret to unwinding when the party is over? A: My secret to unwinding is always a really good glass of wine! I love when a party is over but a few people are still there, usually your sister or your closest friends. It's fun to have a post-party drink with your nearest and dearest.

chapter fifteen

Halloween

> "When black cats prowl and pumpkins gleam, may luck be yours on Halloween."
>
> —Unknown

THERE COMES A TIME at the end of every October when the world gets a little spookier. Cool winds eerily blow fallen leaves around the streets as hosts of little witches and goblins take to the night in search of . . . candy! With so much fun and excitement in the air, it's no wonder Mermaids love this time of year to trick *and* treat.

To bring out the inner child in all your friends, make like the Peanuts gang in *It's the Great Pumpkin, Charlie Brown*, and host a pumpkin-carving party. Ask guests to come dressed in costume and decorate your venue with miniature pumpkins, bouquets of mums, and black, orange, and silver candles (for a spooky glow). At each place setting, roll out white or brown craft paper (located in your treasure chest) and set out a medium-sized pumpkin, a set of carving tools, and permanent markers. Invite your guests to carve pumpkins while they sip Oktoberfest brews, nibble on bowls of roasted pumpkin seeds, and listen to the soundtrack from *The Rocky Horror Picture Show*. After the carving is complete, have contests for the ugliest, prettiest, most creative, and scariest pumpkin.

While guests are mingling and admiring their work, gather up all of the pumpkin "innards" and divide them into zip-top bags. Drop those bags in brown paper lunch bags (which you can decorate or leave plain, and fasten with an orange sticker or ribbon), insert a recipe card for homemade pumpkin bread, and send guests home with them, along with the pumpkins and carving tools, as a great parting gift. Traditional activities like bobbing for apples and face painting are also fun for the kids, just make sure to have prizes for best costume and best apple bobber.

Fall Flowers

Fall in love with fall flowers! Great arrangements with flowers of this season can be created from: Roses, amaranthus, dahlias, oak branches, Calla lilies, cockscomb, cosmos, hydrangeas, and kangaroo paws.

Pumpkin Carving Ideas

- The Preppy Pumpkin: Monogram it!

- The Picasso Pumpkin: Fashion it after your favorite artist's work, from Degas to Dali.

- The Pretty Pumpkin: Make like a makeup artist and carve big, dramatic eyes and eyelashes and a pouty mouth, and use colored markers and glitter paints to add some color.

- The Plain-Jane Pumpkin: Simple triangles for the facial features and a tealight inside? Still special!

Here are four ways to sweeten up your next Halloween party:

Invitation Idea. For a spooktacular-and-swish invite, send miniature dust-brooms tied with orange and black ribbon or twine and affix a hang

RECIPE BOX

Pumpkin Bread

1 (15 oz) can pumpkin puree*

4 eggs

1 cup vegetable oil

2/3 cup water

3 cups white sugar

3 1/2 cups all-purpose flour

2 t baking soda

1 1/2 t salt

1 t ground cinnamon

1 t ground nutmeg

1/2 t ground cloves

1/4 t ground ginger

Preheat the oven to 350°. Grease and flour three 7 x 3 inch loaf pans. In a large bowl, mix together the pumpkin puree, eggs, oil, water, and sugar until well blended. In a separate bowl, whisk together the flour, baking soda, salt, cinnamon, nutmeg, cloves, and ginger. Stir the dry ingredients into the pumpkin mixture until just blended. Pour into the prepared pans. And bake for about fifty minutes. Loaves are done when a toothpick inserted in the center comes out clean.

*Mermaid twist: When you send guests away with those leftover pumpkin innards, tell them they can use those instead of pumpkin puree. Simply blend in a food processor to puree, and then use the leftover seeds to roast.

tag that invites guests to *"Come fly with us this Halloween!"* The cheap-and-chic hostess could entice guests by emailing a Halloween-themed invite, or ask kids to make the invitations from colored construction paper and cut-out shapes of bats, ghosts, and witches.

Signature Cocktail. For a cheap-and-chic way to serve a large crowd, offer a "Witches Brew" punch. This can be served in a large black plastic cauldron, which can be easily found online or at Halloween supply stores. This will look even spookier when you serve your ice cubes filled with candy spiders or bugs. Light-up cubes have made a comeback as well! Dress up your bar by filling clear martini glasses with colorful candy corns for guests to nibble, which also makes a pretty display.

Delightful Décor. Transform your entire venue into a haunted house! For the spooktacular-and-swish haunted house, buy or rent a few fog machines to blow outside and make the entrance to your home appear more mystical and

spooky. The cheap-and-chic haunted house can achieve the very same effect by using some dry ice. Decorate your "haunted house" with dead flowers, fake tombstones, and wrought-iron gates. Project a silent, scary movie on a white wall in the main room of the house, such as *Nosferatu*. Have one of your dry ice displays placed on the bar in glass beakers or safe containers. To keep it smoking all night, slowly pour water over the dry ice every now and then. Lay cobweb tablecloths (you can buy fake cobwebs or use an old hammock or fishnet to create this look) across your buffet tables and bar area, and create a wreath for your door made from black feathers, rubber bats, and fake blood. You could get a few hay bales to spread outdoors, or inside your home, and cover them with black or burlap fabric for extra seating for guests. You can also stack hay bales to make different structures, such as a buffet table, a bar, or even an entire haunted house structure by using fabric to cover the top and lots of LED candles to add an eerie light. Hire local actors to come to your house dressed as goblins and ghouls, and send the agile ones up into your trees as "tree creatures" to scare guests as they enter and exit the party. Make a mystery maze, if you have a garden or yard that will allow it, and cover your trees and bushes with more cobwebs, or create the same effect by cutting toilet paper into ragged edges and draping over bushes and trees. Music is key for a party like this. When Mermaids & Martinis hosted a kid's Halloween party in NYC, Mermaid Jamie created a *fin*Tastic playlist of soundtracks from *Ghostbusters*,

The Addams Family, and from Michael Jackson's album *Thriller*. All were family-friendly and fun. We also layered into the playlist recordings of creaking doors and stairs, cackling laughter, and howling wind sounds that we found online. Don't forget to tune your TV to a static channel (or download this online) for a creepy, *Poltergeist* effect.

Fun Favors. Gather a bunch of movie classics like *Bride of Frankenstein*, *The Shining*, and *Rosemary's Baby*, as well as some family-oriented ones like *Practical Magic* and *The Legend of Sleepy Hollow*, along with a mixture of pumpkin seeds, popcorn, and candy corn tied together in a bag with a note: *"Hope you had a scream!"*

> **RULE OF FIN:**
> *Keep in mind when hosting a Halloween party for all ages you don't want your décor to be too scary, too racy, or too boring.*

Spooky Soirees

So you want to host a scary party but Halloween is still months away? Never fear! Here are a few frightfully chic ideas that will take your next party to the full moon, even if it's only June. Use these ideas as the building blocks of your next party, and remember that the possibilities are endless.

> **RULE OF FIN:**
> *Trick-or-treating can be fun for both littles and adults. Make sure every guest leaves with a bag filled with something sweet.*

Eat, Drink, and Be Scary

Scare your guests into attendance with a bloody-finger "don't forget" invitation. This invite is easy to create: Buy a bunch of rubber (or candy) fingers covered in fake blood (sold at most party stores and online) and tie a red ribbon or piece of string around the middle of the finger. Affix a hole-punched card to the red string with the party details. A cheap-and-chic (and really cute) alternative can be made by printing the party details with an image of a finger (you can trace your own) on a flat card. Punch holes around the edges and string a red ribbon through the card.

RECIPE BOX

Blood-Red Sangria
    1 bottle "blood" red wine (your preference)
    2 cups ginger ale or club soda
    1 orange cut into wedges
    1 lemon cut into wedges
    1/4 cup sugar
    few drops of grenadine syrup
    (optional, for darker "blood-like" color)
    gummy worms, gummy bugs, or spooky
    hard candy

Pour wine into a pitcher, squeeze the juice from the lemon and orange wedges into the wine. Toss in the fruit wedges (leaving out seeds, if possible) and add sugar. Chill overnight. Add ginger ale or club soda, grenadine syrup, ice, and gummy candy just before serving.

Try this cheap-and-chic drink glass garnish that will save you time and money: rim the glasses with red sugar (granulated sugar dyed with red food coloring) and garnish with a set of plastic vampire fangs.

"Blood-Red Sangria" anyone? Make this signature cocktail and scatter some plastic eyeballs in the punch bowl for a bit of fearful fun!

Thank your guests for sharing and scaring with "petrifying pumpkin seeds." These seeds are an affordable party favor that can be made with leftover seeds from the pumpkins your guests carved. Cook up some different flavors by tossing washed seeds with your favorite spices and flavors (salt, paprika, and parmesan cheese work well) and bake at 350° for about thirty minutes. Place labeled bowls and baggies on a table so your guests can make their own delicious and healthy goody bag.

The Macabre Masquerade
This is a grand affair. Make it Venetian inspired, and ask guests to come dressed in their most outlandish, over-the-top ensembles. Use vibrant masks as centerpieces, or consider asking guests to decorate their own papier mâché masks with feathers, glitter, and sequins you provide. This is a great party activity. Fill your house will lots of black and gold balloons, and create a fabulous dance floor by renting flooring, or sectioning off an area of the party. Ask a fortune-teller to dress up and do readings for guests.

Kill 'em with kindness! If you are having a sit-down dinner, consider using "Poison Apples" as place card holders by making an incision in a red apple and placing a black place card inside. Or, set up your chalkboard (in your Mermaid treasure chest) next to a basket near the door lined with a black cloth and fill with a bunch of red "Poison Apples." Write a personalized thank-you

message to your guests with red chalk in your "creepiest" handwriting, like "RIP: Revel In Peace," to send them on their way.

The Devil Wears Prada Party

Host a "*The Devil Wears Prada*" party for all of your posh gal pals! Welcome your guests with a tray of "Runway Royales." Just splash some Crème de cassis in each glass of bubbly for a spooktacular twist on a Kir Royale. Set up your bar to resemble a fashion editor's closet. Download and print out your favorite high-end fashion labels and designer logos and paste them onto wine and champagne bottles after soaking the original labels off. What guest wouldn't love being served "Prada Prosecco" or a glass of

"Missoni Merlot?" For a devilish look, the hostess should wear all black with a hint of "runway red" and ask guests to dress up as their most exaggerated version of a "dead" fashion trend or style. You will have some great pictures of some scary trends from the past and present. Hire a makeup artist to give guests supermodel looks at the party. Don't forget to give those leading ladies in your life a treat! A bottle of black nail polish for a Prada-like party favor, or homemade devil's food or red velvet cupcakes are sure to be a huge box office hit. Set up an oversized designer sketchpad next to a stack of blood-red lipsticks for the fashionistas to write their favorite fashion tip to the host before they click their Louboutins and disappear to discover the next big trend.

Whether you want your Halloween to be spectacular-and-swish, cheap-and-chic, or a perfect balance of the two, find your inner Mermaid, call on your creative spirits, and start plotting that bewitching bash.

chapter sixteen

Thanksgiving

> *"A happy life is made up of little things—a gift sent, a letter written, a call made, a recommendation given, transportation provided, a cake made, a book lent, a check sent."*
>
> **—Carol Holmes**

THANKSGIVING is one of my favorite times of the year—it is so full of warmth and tradition. Families and friends gather to share their gratitude for life's abundant blessings. Most families have at least one Thanksgiving tradition. Some play games (my family loves charades), others play sports (it *is* football season, after all), and some just tell stories. Building a Thanksgiving celebration around family and tradition is a surefire way to make the holiday glorious.

If you don't already have one, create a tradition! Borrow my family's tradition and play charades after dinner. It's a great way to connect after a long dinner and get back some of your energy! Or, if the weather permits, host a touch football game outdoors. I have a friend whose family loves to play "Thanksgiving Twister," which is especially tricky with a full stomach. Or, "Pin the Feathers on the Turkey" is a great game for the kids. Another fun tradition is to have your guests write anonymously on a piece of paper what they are most thankful for. Put all of the pieces in a paper pilgrim hat. After dinner, while everyone is still at the table waiting for dessert, pass around the hat and have each person pull one out and read the message out loud. Then, ask guests to guess whose note it is. This is a great way to share with everyone why you are filled with gratitude during this holiday.

> **RULE OF FIN:**
> *Be thankful for the traditions that you share with others, and make sure to tell at least one person at the party why you are thankful for them.*

Here are four meaningful ways to make your next Thanksgiving memorable:

Invitation Idea. Mail every guest a blank thank-you card along with the invitation. Ask your guests to fill in the thank-you note with what or who they are thankful for this year and bring it to the Thanksgiving celebration. Sometime during the party, they can share what they wrote.

Signature Cocktail. Apple cider and spiced rum not only warm the belly but they also make your home cozy and fragrant. There's nothing like a warm, spicy drink during the Thanksgiving season. Try our "Gratitude Goblets" or a "November Dream" cocktail!

Delightful Décor. Give chilly guests a warm welcome with mulling spices brewing on the stove and a tray of "Gratitude Goblets." Let everyone know where he or she is sitting with colorful feathered place cards. Or, you could create a place card for each person (and include why you are thankful for that guest, signed by the host!) You will want to keep the table setting minimal since there will be so much food, which is the hallmark of a great Thanksgiving party. You can also place different sized gourds at each place setting, make an incision and slide in guest place cards (or hollow out those gourds and place

---

RECIPE BOX

November Dream
3/4 cup frozen cranberries
1 1/2 oz bourbon
1 oz cranberry-honey syrup
cinnamon stick
bag of non-frozen stemmed cranberries

Fill a Collins glass three-fourths of the way with a mixture of crushed ice and frozen cranberries. Pour in 1 1/2 oz. bourbon and 1 oz cranberry-honey simple syrup.

Garnish glasses with three cranberries tied by their stems to a long, thin cinnamon stick.

Cranberry-honey simple syrup: Boil one part water, one part honey, and one part cranberries. Strain out the solids. Refrigerate the syrup.

---

tealights inside of each to add a lovely glow to the room). Decorate the room with flowers like dahlias and ranunculus or create centerpieces by collecting the beautiful leaves and pinecones that may be right outside your doorstep! Another idea would be to light lots of ivory pillar candles of all heights and place them along the center of a long table or clustered in the center of a round table. Order wishbones online (luckybreakwishbones.com) and spray-paint them silver or gold or other autumnal colors. At the end of the meal, each person can break a wishbone to make his or her wish.

Fun Favors. Set out cute to-go boxes for guests to take home leftovers. Include recipe cards that you have pre-printed for things like turkey soup, turkey quesadillas, and creative twists on traditional turkey and cranberry sandwiches. Remember the thank-you card invites? Mix up the cards and have everyone take home a random card along with a mini bottle of Wild Turkey whiskey. They can sip while they read and remember this great holiday.

For a great host gift, consider a pretty gravy boat or mulling spices. To be spec-and-swish, break bread with the host in style! Bring a magnificent, artisan loaf of bread. I love to set my table with a beautiful piece of edible art work.

While Thanksgiving is steeped with tradition—it can also be quite fun to switch things up every few years or so! For a twist on Thanksgiving, you could serve individual

RECIPE BOX

Gratitude Goblets (serves 6-8)

Mulled apple cider and spiced rum
1 gallon of apple cider
1/2 bottle dark rum
1/4 bottle butterscotch schnapps
1 Muslin bag
2 cinnamon sticks
1 t nutmeg
3-4 pieces star anise
2 red Gala apples

Take a muslin bag, put one level tea-spoon of nutmeg into the bag. Then, add 2 cinnamon sticks into the bag and the star anise and tie. Pour a gallon of apple cider into a pot and put on low heat. Drop the muslin bag into the pot. Just before the cider comes to a boil, take the pot off the heat. It should be warm (not boiling). Then, add the rum and butterscotch schnapps. Remove the muslin bag. Pour the cider into goblets. These can be mugs, glass goblets, etc. Garnish with an apple slice.

Cornish hens or roast chickens to guests. Or, you could prepare a coastal-themed dinner if you are hosting by the shore. If you live somewhere urban—delivery is always an option! Even a Chinese takeout or Indian-themed buffet could be fun, and you will have loads of time to kick up your feet after dinner and connect with your guests by not having to hover over the dishwasher.

If you are sticking with the classic turkey dinner, try roasting one Mermaid style. Chef David chimes in on the best way to roast and host:

Roast Turkey
Start with the best quality turkey you can find, such as organic and free range. Turkeys under fifteen pounds tend to cook better than larger ones.

thank you.

To prepare the turkey for roasting, first remove the giblets (save for gravy or stuffing). Next, rinse the bird inside and out and pat dry with paper towels.

If you are stuffing the bird, stuff it loosely, allowing about 1/2 to 3/4 cup of stuffing per pound of turkey. Brush the skin with melted butter or oil. Tie drumsticks together with string (for stuffed birds only). Insert a meat thermometer into the thickest part of the thigh. The thermometer should point towards the body, and should not touch the bone.

Place the bird on a rack in a roasting pan, and into a preheated 350° oven. Start taking temperature readings with a meat thermometer, inserted deep into the thickest part of the turkey breast and thigh. You want a resulting temperature of 175° for the dark meat (thighs and legs) and 165° for the white meat (breast). The temperature of the bird will continue to rise once you take it out of the oven, so take it out when the temperature reading for the thigh is 170°, and for the breast 160°. If you don't have a meat thermometer, spear the breast with a knife. The turkey juices should be clear and not pink.

Bake until the skin is a light golden color, and then cover loosely with a foil tent. During the last forty-five minutes of baking, remove the foil tent to brown the skin. Basting is not necessary, but helps promote even browning.

Enjoy!

chapter seventeen

Winter Holidays

> *"The Holidays are a time of year when everybody wants their past forgotten and their present remembered!"*
>
> **—Unknown**

YOU CAN ALMOST SMELL IT. Winter is here, and there's an undeniable electricity in the air. Everyone is a bit happier, a bit kinder, and a bit more compassionate or loving. Snow is starting to fall, temperatures are dropping, and the days are growing shorter. It's that special time of year when miracles happen and celebrations are the routine sounds of the season. Holidays should be a total release, free of stresses and full of spirit. Why? Because it's the high point of the year for parties. Everyone attends at least one party during the winter season: Office holiday parties, Christmas parties, Hanukkah parties, carol sing-alongs, potlucks, cookie exchanges, Secret Santa parties . . . and all before New Years Eve! Whether you observe Kwanza, Christmas, Hanukkah, or no particular religious holiday at all, there is an abundance of ways to feel the celebratory spirit this winter. At the base of all these special days are the same principles: Compassion, generosity of heart, forgiveness, and love. When these principles are incorporated into your seasonal celebrations, you are sure to have a great time.

So what are some great ways to celebrate? Ask friends and family to get together to visit a shelter to serve others for a day. Inquire at your church or a local non-profit organization about their gift-giving policy, and if it is permissible, start a group online or ask guests to bring along wrapped gifts for those who cannot afford any this year. Host a "sELFless" party to wrap and revel with friends who become "elves" for the day with you. Choose a local charity, and in-vite your friends over for cocktails to help fill boxes, wrap, and label. You will really feel the holiday spirit when you help those in need.

If purchasing a lot of extra presents isn't something you and your Mermaid friends have the budget for, go cheap-and-chic and ask guests to *"give the gift of YOU!"* At this party, each guest could identify what their friends may be in need of at the time and share a service. For instance, one might offer to teach a cooking lesson, another may offer free legal services, or the relaxing gift of a massage or nutrition consultation. A friend may offer to design a website for another friend at this party, or babysitting services to help friends finish prepping for the holidays. These types of gifts often have more meaning than any material present.

> **RULE OF FIN:**
> *To wrap gifts in a cheap-and-chic way, use craft paper, newspapers, or even construction paper for smaller gifts and tie with twine. Draw a message or stamp something on the packaging. For spec-and-swish wrapping, dress it up! Tie a necklace or bracelet around a smaller gift as "ribbon" and find beautiful pieces of printed papers, samples of chic wallpaper, or pieces of fabric to use as gift wrap.*

One of my favorite parts of the season is decorat-ing! Growing up, my family always decorated our house to the hilt for Christmas. We started an annual tradition with another family, the Greens, where we would travel to a tree farm the day after Thanksgiving to select our Christmas tree. Then, the following weekend, it was on to unpacking my mom's hundreds of ornaments and boxes of holiday décor. Our

Winter Flowers

Roses, bittersweet, amaryllis, protea, orchids, tulips, ranunculus, amarillas, snow balls, dutch lilacs, poppies, acasia, alstroemeria, carnations, chrysanthemums, cyclamen, evergreens, gerbera daisies, ginger, holly berry, lily, Asiatic lily, Casablanca lily, narcissus, pepperberry, phlox, Queen Ann's lace, Star of Bethlehem, statice.

tree trimming was always accompanied by Benjamin Britton's "Carol of the Bells" and some yummy eggnog or a themed cocktail with neighbors or friends dropping by.

Now that I live in New York City, I've taken a few of these traditions and added a little more *me* to them. For instance, one Christmas I decided to have a peacock-inspired tree. With beautiful peacock ornaments adorning each branch, I filled large hurricane vases with peacock feathers to sit at the base of the tree and on tables around the room. I also strung blue lights around windows for a peaceful look. The top of the tree was adorned with a great model of a peacock with the plume fanned out!

Consider incorporating some of your favorite colors or themes into your holiday decorating. Want the ultimate girly-girl tree? Purchase a fake white or pink tree and decorate it with costume rings and necklaces from your jewelry chest, and tie vintage mini perfume atomizers with silk ribbon to the branches. Place a white cashmere French beret on top with a large gold star pinned to the side of the beret. Sprinkle little faux diamonds around the bottom of the tree and on the fireplace mantle. Fishnet stockings in black or white will look lovely hung on the mantle by large green velvet bows. Dress up your wine and bubbly bottles when having the girls over with precious fur stoles. And I just loved hanging mistletoe made from silver disco balls and holly for the ultimate girls' holiday party last year. Really, anything goes! Just so long as it puts you in the celebratory mood every time you look at it.

My friend Dean really knows how to celebrate the season. He is known for his annual holiday party in Los Angeles where the guest list reads like a "who's who" at a celebrity red carpet event. One year, he actually repainted his house like a candy cane!

Remember to book these folks well in advance— this is peak party season, after all. If you are looking to stay cheap-and-chic, ask friends to lend a hand with the party. Most will gladly spend a little extra time with you making sure the event is a success.

Dean transforms his California dreamin' den into a dreamy North Pole den for his guests to open presents with "Santa" (aka Dean!).

I'm convinced one reason so many people have parties during the holiday season is because the decorating is already complete. If you have already adorned your home for the season, then inviting folks over to make merry just seems like a natural next step. Whether you want your event to be for adults only, or for families, to include gift giving or not, to be a cocktail party or a full-fledged dinner party, allow yourself to really jubilate by hiring people to add the little touches: hire a pianist to play Christmas carols, have your bartenders dress up as snow fairies or mixologist elves, and hire a waitstaff to help with cleanup and to re-plenish food and drink throughout the evening.

> **RULE OF FIN:**
> *Let old traditions inspire new ways to celebrate.*

No matter how you celebrate this holiday season, here are four inspirational ways to make your season a little merrier and brighter:

Invitation Idea. Traditional holiday cards are a great way to invite guests to your party. Or, you can create your own custom invite with photos of your family or friends. If your event is an annual affair, create a photo invite with pictures from the previous year's bash. Guests will love reliving those memories as they anticipate coming to your party this year.

Signature Cocktail: Make sure guests are feeling the spirit of the holidays by serving Midnight Snowglows, Mistletoe Egg Nogs, and Candi Cane Coolers.

Delightful Décor. Use your regular holiday decorations as inspiration for the party. You probably won't even need to add much to them. You could create a flower arrangement from the season with amaryllis, evergreens and fir. If you have a fireplace, build a fire, or fill the bottom of it with lots of glass candles. If not, consider downloading a crackling fireplace to play on your TV.

Fun Favors. A classic or themed holiday or-nament will remind guests every year of your spectacular soiree. Holiday "Crackers" are a fun tradition too. These originated in London and were meant to look like street wrappers. They are simply a cardboard tube wrapped in a festive twist of paper. The cracker is meant to be pulled by two people (or one person can pull each end) and the cracker will split open while making a loud "Crack!" noise. These are usually pulled at Christmas dinners or holiday parties. You can buy them pre-filled with treats or fill them yourself with trinkets, meaningful

RECIPE BOX

The Midnight Snowglow
2 oz Kahlua
hot chocolate
dollop of whipped cream

Make a pot of homemade hot chocolate or use store-bought, and pour into a glass with the Kahlua and stir. Add a dollop of whipped cream. Garnish with an After Eight mint for a frosty finish to your Snowglow.

The Mistletoe Egg Nog
1 cup eggnog
1 1/2 oz vodka
dash of cinnamon

Mix together and sprinkle a dash of cin-namon on top. Garnish with a lipstick kiss on the side of the glass!

Candi Cane Coolers
Named after my dear friend, Candi Maher, who always *loved* the spirit of the holidays.

2 oz vanilla vodka
1/2 oz Peppermint Schnapps

Serve in a rocks glass over ice. Garnish with a mini candy cane or rim the glass with crushed candy canes.

notes, lottery tickets, sweets, or small toys. An easy way to make these at home is with a cardboard toilet paper roll and tissue paper. They are sure to put a smile on your guests' faces.

Twelve Days of Christmas

I love this idea for a Christmas party: Celebrate the "Twelve Days of Christmas" with twelve consecutive nights of gathering with friends, inspired by our friend, Mermaid Shelley.

Mermaid Memory
Mermaid Shelley, Jamie's Mom

Our "Holiday Loop" party started as a progressive dinner party with a group of my very special friends. Then we decided to have a theme to coincide with each year. The year Jamie and Josh married, we had a wedding theme. This year is our 14th year, so our theme is "14 Karat Gold." Carrot cake will be the featured dessert, all of our centerpieces will be spray-painted gold, and of course, we will wear gold attire. Happy Looping!

How does it work? Friends volunteer their homes as a "stop" on this twelve-night holiday loop. Each night's theme is based on one of the days from the song "The Twelve Days of Christmas," and each host creates a menu, cocktail, décor, and even attire based on the theme. If you are a very ambitious Mermaid, you could host the entire affair at your home for a long and lovely "Twelve Days of Christmas" dinner party, or try to incorporate all into a few stops on one evening. Here are some ideas for each day, to get you started:

- *First Night: A Partridge in a Pear Tree.* Serve roasted partridge for dinner followed by pear tarts. Decorate with miniature pear trees or large hurricane vases filled with pears.

- *Second Night: Two Turtledoves.* Serve a dessert bar of chocolate turtle candies and Dove ice cream bars.

- *Third Night: Three French hens.* Serve Cornish hens paired with a festive French wine tasting of three different vintages.

- *Fourth Night: Four Calling Birds.* Remember calling cards? The digital age has all but wiped out this old-fashioned party tradition. Well, calling cards are back! Every guest gets a calling card on this night that is themed to the personality of the person.

- *Fifth Night: Five Golden Rings.* Serve canapés that are round in shape (such as mini quiches or mince pies) in sets of five on beautiful gold-leaf paper on trays, or place multiple clusters of five golden tea lights all along your tables.

- *Sixth Night: Six Geese a Laying.* For a cute and creative centerpiece—spraypaint a bunch of eggs gold and arrange them in glass vases on top of some brown raffia, it will look like the perfect holiday "nest."

- *Seventh Night: Seven Swans a Swimming.* It is said that swans mate for life, so this could be a fun way to celebrate the couples in the room. Maybe there is a newly en-gaged pair you could toast, or honor the couple that has been married for the longest amount of time.

- *Eighth Night: Eight maids a milking.* Serve fresh-baked cookies with milk served in shot glasses for guests to dip and sip.

- *Ninth Night: Nine ladies dancing.* Host a DVD viewing of Radio City Music Hall's Rockettes. Or, rally the kids to create and rehearse a dance that they can perform at the end of the party.

- *Tenth Night: Ten Lords a Leaping.* Host a viewing of *The Nutcracker* ballet, or have this classic playing in the background at your party.

Friends of mine invited ballet students from their local performing arts school to perform scenes from the Nutcracker at their party.

- *Eleventh Night: Eleven Pipers Piping.* Welcome friends to your home with a live bagpiper at the entrance, or play a beautiful soundtrack of bagpipers. Alternatively, host a cake-baking party and everyone gets their own personalized bakers hat, apron, and "cake piper."

- *Twelfth Night: Twelve Drummers Drumming.* Serve chicken drumettes for an hor d'ouevre, play music from a famous drummer like Ringo Starr of the Beatles, or another band with an iconic drummer. Or, if you have the video game Rock Band, everyone can play, and the winner takes home a prize. For dessert, you could bake a "pa-rum-pa-pum-pum" rum cake.

Winter Woodland

This party will have guests dreaming of walking in a winter wonderland. For this event, it's all about putting the whimsy into winter. For a spectacular-and-swish invite, send guests a cedar wood plank with invite details written or stamped in ink directly on the wood and dec-orate the edges with blue and white "snow" crystals. These planks are usually used to cook salmon and can be purchased at the hardware or

woodchips and hand-cut snowflakes which can be easily made from white coffee filters.

Guests will feel cozy inside while sipping the "Snowgoose" signature cocktail, which is simple to make.

RECIPE BOX

The Snowgoose (makes 1 pitcher, serves 6-8)
3 (12 oz) bottles hard cider
1 bottle apple brandy
1 apple, cut into slices
cinnamon sticks
ice

Mix hard cider and apple brandy together into a pitcher. Fill glass cider mugs halfway with ice. Pour "Snowgoose" signature cocktails into mugs. Garnish each mug with an apple slice and cinnamon stick.

grocery store in packages. A cheap-and-chic option is to mail wooden popsicle sticks with details such as the "what," "where," "when," and "why" written on each stick. Place the sticks in a brown recycled envelope or box and fill with

For some delightful décor, bring on the plush plaid. You can even make plaid runners or tablecloths by simply buying fabric by the yard at a fabric store, or consider using a plaid wool blanket or throw. Pull out more of your big, warm, and cozy throw blankets and floor pillows, and scatter them on floors and furniture to create a log cabin mood. Faux fur rugs and throws are easy to find these days in different styles and shades like "fox" and "bear"—and will add a lush look to the room. Centerpieces made from pinecones and fir leaves will add a fragrant touch. If you don't have a working fireplace, use bonfire-scented candles, and play a crackling firewood DVD on the TV. Create a replica of a moose head with antlers to hang over a fireplace or mantle out of brown cardboard or papier mâché. If you are really feeling crafty, drill holes in a real log to hold tea light candles. Make your menu meaningful by filling your buffet table with items like "magic mushroom" appetizers and themed frosty cocktails. Serve an icy blue "Lake" punch with snowflake-shaped ice cubes to warm up a larger crowd. Spray-paint ordinary wooden deer (found at craft stores) colors like winter blue and metallic silver. Place "winter fairies" and sprites in unexpected places to keep guests surprised and entertained all night long.

Your guests can keep the fire burning well after the party with their party favor—a stack of firewood wrapped in a brown craft paper and tied with twine.

> **RULE OF FIN:**
> The "plan-ahead" Mermaid will shop right after the holidays, when décor and gifts are 50-75 percent discounted, and save them in her "treasure chest" for the rest of the year.

White Elephant Party

Mermaids & Martinis hosted a "White Elephant" party in a beautiful venue called the "White Room" at Soho House, in New York City. Jamie and I spray-painted hundreds of circus-style peanuts gold and placed them in glass hurricane vases with bases of fake snow. We also scattered the snow and gold peanuts along the bar and cocktail tables and brought in a beautiful white ceramic elephant to hold the presents. You can host your own "White Elephant" party with a few of these touches.

The primary purpose of a "White Elephant" party is a gift swap. Everyone brings a present (which can be a good present or a "gag" gift, depending on the host's preference), and then everyone participates in a game of chance to determine what present they take home. To play the game, each guest draws a number, and when it's their turn, depending on their number, guests may either "steal" a gift from a person who has selected before them, or they may select and unwrap a new gift. The game ends when each person has had a turn. There are many variations of this game, and it's always a fun time.

Another idea for a swap party is a variation on the good old "Yankee Swap." This has been a tradition in my family for years. Both of my parents come from large families—my mom is one of eight kids and my dad is one of five kids. Once their siblings started having kids and those kids had kids, well, gift giving got a little pricey. So, we started a tradition of "Yankee Swap." How it works: everyone buys a gift at a set budget, but no one knows for whom they are buying for. Then, at the party, we each draw numbers and, on our turn, select a wrapped present to open. It can be pretty funny to see who ends up with what gift.

The funniest gift swap I ever went to was at a holiday party hosted by my friends Stefi and John. They invited all of their guests to look through their homes and bring over something they no longer wanted. Basically, it was a "Dump the Junk" party! When we arrived at their place, all of our unwanted gifts were thrown into a pile and we proceeded to play "White Elephant." It was great fun to watch one guest end up with another's discarded Weight Watchers food journal. Another guest had actually gift-wrapped a bad review he received from his boss at a former job! We read part of that one out loud to the group. Needless to say, it was a memorable night.

Hanukkah Party

"Colorful candles burning bright, each lit on eight very special nights."

—**Author Unknown**

Miracles happen every day. This is the time of year to embrace life's many miracles. Hanukkah has many beautiful aspects, including the ideal of forgiveness, the lucky number eight, and the blessing of miracles. Hanukkah, also called the Festival of Lights, has its origins in the 2nd century BC, when the Hebrews prepared to rededicate their temple by relighting the "eternal flame," after driving out their oppressors. They had just enough consecrated oil to burn for one day, but the oil miraculously lasted for eight days until new oil arrived to fuel the flame. The rededication of the temple after it was defiled could remind us that each of us is a temple with a spiritual presence in our hearts.

In honor of the miracle of Hanukkah, asking guests to recount miracles is a wonderful way to start table talk. You can even purchase books of miracles to distribute to guests at the party. Reading some of these miracles aloud will surely inspire and hearten your guests. Consider setting out little place cards around the table that explain the meaning and significance of Jewish traditions like the dreidel, Hamsa, and Star of David.

Here are four ways to celebrate a meaningful Hanukkah:

Invitation Idea. Invite your guests to celebrate the Festival of Lights with you by sending them a homemade matchbox. Use midnight blue paper and a metallic silver ink star stamp to

decorate the matchbox. Write party details on the back of the box or include them on a folded piece of paper inside. You can find larger cardboard matchboxes online at any art supply store.

Signature Cocktail. Keep the traditional Hanukkah colors throughout your party palette with this specialty cocktail:

RECIPE BOX

Blue Martini (serves 2)

3 oz gin or vodka

1/2 oz dry vermouth

1 t blue Curaçao

1 t fresh lemon juice, strained

Shake all ingredients in a cocktail shaker filled with ice. Strain into two martini glasses, and garnish with lemon twists.

Delightful Décor. Fill hurricane vases with cheap-and-chic plastic dreidels or silver candy gelt coins for centerpieces, and sprinkle extras around your table or bar. Or, be spec-and-swish by investing in a variety of Menorahs from silver and gold, to hand painted or rustic. They will look beautiful when lit and strewn down your table. And, of course, have candles, candles,

candles! Why not play a CD by The Macabees at your next event?

Fun Favor. Send your guests off into the starry night with sparklers. I've even seen some in the shape of the Star of David or a Menorah. A Hanukkah tradition includes eating jelly donuts called Sufganiyot, which make for a fun treat on your table.

Holiday "X"

Even if you don't observe any particular religion, there are still plenty of ways to celebrate the season with friends and family. Here are some of my favorites:

Create a "Giving Tree." Find a way to give back on any budget. This is something you can do with friends of all religions. Collect unwanted clothes to donate, or cook, bake, and gather food for a less fortunate family or neighbor, or donate to a mission. Anything that gets friends and family together to do something good for someone else is a great way to celebrate the season.

Chestnuts Roasting on an Open Fire. Purchase a bag of chestnuts, and use them in every aspect of your party-planning. Make an incision in the chestnuts and use them as place card holders. Then, make a large chestnut centerpiece for your table that features fire-scented candles.

The signature cocktail can be flavored with a nutty liqueur, and you can serve dishes like roasted chestnuts on toast points for an appetizer, chestnut gnocchi and a roast chicken or turkey paired with chestnut sauce or stuffing. Finish with warm chestnut chocolate chip cookies.

Hotel Holidays. Some people shudder at the idea of leaving home for the holidays. But exploring a new destination can be a very spiritual experience! Discover a Roman holiday in Italy, the holy essence of India, or even just a peaceful weekend drive out to the country. Celebrating with family and friends in a new destination can really bring to life the hidden qualities and energies of another city or country. For instance, I know people who travel to New York City on Christmas morning just to visit St. Patrick's Cathedral, and drink eggnog under the grand tree in Rockefeller Center. Wherever you find yourself during the holiday season, keep the spirit in your heart!

Dean Banowetz is known as the "Hollywood Hair Guy." His flair for hair certainly compares to his flair for entertaining. A beloved host, his parties have become true Hollywood legends. Here are a few tips from one of the finest:

Q: What's the best supplement to a party?
A: When I have a party, everything has to go together. Remember, *love is in the details*. Food is also beyond fantastic. I always use the same chef to cater my parties, and the only guideline I give him is, "I want my guests to forget about everything at the party except the food." I also love games, which are my specialty because I am all about being in character and creating an environment. Decorations are important, too. I say, "It is never done until it is *overdone*." I love to paint my house to match my gift wrap. When you think you have too much, add more. I am not happy unless people's jaws are on the floor. I want to make sure they are never going to forget my parties, and I want people to want to come back to my parties.

Q: Who are some of your favorite guests or types of guests?
A: My favorite guests are ones who RSVP on time and are willing to participate in all of the activities and events. I also love guests who like to mix and mingle.

Q: What is your favorite thing to do when preparing for an event?
A: No detail is too small for me. I love to make a fantasy list of over-the-top, crazy ideas, and then I try to make them realistic. For example, a party theme could be as basic as a cookout. But taking it to the next level is key. So, pick fifteen or so friends and tell them to bring a change of clothes to spend the night if they drink too much. When they show up at the party, have ten or fifteen pup tents set up for them to sleep in. They'll go crazy and think it is fabulous, but then you take it up another notch. Hire a caterer to come in the morning to make custom omelets for them.

Q: What has been your favorite event to attend or host, and why?
A: I love a fabulous Christmas party because no one usually remembers the Christmas party they went to last year.

Q: What makes a party a memory for you?
A: My favorite things to have at my parties are a photographer, a bunch of disposable or Polaroid cameras, or a photo booth (or, in my case, photoboothless.com) so my guests have a take-away memory. If I am having a dinner party, I want the table to be especially decorated. Under each placemat is a zip-top bag that guests can use to take what they want from the table, as long as it fits in the bag. It is *all* about a take-away! Because then every time a guest sees that item, they think of me.

Q: What's your "Rule of Fin"?
A: A host gift is a must, and if there is a specific theme, follow the rules of the host. Also, smile a lot, and remember, it is a party!

Q: What is your secret to unwinding when the party is over?
A: I always include the party-over time in the invitation. It helps me be respectful of the neighbors, and it is great for helping me manage the time of the folks I've hired. After everyone leaves, I love to have something to eat because I usually don't eat during the party. Then, I take a hot shower, and I relax with a glass of wine.

chapter eighteen

A Theme for Every Party, and Every Party Has Its Theme

"I don't know a lot about politics, but I can recognize a good party when I see one!"—Mae West

ALL PARTIES REQUIRE A THEME—even if it's just in the selection of foods you choose to serve. Remember my first party? The Las Vegas buffet? I was so overly excited about the party that I overwhelmed my guests by serving all kinds of dishes from pork sliders to petits fours. It made absolutely no sense because it had no unifying theme.

While I'm a true believer in living the theme all the way from my shoes to my up-do, I also love getting others involved in the mood. When I was in college, I signed up to take a bartending course. Even back then, I loved mixing cocktails and serving them to happy guests! Well, the night before my first class, I invited everyone who lived on the first floor of our apartment building to gather for a viewing of *Cocktail*, the movie starring Tom Cruise. I played the part of bartender and had a great time mixing drinks for everyone. It really put me in the mood for class the next day.

Every time I travel to my favorite city in the world, Paris, I watch a few of my favorite French movies the week before to get into my Frenchie frame of mind. I invite over a fellow Mermaid to open a bottle of French champagne, and pack my suitcase—which always becomes a party in its own right! By living the French theme, saying *bonsoir* is never easier!

Another example of living the theme is when I recently visited an ashram. Before the trip, I decided to make a pact with myself (my higher self, of course) to not watch any television, and to cleanse my diet. I bought a bunch of great meditation downloads for my iPod to listen to on the plane and boat ride there. It was much easier to ease into ten days of yoga and silence when I had lived the theme before. And it really helped me get the most out of my trip, so I could spiritually bring even more back home with me. If you live the theme from head to toe, you and your guests will always be in the

Mermaid Memory
Mermaid Valery

Not long ago I had the joy of helping my cousin Hilary plan my sister Kirsten's bridal shower. Hilary and I had chosen a sunflower theme for the shower (Kirsten's favorite flower). We adorned the venue with beautiful sunflowers and used yellows, golds, and browns for all of the place settings, linens, china, and centerpieces. The day of the shower arrived, and the bridesmaids began to gather. As they were taking in our sunflower heaven, Hilary exclaimed, "Don't forget, LIVE the theme, ladies!" Even though many of the girls looked confused, I didn't even flinch. Because I've known her my whole life, this statement came as no surprise. I can happily say that all of the party guests still rave about our successful sunflower soiree! I also love to entertain, and often follow Hilary's Rule of Fin when hosting parties. After all, the theme really is the keystone of a party. It's what makes sense of all the decorations, the food and beverage choices, the music, and sometimes even the host's attire. Here's to living the theme!

mood for a great party. So, the next time you channel your inner Mermaid to plan the bash of the year, *LIVE THE THEME!*

Here are some popular theme ideas to get you started:.

Breakfast at Tiffany's

"Well, when I get the mean reds, the only thing that does any good is to jump in a cab and go to Tiffany's. Calms me down right away. The quietness and the proud look of it; nothing very bad could happen to you there. If I could find a real-life place that'd make me feel like Tiffany's, then . . . I'd buy some furniture and give the cat a name!"

—Holly Golightly

This is a great party theme for a group of your closest, not-afraid-to-hug-you-really-tight kind of friends. It's a brunch, which always invokes a warm, intimate energy. Best of all, this event is not that hard to pull together—you really

can host this party on any old Saturday or Sunday with little preparation. Serve up your own version of Breakfast at Tiffany's, throw on a little black dress, and remember, don't invite any Super Rats!

Invitation Idea. Write the lyrics from the movie's theme song "Moon River" on a note card, or email a great vintage shot of Audrey inscribed with the details of your event— after all, she is pretty hard to say "no" to! You can invite ladies to dress up in their favorite "Audrey" look.

Signature Cocktail. Serve Holly Golightly's: Champagne, of course! You could also dress up your bubbly with a splash of orange juice or peach puree, adorned by a faux pearl stirrer—

which is the perfect twist on a classic mimosa or Bellini.

Delightful Décor. Welcome guests to your home by hanging a large ream of Tiffany robin's egg blue colored paper to your front door adorned with a large white bow to resemble an oversized Tiffany box. Buy long strings of fake pearls and lay them across the table, make "trivets" by weaving them around breadbaskets piled high with warm croissants and around your serving platters. For this party, go mad with the pearls, darling! Have them dripping everywhere—from chandeliers, strung along wall mouldings, hanging off of chair backs, and overflowing out of vases filled with white flowers. Place little Tiffany blue boxes on white plates as place card holders with name cards slipped underneath the boxes, and place a few chocolates inside. Create

a "Tomato" centerpiece in honor of Holly's weekly visits to "Sally Tomato" at Sing Sing. Brighten up the brunch with a game! Pass around cards and ask each guest to answer questions related to the movie like, *"What would you have named Holly Golightly's cat?"*

Fun Favors. Send guests home with a mix of different copies of this classic Truman Capote book, from vintage books to newer copies. You could also send guests home with a pair of inexpensive oversized black sunglasses and a two-pack of aspirin.

Sunday Jazz Brunch

Breakfasts are a tall order. Recently I hosted a breakfast event for fifteen ladies. Now, women have different tastes when it comes to breakfast: soy milk vs. skim, egg whites vs. regular, and the list goes on and on. So, we made it simple by going to the market and buying a large selection of baked goods, eggs, and toppings for made-to-order omelets.

Coffee might be one of the most important parts of a brunch, and everyone has an opinion on a good cup of coffee. I think freshly-ground beans paired with good, filtered water and prepared in a French Press makes the best coffee. My friend Alethea introduced me to the electric kettle when I was visiting her in

Paris. It really does boil water faster than the time it takes you to pull out all the fixings for the coffee! No matter your preference, your guests will thank you for offering them a little caffeine pick-me-up.

Here are four ways to host a memorable Sunday brunch:

Invitation Idea. *"Feeling kind of blue? Brighten-up and join us for a brunch set to jazz music."* Inscribe this on a jazz-themed invite, and guests will be tooting your horn.

Signature Cocktail. Serve an "Ella so Smoothie!" Smoothies are a great idea for brunches. Healthy fruits, milk, ice, and frozen yogurt make a delicious treat. Pitchers of fresh-squeezed orange juice and bloody mary's are also a great addition to a brunch.

Delightful Décor. Jazz music and a mellow vibe are key. Set your guests' places with sections from *The New York Times*. If one of your guests just loves sports, set his place with the sports section. His wife likes staying on top of all the cultural happenings around town? Outfit her place setting with the arts and leisure section. Take individual whole eggs and place them in egg cup holders for the place cards—draw the guest's caricature or name right on the egg! We all know how

wonderfully energized one can become by merely sniffing the aroma of coffee. Fill low glass vases with fresh coffee beans and white pillar candles, and you've added a lovely, fragrant light to your brunch.

Fun Favors. A copy of Miles Davis' *Kind of Blue* album.

Preppy Party!

"People ask how can a Jewish kid from the Bronx do preppy clothes? Does it have to do with class and money? It has to do with dreams." —Ralph Lauren

A few years ago, I attended a party where everything seemed to be growing plaid and navy. There were embroidered sayings all over the joint, and a friend of mine actually asked if he missed the memo on a pink-pants convention. Well, I must admit, at times I just love myself a little alligator, and draping a cardigan over the shoulders can be an art form in itself. Here are a few "pearls" to inspire your next preppy party:

Invitation Idea. Monogrammed invites, of course! Nothing says preppy like the monogram.

Also, look for invitations that offer plaid, argyle, or madras prints. Guests can take fashion cues from the invites.

Signature Cocktail. The Blue Whale: A stiff "G & T" made with Bombay Sapphire Gin and tonic water. Garnish with a white cocktail onion. After only a few of these, your guests are sure to have a whale of a time. Serve with seersucker cocktail napkins.

Delightful Décor. Ask hired help to dress in preppy attire and have them pass classic Gibson martinis atop tennis rackets to guests, and serve up snacks like chips, nuts, and pretzels in tennis ball tins. Your tabletop fabric should be seersucker or plaid, and everyone must be invited to wear their best whites, pinks, lime greens, and navy. Don't forget to make the lawn a part of your décor. Have games like boulé and croquet ready for play. Tennis court? Definitely time for a match. Poolside? Serve drinks at a "swim-up bar."

Fun Favors.
Embroidered flasks.

*fin*Tastic idea:
You can easily make a swim-up bar by placing a festive tray of beverages on an oversized pool raft and set it to "sail" in the pool.

For a few years, I was lucky to be invited to the Sundance Film Festival. I made some really great memories there. One of my favorite memories was going to a dinner and sitting near Robert Redford and his daughter Amy. I could not stop staring at him because he is still just as gorgeous as he was in *Barefoot in the Park*. He appeared to be one of those men who is so unbelievably comfortable in his skin that he just exudes this calm, peaceful "nothing to prove" aura. Being at Sundance really transports you to a new place. It makes me want to throw a party and invite every celebrity under the snow! I've found myself sipping a beer next to quite a few big stars out there—talk about blockbuster memories.

Film and Television Awards Season

"We want to thank all of you for watching us congratulate ourselves tonight."—**Warren Beatty**

And the winner is . . . the Mermaid! You can choose from any of the big awards shows for this silver-screen event. The Oscars, the Emmys, the Golden Globes, or the Screen Actors Guild awards will provide the perfect backdrop for your star-studded evening. Whatever you decide, make it a red carpet night and treat your guests like superstars. Invite your guests to wear black tie if it's an Oscar party, or festive casual attire if it's one of the other shows.

Invitation Idea. Send your guests a ballot and ask them to select their pick of winners in advance. A cheap-and-chic option is to do this via email. Collect the answers a few days before your event so you can organize the submissions in a format that will be quick to tally throughout the night.

Signature Cocktail. Design your cocktails around the big celebrity nominees. Maybe the "Julia" is a red, fiery drink, or the "De Niro" is a timeless version of a classic Italian Negroni, served straight up.

Delightful Décor. Roll out the red carpet! I rent or buy these for events all the time, and they come in all colors from traditional red to pink, gold, or printed motifs. But, if you don't want to invest in a real red carpet, look for some inexpensive red fabric that can be cut or folded to mimic a red carpet. Take digital photos of your guests early in the evening, and then take a few minutes to print them out on glossy photo paper during the party. Hang the photos on a wall or bulletin board, and don't forget to ask your guests for their autographs! You will have your own Walk of Fame by the end of the party.

Fun Favors. The photos double as fun party favors with take-home frames. A cheap-and-chic option is mini boxes of popcorn, or boxed movie candy tied with a ribbon and a pair of movie vouchers so guests can enjoy a movie night on you.

Meet Me at Tony's

> *"You've gotta be original, because if you're like someone else, what do they need you for?"* —**Bernadette Peters**

I grew up listening to musicals, so I find myself always looking for a happy ending. Sometimes life is not so—you can't always be the leading lady accepting the little gold statue. Sometimes you may feel like the unfortunate chorus girl waiting for her next big break. Whatever your current role

---

I once worked for a magazine that was very involved with an independent film festival hosted in Napa Valley and Sonoma, California. Traveling to the wine country in California was breathtaking and beautiful enough, but hosting *al fresco* films under the stars, right on a vineyard, was heaven. Watching our guests sip rare vintages under a starry night sky while viewing a film projected on the side of a wine cave on a serene and breezy evening was *fin*Tastic!

You can recreate this feeling with your own outdoor movie night. Buy or rent a projector, spread out blankets and pillows on your lawn, serve casual drinks and appetizers, and watch guests relax into an evening of film and fun. You can also go spec-and-swish by ordering matching chaise lounge covers for this event. Have them monogrammed with the date or name of the event or film, then set up the chairs "theater style" and label them by row numbers. Equip each one with a blanket, pillow, and cup holder so the audience can enjoy a libation or two. Tell guests to take their own chair home as a reminder of the fun they had at your festival.

it's a *Mary Poppins* party, and you fill your venue with upside-down umbrellas hanging from the ceilings (use the same adhesive peel-and-stick hook trick as I suggested for your paper moon lanterns), and make it a desserts-only fete by serving "spoonfuls of sugar"—i.e., sweets by the pound! You could easily turn a *Rock of Ages* party into a karaoke-themed event. Celebrate both acts of the hit *Grey Gardens* by serving champagne alongside a centerpiece made from a pyramid of canned corn. The show *Hair* could become a groovy, Woodstock-styled party. Whatever it is, channel your Idina Menzel, Kristin Chenowith, or Tommy Tune and break out some of those great musical soundtracks for inspiration. This party should definitely have "Acts," so think about serving a "first act"-themed cocktail and hors d'oeuvres followed by the second act dinner course, and a grand finale dessert!

Invitation Idea. Write up party details in theater "speak," such as *"Curtain call is at 8 PM!"* Some musical theater can be quite campy, so if you really want to go all out, why not send a small white plaster "cast" with the event details written in permanent marker alongside, *"Break a leg!"* Your guests could bring their cast to the party to get autographs and personal notes from everyone, which makes for a fun favor.

Delightful Décor. Dig out old playbills, or download playbill covers online. Photocopy

may feel like, Mermaids learn to enjoy all the moments we can. A party celebrating the Tony awards can make for a great, happy finale!

Choose your favorite musical (*A Chorus Line* was always one of my favorites) and let it inspire the theme of your party. Or, build your theme around whatever musical is hot at the moment. Maybe and paste them on serving trays and hang them around your venue. Purchase some top hats, spray-paint them silver or gold, and hand them out to guests to wear. Place extra top hats overturned on your tables and fill them with vases of flowers or popcorn for show-stopping centerpieces.

Signature Cocktail. For this kind of event, I like a great champagne punch titled "The Encore," because everyone will be going back again and again for another glass. Tip: Use a good champagne or sparkling wine for the punch, and then all you need is ginger ale and some strawberries.

RECIPE BOX

The Encore
  1 bottle of champagne
  1 2 liter bottle of ginger ale
  2 10 oz packs, frozen strawberries
  (partially thawed)
In a large punch bowl, combine the champagne, ginger ale and strawberries. Stir gently. Before serving, add ice and stir again.

Fun Favor. Send guests home with the movie or book version of a show, or the CD. The top hats also make great party favors.

Cinco de Mayo or Taco Tuesday

"Tell me who your friends are and I'll tell you who you are." —**Mexican Proverb**

What is it about Mexican restaurants that seem to make everyone happy? Is it the flavorful food or the festive red-hot bowls of salsa and queso on the tables? Or maybe it is the lively music that makes you want to spring out of your chair, grab a guapo, and salsa with him!

Here are some of my favorite ways to take a quick and caliente trip south of the border:

Get ready to fiesta by draping a brightly colored printed shawl over your couch, or roll out white craft paper on your table and use Mexican-inspired paint pens or bright, colored markers to label everyone's seat or draw fun images. Create centerpieces by filling glass vases with lots of green and red chili peppers. You can also line the exterior of the vases with those peppers and place a colorful bouquet of flowers in the center, and don't forget the piñatas! The final touch: drape sombreros on the backs of all of your chairs. Don't have any of these items on hand? Check out dollar stores or online party retailers like Oriental Trading Co. Remember to take

a couple of those sombreros and place them upside down on your table. The insides of the hats are great holders for wooden bowls of salsa, queso, and guacamole. You can even spread tortilla chips or colored tealights all along the rim of the sombreros.

Pick up some cheap-and-chic limes to use as place card holders. Or, take some of those extra chili peppers and slice them to hold place cards. If you really want to splurge, create a "Guacamole Bar." Invest in a bunch of stone ground bowls to make homemade guacamole. Each guest can use a bowl to mix his or her own to taste. Flavored Mexican hot chocolate tablets make great party favors.

Your guests will be ready to fiesta from the moment they receive the invitation, and they will be talking about your party for many May 5th's to come. And all because you made a few easy and inexpensive moves to transform your home into a hacienda.

Guacamole

Remember, some like it hot! Serves 2-4.

2 ripe avocados
1/2 red onion, minced (about 1/2 cup)
1-2 serrano chiles, stems and seeds removed, minced
2 T cilantro leaves, finely chopped
1 T fresh lime or lemon juice
1/2 t coarse salt
dash of freshly grated black pepper
1/2 ripe tomato, seeds and pulp removed, chopped

Garnish with limes, red radishes, or jicama. Serve with tortilla chips or soft flour tortillas.

1. Cut avocados in half, remove pit. Scoop out avocado from the peel, put in a mixing bowl.

2. Using a fork, mash the avocado. Add the chopped onion, cilantro, lime or lemon, salt and pepper and mash some more. Chili peppers vary individually in their hotness. So, start with half of one chili pepper and add to the guacamole to your desired degree of hotness. Keep the tomatoes separate until ready to serve. Remember that much of this is done to taste because of the variability in the fresh ingredients. Start with this recipe and adjust to your taste.

3. Cover with plastic wrap directly on the surface of the guacamole to prevent oxidation from the air reaching it. Refrigerate until ready.

4. Just before serving, add the chopped tomato to the guacamole and mix.

Invitation Idea. Spec-and-swish: mail stone bowls with a recipe card for homemade guacamole. On the back of the recipe card, include your party details. For a cheap-and-chic option, go for brightly colored invites that beckon guests to come and olé the night away.

Signature Cocktail. "Stella's Sunset," which my friend Stella created. It's amazing, and so easy to make. Pour 2 oz of Patron over ice in a rocks glass; then, pour Limonata over the tequila and ice. Stir and garnish with a small red chili pepper.

Delightful Décor. When decorating for this kind of party, you can go loco without even downing a few tequila shots. In addition to the throws and sombreros, consider placing fake mustaches at the place settings for the men, and red paper rose hair "wreaths" (Frida Kahlo style) for the ladies. Music is also important. Find a great album, or hire a live Mariachi band to come to your home.

Fun Favors. Mexican hot chocolate tablets, sombreros, mustaches, and the paper flowers—let your décor double as party favors!

RULE OF FIN:
If an avocado does not "bounce back" to the touch, it is not ripe. Keep pits in your guacamole to keep it fresh and prevent browning when you store in the refrigerator.

*fin*Tastic Idea: Celebrate another Mexican event in style with an *"El Dia de los Muertos"* party, a *"Day of the Dead"* party.

This is a traditional celebration to honor relatives who have passed and is typically celebrated on November 1st or 2nd of each year. Memories are shared and stories are told. Décor ideas are hand painted papier mâché skulls and toy skeletons, as well as candy, flowers, and mementos. Shrines are built with pictures of those who have passed, and tokens are placed there to remember them by. Have fun honoring those you have loved by serving their favorite dishes and cocktails, playing their music and decorating in their style. This day is meant to be sentimental and fun.

New England Shore Dinner

"If you're fond of sand dunes and salty air
Quaint little villages here and there
You're sure to fall in love with old Cape Cod

If you like the taste of a lobster stew
Served by a window with an ocean view
You're sure to fall in love with old Cape Cod

Winding roads that seem to beckon you
Miles of green beneath a sky of blue
Church bells chimin' on a Sunday morn
Remind you of the town where you were born

If you spend an evening you'll want to stay
Watching the moonlight on Cape Cod Bay
You're sure to fall in love with old Cape Cod"
—Sung by Patti Page

I grew up in New England and spent a few summers away at an overnight sailing camp in Chatham, Cape Cod. My first memories of lobster rolls and salty air will always stay with me, and although now I spend a lot of my vacation and summer weekends on the east end of Long Island, nothing compares to those New England summers of my childhood. This party theme evokes all that is grand and wonderful about the

New England summer, and can be created in any part of the country!

Invitation Idea. Send your printed invitation with two lobster claws on either side "holding" the invite. Clever copy could read: *"Just Be-Claws it's Summer"* or *"Lobster-Bake Bash!"* The invitation itself should have a nautical or summery theme. You might even find old sea maps online that you can print out and overlay the details of your party.

Signature Cocktail. Serve a crisp, white summer wine from a local vineyard, or a refreshing summer ale from Boston, Maine, or another New England locale. Fill colored beach pails with ice to hold your beers, wine, soft drinks and water, which will pair well with your lobster dinner or clambake.

Delightful Décor. Send the kiddies out to the beach to collect items for your natural centerpiece. Spread black and white newspapers along

*fin*Tastic Idea: If you really want to be spec-and-swish, what about hosting a "Mermaid Watch" party? Do some research online and print old maps that show where sailors used to try to locate mermaids. Place long brass telescopes in the center of the table. Create a mini "Row Bar" by using a dingy or old row boat (paint the name of the theme of your party on it, or, for a less permanent option, use decals to display a themed message) and fill one half of the boat with ice and beverages, and use the other half for a raw bar that features a variety of shellfish. Strategically position lobster pots on either side of the boat and fill them with large pillar candles to keep your "Row Bar" alight as the sun goes down.

How to Put Together a Traditional Lobster and Clam Bake

Getting Started: Choose a great location outdoors, select and purchase your ingredients, plan out the cooking, and pick your sides.

Ingredients (per person):
1 lobster
1/2 lb. shellfish, including any or all:
mussels, oysters, clams, steamers
1/2 lb. sausage
(linguica, kielbasa, or andouille recommended)
1/2 onion, cut into quarters
1 ear of corn
2 cans beer or water

Directions for cooking your clambake in a pit or on the grill: First, dig a deep, wide pit and fill the pit with charcoal. Then, light your fire, and surround the coals with medium and large rocks. Do not cover the charcoal because you could put the fire out. Let the rocks heat up. When they are hot enough, a drop of water will evaporate on them. If using a charcoal grill, remove the grate, and follow the same instructions as for a pit. When the coals are burning brightly, begin layering your ingredients. First add a layer of seaweed, then clams/oysters, then more seaweed, then linguica/sausage (if using), then more seaweed, potatoes, corn, lobster and more seaweed. Finally, add a layer of wet burlap that you've soaked in beer to help seal in the moisture.

Note: If using a grill, you won't need the burlap and can simply close the top. Cook for approximately one hour.

Serving suggestions: Serve your seafood alongside small ramekins filled with melted butter so everyone can dunk their steamers and lobsters. Lemon wedges can be squeezed over all the seafood. Nothing completes a clam bake or lobster bake like delicious New England clam chowder, coleslaw, and corn on the cob.

the table (which is hopefully outdoors) to be cheap-and-chic, or roll out your brown craft paper and spread out an old hammock on top for a tablecloth that resembles a fish net. Tie your napkins with rope or twine in the shape of sailor knots. At my sailing camp, the figure eight was the first knot I learned, and I have put it to good use at the dinner table (if not at sea). Don't be afraid to bring the indoors outside! You can create an outdoor room from scratch. I had

Mermaid Memory: *Mermaid Hilary*

One summer weekend, my friend Annie and I were at the beach preparing for a barbecue with friends. Annie is a real-deal Mermaid. She's the kind of girl you always want to borrow something from, and not because she buys everything that is trendy and expensive. Annie really knows how to treasure shop, and she finds some real gems. Inevitably, if you ask Annie where she bought something, her reply will be, "It was my grandmother's," or "Oh, this? I just bumped into this at a little boutique." Not only does Annie have a real knack for putting together an outfit and making it look delicious, but Annie also has a real knack for making ingredients come together in a delicious way. For our barbeque, Annie made this *fin*Tastic salad dressing. It was healthy, memorable, and easy. And, now I use it all the time. At your next summer soiree, try this out:

Annie's Amagansett Dressing
Combine 1 T of Grey Poupon mustard, a drizzle of honey, and the juice of a whole lemon. Mix well. Then pour in an equal portion of olive oil. Mix again and serve. Easy, healthy, and dee-lish.

a beautiful jute rug in my old apartment. When the time came to get a bigger rug for the room, I turned my old jute rug into the perfect base for a beach picnic party. This idea can work for any rug or piece of furniture that you think has seen its last day in the sun. If you have the means to store these pieces, you can repaint them, or personalize them to give them a second life.

Fun Favors. Cheap-and-chic: little silver tins placed at each setting and filled with lobster bibs, oyster crackers, wet naps, small jars of cocktail sauce, and tins of Old Bay seasoning. Spec-and-swish: monogrammed boat bags filled with lush beach towels.

A Night in Paris

"If you are lucky enough to have lived in Paris as a young man, then wherever you go for the rest of your life it stays with you, for Paris is a moveable feast."

—Ernest Hemingway

Every night in Paris is an event. Dinner on an ordinary Tuesday night means making a trip to the local fishmonger, then on to the boulangerie for a freshly baked baguette, the patisserie for macarons and sweets, the vintner's for wine, and the flower cart for flowers! If ever a city believed in the small details, it is Paris. Next time you want to recreate a slice of Paris, here are a few tips I have learned:

Invitation Idea. Nothing says "French" to me like a beautiful soufflé. I once went to a restaurant in Paris near the Eiffel Tower where everything on the menu was a soufflé. Consider a soufflé-themed party with an invitation that asks guests to, *"Please come and soufflé with me!"* You could start with a cheese soufflé, followed by a chicken and mushroom or fruit de mer (seafood) soufflé, and finish with a chocolate, hazelnut, or even chestnut soufflé. Magnifique.

Or, perhaps the Moulin Rouge is more your speed. Invite guests to your affair with red and gold invitations that feature a spinning windmill or pin wheel on the front with the event details.

Signature Cocktail. For the soufflé-themed party, try the "Chestnut Magic." Pour Marrone Roasted Chestnut Liqueur over ice for an aperitif. You can also add a splash to a cup of coffee for a delicious post-soufflé nightcap.

For the Moulin Rouge party, serve the "Can Can." Mix two parts Domaine De Canton French Ginger Liqueur with three parts gin. Garnish with candied ginger and a cucumber slice. Serve in a chilled martini glass.

Delightful Décor. These ideas will work for both the soufflé-theme and Moulin Rouge theme because they are so evocative of Paris. Create a tower of macarons. Hire Lido dancers to perform at your bash. Go online and print the old French ads for the Moulin Rouge. Frame these and place them around your venue. Use empty champagne and French wine bottles as vases for flowers. I also love a champagne tower. It was at my friends' Alex and Alethea's wedding in a town called Fontainebleau, just outside of Paris, that I first saw one. Stack a bunch of champagne glasses in a tower. When you start pouring the champagne from the top, it trickles down like a beautiful cascade of bubbles.

Fun Favors. For the soufflé-themed party, send guests home with a soufflé pan or a bottle of great French wine.

For the Moulin Rouge party, a cheap-and-chic favor is pasties for the ladies (and the guys will thank you, too).

Kentucky Derby Party

"I didn't want to just come to the Kentucky Derby to say I was in the race."

—Michael Matz

203

Whether you are from a red state or a blue state, from the Deep South or Denver—everyone looks forward to the Kentucky Derby at Churchill Downs, held annually on the first Saturday in May. This gorgeous and grand horse race is the perfect reason to get friends to gather and cheer for their picks. If you are lucky enough to be there in person—hats off to you! (Or perhaps I should say, "Hats *on* to you!")

I met Betty Baird Kregor, a beautiful blonde Mermaid from Kentucky, while in the Bahamas. She was vacationing at a neighboring hotel with her stunningly beautiful family. It's amazing what you can learn about someone if you are open to just starting a conversation. It turned out she is a golf pro, mom to equestrian daughters, and was on Oprah! I told her how I'd always wanted to host a true, old-fashioned Kentucky Derby Party, and she was full of advice. We became Facebook friends, and I'm continually inspired by, and following her every Southern move online. To Derby like the true South, you must serve mint juleps made with Kentucky bourbon. I've actually named one of my signature cocktails "The Baird" in honor of the lovely Betty. Mermaids are off to the races with these fabulous ways to host your own "Day at the Derby" party!

Invitation Idea. Create and send out betting sheets that feature the details of your event. Ask your guests to bring them to the party with their top horse picks for the chance to win prizes. Real betting sheets usually aren't available until a day or two before the Derby. Don't forget to include: "Derby Attire," big hats and big appetites.

Signature Cocktail. Get into the spirit of the South by serving mint juleps accompanied by mini pecan pies. We love serving up two versions of this classic cocktail, one called "Minty" and the other "The Thoroughbred." ("The Thoroughbred" was for our guests who craved a little less mint and a little more bourbon.) Your guests might also like "The Baird," or they might prefer a menu that's more "down and derby," like frozen bourbon slushies and buckets of Kentucky Fried Chicken! If you plan ahead, you can order authentic monogrammed mint julep cups from numerous online vendors, which will make your guests feel like they are sitting right on "Millionaire's Row."

Delightful Décor. You don't need to be at Churchill Downs to feel like you're running for the roses. Dress your table with a bed of roses by cutting tons of red rosebuds and placing them along the center of your table. Buy a separate bouquet of miniature red rosebuds and use them to create horseshoe shapes for the corners of large white or silver serving platters. Go to the hardware store and purchase some brass rings or horseshoes, which will look great as napkin rings or "coasters" fitted around your glassware. Buy two or three traditional black velvet riding hats (or

RECIPE BOX

Minty and The Thoroughbred (serves 2)
  20–30 mint sprigs
  1 cup sugar
  1 cup water
  3 oz bourbon

Prepare mint simple syrup by dissolving 1 cup of granulated sugar into 1 cup of boiling water. Crush 10–12 mint sprigs in the syrup to release mint essence. Allow to cool completely (about one hour). Place 1–2 T (or to taste) of the mint simple syrup into a julep cup. Add the bourbon, fill with crushed ice, and stir until the glass becomes frosty. Garnish with a mint sprig. For "The Thoroughbred" variation, add an extra 1 oz of bourbon to each glass.

The Baird (serves 1)
  2 oz rum
  mint leaves
  strawberries
  simple syrup

Pack the bottom of a julep cup with a few mint leaves and strawberries. Pour simple syrup over it and muddle away. Pour rum and fill with crushed ice.

Bourbon Slushies (serves 1)
  1 part Coca-Cola
  1 part bourbon

Blend the Coca-Cola and bourbon with lots of crushed ice. Serve in a glass mason jar and enjoy!

plastic to be cheap-and-chic), overturn, and place white bowls inside filled with appetizers like chips, dips, and nuts. While you are at a local tack shop (or logged onto eBay), buy a pair of black riding boots.(Rubber boots are available on the cheap and are even better suited to planting.) Fill each boot with a lovely green topiary tree and place the pair at the door to greet guests. Big, beautiful hats are a requirement. If guests forget, set up a little "stable table" at the party with plenty of plastic derby hats, found at your local party supply store. Lay out beads, feathers, flowers, and glue so guests

can decorate and write the names of the horses they are rooting for. Finally, go to a thrift store or search online for some beautiful and budget-friendly hats. Hang them throughout your home, on the backs of doors, and on your front door, or offer them as prizes to those lucky bettors.

Fun Favors. Much of your décor can double as party favors, including the hats and roses. Or, you can order monogrammed Southern-style paper fans to give to guests. Guests will look oh-so-gracious leaving your soiree with fans in hand.

Feng Shui Fetes

"Be not afraid of growing slowly; be afraid only of standing still."

—Chinese Proverb

My feng shui architect R.D. Chin helped transform my living space and, therefore, my life! He visited my apartment and helped me uncover the areas that were "blocked" energy-wise. First, he laid out the Chinese traditional Ba-gua. A Ba-gua is what you use to define the "corners" of your home, usually broken down by wall. So, my apartment had the Travel Wall, Career Wall, Wealth and Power Wall, and the Wall of Creativity. My travel wall "worked" almost instantly. After we feng shui'd I scored a free trip with fellow entrepreneurs to London on a private charter! Then the career wall started to kick in when Mermaids & Martinis gained a lot of momentum in a short amount of time. The other walls are still taking shape! Consider hosting a feng shui fete to enjoy some chic chi and share that good energy with friends.

Invitation Idea. Send your invite on Chinese red paper or bamboo paper and print a yin/yang symbol on the invite.

Signature Cocktail. Serve a Chi-Tini. Pour 3 parts sake and 1 part PAMA (pomegranate flavored liquor) into a glass, hit the side of the glass with a spoon to mix the liquids, and serve in glasses that are chilled. Have bamboo drinking straws ready! You can also keep it simple by serving sake in classic authentic sake cups alongside Sapporo beer.

Delightful Décor. Chinese foo dog centerpieces and polished black river stones will set the

Nine is a very auspicious number according to feng shui. I asked R.D. for some tips on hosting a *fin*Tastic feng shui fete, and he sent me nine possibilities:

- Colorful Chinese envelopes with a dollar bill or money gift make a great party favor. These red envelopes are used for auspicious and happy occasions. When you buy red envelopes, please check the Chinese character to make sure the envelopes match the theme of your party!

- Small Chinese take-out boxes filled with chocolate-covered fortune cookies, with a Chinese coin attached to a red ribbon on the boxes are fun takeaways for guests.

- Small earth crystals, such as heart-shaped rose quartz crystals, in a decorative silk pouch for love and protection will make a meaningful gift for guests.

- Another great gift idea is jade bracelets, which protect the body and spirit.

- For décor, string lights made with colorful Chinese lanterns that symbolize "Good luck!"

- Give a gift of fruit, such as oranges and clementines, which symbolize a "Wish for good fortune and new beginnings."

- Get a deck of I-Ching cards and read them with your friends to gain insights for your problems.

- Ba-gua mirrors symbolize "protection" from sharp corners and unwelcome neighbors. Purchase these for guests to take home.

- Gift a feng shui consultation as part of a surprise raffle!

right tone on a table. You can also create a large centerpiece of clementines and a bamboo plant. Serve your food right out of Chinese take-out boxes with ivory chopsticks and insert personalized "messages" into each guest's fortune cookies. Add a spec-and-swish flair to the event by inviting a Bonsai artist to teach a master class at the party and each guest can create their own Bonsai scene to take home.

Fun Favors. How about R.D.'s book? It's called *Feng Shui Revealed*. Or consider sending guests home with soy candles or a small lucky bamboo plant.

I Love a Luau

"Hele mei hoohiwahiwa!"
—"Come celebrate!" in Hawaiian

I love a good luau. Traditionally, a luau is celebrated by roasting a whole pig as the centerpiece of the event. Practically, this is not so easy to do! My friends hosted a beautiful luau complete with a whole pig, including an apple in its mouth. Impressive as it was, my vegan cousin Brittany cried "Poor Wilbur!" Don't be afraid to serve pulled pork sliders in place of the spit and pig, and please, for Britt, consider a few options for the vegetarian guests.

Invitation Idea. Send a lei tied with a hang tag or card with event details. Invite guests to wear their best Aloha shirts and tropical-inspired dresses. As the hostess, hunt and gather for a retro-chic Muu-Muu and dress it up with a modern belt and jewelry.

Signature Cocktail. Serve "Tropical Tiki" punch, "Coconut Coladas" and Mai Tai's in bamboo mugs or glasses that look like totem poles. You can find these on eBay or at other online vendors. My parents and I used to have Friday night dinner "dates" when I was a kid. There was this one restaurant we would go to where you'd get these great Buddha ceramic mugs, and some of which were made to look like totem poles or bamboo trees. I found a bunch of these recently on eBay for my next luau-inspired party. Fun drink umbrellas are a must with these cocktails:

Tropical Tiki: This is a super easy punch recipe. Just pour equal parts of guava juice, passion fruit juice, and pineapple juice into a punch bowl and add a bottle of prosecco. Then, add lots of ice.

Coconut Colada: This drink is inspired by Cyril's Fish House, a great beach shack in the Hamptons famous for a frozen drink called a "BBC" (Banana Colada made with Bacardi and Baileys). This twist is a frozen colada made with Coco Loco coconut milk, Baileys, Malibu Rum and ice. Blend equal parts and sprinkle shredded coconut on top of the drink. Add a piece of coconut for garnish.

Delightful Décor. Light a few tiki torches to outline your venue, and create large arrangements of colorful, exotic flowers like orchids. Place tall arrangements of green monsterra leaves in floor vases to set the right mood. Create a tiki bar and deck it out with hollowed-out coconut shells

The Way to Lei

Adults: Use real flowers (orchids are beautiful) or string your leis with shells and beads.

Kids: Use construction-paper flowers, popcorn, and candy to make kid-friendly leis. If you set all of the supplies out on a table, kids will have a blast making their own leis.

Want an easy lei? Order silk leis online.

filled with tea lights. Buy some grass skirts to drape around your tiki bar and your buffet table. In Hawaiian, the word "luau" means feast! In addition to the tradition of a whole pig, create "pu pu" platters ("pu pus" are the Hawaiian word for hors d'oeuvres) with items like coconut shrimp and grilled chicken teriyaki and pineapple skewers served on large platters made of shell. Play Hawaiian music, or hire a ukulele player to play live music. Or, to be really spec-and-swish, hire a couple of professional hula instructors to give lessons to guests throughout the night.

Fun Favors. Send guests on their way with one of those vintage glasses you bought on eBay, a DVD on how to hula, or be cheap-and-chic and send them home with a bag of macadamia nuts.

The Wizard of Oz

"Oh, you're the best friends anybody ever had. And it's funny, but I feel as if I'd known you all the time. But I couldn't have. Could I?"

—Dorothy

Take an unforgettable trip to the Emerald City with friends and family. *The Wizard of Oz* is one of those movies you are never too old to enjoy, no matter what your age. Make your menu meaningful, and serve beef "tornadoes" paired with yellow-brick potatoes and emerald greens. All of your desserts should be munchkin-sized, of course. A rainbow themed ice cream bar or an array of rainbow-colored popsicles makes a great dessert for adults and kiddies alike.

Invitation Idea. Play on some of the memorable lines of the movie with your invitation wording. *"If you have a heart, a brain, and lots of courage, please join us in Oz on April 12 at 3 PM sharp. Latecomers will be left in Kansas."*

Signature Cocktail. Serve the "Ruby Red," a martini made with Absolut Ruby Red vodka, grapefruit juice and a splash of grenadine. Rim your glasses with red sugar crystals (red food coloring and granulated sugar). "Flying Monkeys"—frozen banana and chocolate smoothies—make cute mocktails and kiddie drinks.

Delightful Décor. A scarecrow at the front door to greet your guests is a must! Go to the lumberyard or home improvement warehouse and get enough bricks so that you have one for every guest. Paint them yellow, and, when they are dry, write each guest's name with a sharpie or a thin white paint pen. These will make memorable place cards. Hang signs from doors in your house that say: *"There's No Place Like Home."* Create beautiful poppy centerpieces for your table, but don't let the poppies lull your guests into a deep sleep. Instead, keep your guests energized with upbeat background music, like the soundtrack from *Wicked*. Want to invite Glenda the Good Witch to wave her wand at your party? Purchase a couple of bubble machines and keep them running during the party. Hiring a bartender? Have him serve the signature cocktails from old-fashioned tin oil cans (you can find these at kitchen supply stores, typically used for olive oil) and decorate your bar with a couple of large hourglasses.

Fun Favors. A "Hot Air" balloon can easily be made by taking a large basket and lining it with cloth. Place it on the floor near the main door of your home or venue and tie a couple of homemade "sand bags" to the sides, then tie an oversized helium balloon to the top of the basket's handle. Fill up the basket with party favors (pairs of red slippers, maybe?) and send guests away on their yellow brick road to home.

Hey Baby, What's Your Sign?

"You are made of stars."
—**Serbian Proverb**

Everyone loves to check their horoscope, whether they take it seriously or just enjoy the entertainment. Zodiac signs have a lot of cache. So why not host a party that captures the mood and feeling of horoscopes? This party theme can be held any time of the year.

Invitation Idea. Print everyone's individual horoscope, which you can find at any number of websites online, on their invitation. Then, personalize the wording of each invite (if your party is small). For example, *"Hello, King of the Zodiac. You are invited to explore your Leo potential on August 2nd."* If your party is large, send a generic invitation, but still try to include each individual's horoscope.

Signature Cocktail. Serve "Lucky Stars" or "Scorpion Bowl" cocktails. Fun culinary delights can be themed with cute signage on a menu card or buffet table like: Virgo Veggies and Cancer Crab dip, or S'Pisces grilled chicken and Capricorn on the cob.

Delightful Décor. Hire astrologers to do readings for guests. Decorate your tables with crystals and zodiac symbols. If the party is indoors, use constellation floor lights to spray a constellation on the ceiling. If outdoors, the sky is your décor!

Fun Favors. Send each guest home with a charm of his or her birthstone, or with bath salts customized to their own star sign!

RECIPE BOX

Lucky Stars: Puree one star fruit; Divide the juice among six champagne flutes. Top with champagne or sparkling wine. Garnish with a star fruit.

Hello, Not Goodbye

"It's not where, but who you're with that really matters. And, hurts not much when you're around."

—The Dave Matthews Band

Send off friends and family in style! Everyone loves a great farewell party. And, your friends will have happy memories to remember you by until the day when you can say "Hello" again.

Invitation Idea. Use a passport holder, boarding pass, or even a luggage tag as the template for your invitation. Print the details of the party right on the boarding pass, or on a piece of paper you slip inside a passport holder.

Signature Cocktail. Serve the "Bye Bye Baby," which is a dirty vodka or gin martini with three olives. You can fasten a little airline wings pin (remember those? You can find a bunch on eBay!) on the stirrer alongside the olives for fun.

Delightful Décor. If you have them, put out some antique travel trunks or suitcases as tables for appetizers and cocktails. A cheap-and-chic alternative is to decorate brown moving boxes with images and photos of beautiful landscapes from exotic destinations cut out of

magazines, or download passport stamps, country flags, and travel symbols from the Internet. Those moving boxes are also the perfect materials to build your own bar—stack them and drape large maps over the top as bar runners.

Fun Favors. Sending guests home with address books will encourage everyone to stay in touch.

Rock the Casbah

"Should I stay or should I rock the Casbah?"
—**A Mermaid quoting The Clash**

My friend Annie celebrated her 30th birthday with this theme. If we could rock the Casbah in the middle of St. Louis, then I'm certain you can do it anywhere! Here are a few ways to bring Mermaids to the Middle East!

Invitation Idea. Take your cue from *Aladdin* and create or purchase invites that feature a genie's lamp. Tell your guests that your third and final wish is that they will attend the party!

Delightful Décor. For Annie's outdoor event, she rented a professional "circus style" tent and a portable dance floor for her party, but you can make these on your own. If you already

own a canopy or "pop-up" tent, you can easily re-cover these in fabrics of any color or prints. Or, string fishing wire from trees and fence posts (connecting the wire between them) and drape your fabric over it to make a tent-like structure. Lay down floor pillows inside the tent (try vibrant prints and colors like red,

orange and gold), string up tons of colorful lanterns, and place candles in copper pots. Serve foods that guests will eat with their hands.

If you want to go more spec-and-swish, invite your guests to feel as if they are in the middle of a whirling suq. Play loud traditional music, adorn your party with brightly colored leather poufs for guests to sit on, set up a large inlaid table for your buffet, and use hand painted ceramic bowls and bronze and silver serving platters for food. Pass finger bowls with scented rose water for guests to rinse their hands in between courses. Hire belly dancers to perform around the party, and have a few hookahs lit and smoking to share with the crowd for fun. Use gold oil lamps if you can find them at flea markets, or you can spray-paint wine bottles gold. Or, order traditional metal "Sky" lanterns online. Fill large hurricane vases with sand and place burning incense sticks inside. To be spec-and-swish, rent a few

fog machines to add a layer of smoke and mystery to the evening. Finally, create a ruby rainstorm by scattering lots of fake jewels on tables and the bar.

RECIPE BOX

The Desert Moon
1 1/2 oz vodka
1 oz peach schnapps
1 oz white cranberry juice
1 oz lychee juice (from a can of lychees)
1 lychee, for garnish

Mix all ingredients together and serve in a martini glass. Garnish with a lychee or a gypsy's pouch (small printed silk pouches filled with foil-wrapped chocolate coins) tied to the stem.

RULE OF FIN:
When sharing a hookah, it is bad luck to put the smoking pipe down in between puffs. You must always pass to the next person until you have finished the hookah.

Signature Cocktail. "The Desert Moon" will have guests in a great, let's-stay-up-and-watch-the-sun-come-up kind of mood.

Fun Favors. "Gypsy's Bells," which are ankle bracelets made of bells to "jingle" the night away on the dance floor, are a festive favor. A cheap-and-chic host gift is incense sticks. Or, go spec-and-swish and give the hostess a ruby-inspired cocktail ring or toe ring.

Destination Celebrations

> ## "If your ship doesn't come in, swim out to it."
>
> —Jonathan Winters

Here are some very quick tips for transporting your guests to another time and place:

- London: Send a wrapped mini box of Cheerios as an invite welcoming your guests. Line your table with glass jars filled with a variety of British Cadbury candies. Serve up a selection of authentic British beers, Pimms cups, and fish and chips wrapped in newspaper.

- Cuba: Use Cuban cigars as décor and as party favors. Cigar boxes as vases for low-cut flowers make lovely centerpieces. Postcards from Cuba make nice place cards. The menu is really fun to create for this party! Pass signature cocktails like Cuba Libres and Mojitos and serve Cubanos as hors d'ouevres, which are little Panini-style sandwiches. Pair your main dishes with black beans and plantains. Finish the meal with a tray of Café con Leches. Decorate your venue with fake palm trees or use large vases filled with monsterra leaves. Set out straw hats on the table for the guys and pairs of maracas for the ladies. The music is key for this party—the drum is a big component in Cuban music. To be spec-and-swish, hire instructors to teach guests classic Cuban dances like the Cha-Cha, the Mambo, and the Rumba.

- **African Sunset:** Channel Peter Beard, the famous photographer who captured much of Africa through his iconic black and white photographs, by downloading images of exotic African animals. If you have been on an African safari, dig up your photos and create a slideshow that can be displayed on a wall or on your TV during the party. Create a menu that features antelope, crocodile, and "Peanut Butter Stew," which is a signature dish from Central Africa. This particular party will take a lot of hunting and gathering, but it sure will be a memory. A great party favor? Order beads, necklaces, and works of art from a tribe such as the Massai, and profits will go to their community.

- **Celebrate the Chinese New Year:** Send guests a pair of ivory chopsticks with an invitation printed on red paper. Have a pair of Chinese slippers waiting at the door for your guests to change into when they arrive. Change light bulbs to red,

and decorate with red fabric. Hang a paper dragon above the table or the entry hallway. Serve Peking duck wraps and a buffet of Chinese themed food items. Send each guest home with an authentic Chinese tea set. These are surprisingly inexpensive at pearlriver.com.

- **Moroccan Magic Carpet Ride:** Create a magic carpet by scattering tons of red and pink rose petals all over the floor. Push a traveling tea cart that holds a variety of beverages on wheels. Your signature cocktail could be the "Marrakech," and you can host a hummus-and-pita bar and screen the movie *Casablanca*. If you can afford to hire a white-tuxedo-wearing pianist named "Sam" for the night, even better!

- **Celebrate the Sun and Sea in the South of France:** Imagine yourself gazing out at the Mediterranean Sea from the deck of the famous Hotel Du Cap Eden Roc in Cap D'Antibes, and let yourself be inspired to throw a party! This menu should be created with the sun and the sea in mind. Serve a beautiful selection of homemade infused olive oils paired with baguettes, a crudités platter, a selection of French cheeses, and a main dish of a whole fish or a varied seafood platter. Bottles of French rosé paired with your dish will be lovely.

Pastis will make the perfect aperitif. A set of Provence-inspired printed napkins make for a great party favor. You will make every guest feel like F. Scott Fitzgerald and Zelda for the night!

- Bollywood Spice: Serve a long bar of fragrant and beautiful Indian foods—from Biryiani to Tandoori with a "Naan" station to load up all different toppings. Centerpieces can be glass vases filled with colorful Indian spices like curry or black lentils called "dohl" placed in jars with white pillar candles. You can place framed Bollywood movie posters on your tables and project a black and white Bollywood film on a wall. Have a henna artist do henna tattoosand place jewels on guests. A stack of traditional Indian bangles could double as napkin rings and party favors. You may even find a bindi on your place card that you can peel off and wear that night!

- Route 66—The American Road Trip: Serve All-American beers with mini burgers and fries, and adorn your place with Route 66 signs. Hang framed maps of the US and postcards of iconic places like the Grand Canyon. Don't forget to display memorabilia from places that true road trippers know about, like the largest ball of twine, the house made of corn, or Wall Drug. Send guests away with photo albums made from recycled license plates.

- Take Me to Tokyo: Serve a signature pink martini with a Hello Kitty sticker pasted to the side of the glass. Fill large wooden sushi boats with different types of sushi rolls. Create place cards and put them in between chopsticks. Make origami flower arrangements, and host a live karaoke contest at your house. Send guests home with copies of *Lost in Translation* or mini bottles of sake.

- **The Pride of Portugal:** I've spent a good amount of time in Portugal, and if there is one thing I can say about the people, it is that they are so kind, humble, and full of *great* pride for their beautiful country. Spread the love and theme your menu "Algarve," which is the southernmost region of Portugal. Serve lots of fresh fish, sardines on crusty bread drizzled with olive oil, and other traditional Portuguese fare like chorizo and peppers and Portuguese sweet bread. Traditional blue and white tiles make great place cards, and a bottle of port is the perfect party favor.

- **Budapest:** For a truly creative invite, make one with an image of a Buddha + Pest, because Budapest is divided by the Danube river into two sides—Buda and Pest. When I traveled there, we stayed on the "Buda," side which is much more traditional, complete with the stunning old-world castle atop a hill. The "Pest"

side is post-Cold War modern and very cool. You could divide your party into the two themed "sides" and incorporate elements into both parts of the event. The signature cocktail can be Attila the Hun, which is simply scotch, straight up! A great party favor is a nicely wrapped bottle of paprika, which is the official spice of

Budapest. Or, consider a nice bottle of Hungarian wine.

- Turkish Bath Bash: In Turkey, the evil eye is meant to ward off evil spirits. People will paint blue "eyes" in their homes and wear pendants around their necks or wrists in the shape of an eye. Host a party where you serve different types of kabobs and dolma, which are traditional Turkish fare, and create a specialty cocktail named "The Bodrum," which is one of Turkey's most beautiful towns located on the Aegean Sea. Make it a martini of your choice and create an "Evil Eye" garnish—a large green olive with a small hole cut in the middle revealing the olive pit. Hang ceramic evil eyes around your home, or decorate the bottoms of your plates and serving platters (by using washable paint or markers) with evil eyes so when guests are done eating their meals, they will have a super-eyes! A spec-and-swish favor is a beautiful "eye" bracelet or necklace. A cheap-and-chic favor is Turkish Bath Salts or Turkish coffee.

- Belgium—I've been Bruges-ed! Visiting Bruges was truly an experience. While I was there, I stayed in the attic of an inn overlooking one of the canals. One night before I went to bed, I was pulling the curtains down on my window and saw two swans gliding by in the moonlight. This city really is one of the most lovely in the world, and just like Bruges, your party should be all about the presentation and the food! Serve mussels and frites, Belgian beers, and lots of *good* chocolate (not the run-of-the-windmill kind!). For décor, everything should be petit, sweet, and reminiscent of Bruges. Lace is one of their traditional products, so use lots of lacy tablecloths and napkins, and also set out framed pictures of canals and river boats. A box of classic Belgian chocolates makes for a great party favor.

- Dock & Dazzle—St. Tropez, Croatia, Lake Cuomo: Create your very own "yacht" party and bring on the glitterati! This party is great for the outdoors, or hosted on a boat. Serve custom "dock-tails" themed "Spirit of the Water," and pass out mini Paparazzi cameras to use during the night. The perfect party favor? A "deck" of playing cards in a monogrammed silver keepsake box.

For any of the above parties, find decals in traditional colors, ones that spell a quote or a saying, or ones that depict a famous tradition about the country you are celebrating and highlight them on a wall or table for your event. Remember, they peel off easily and are a quick, cheap-and-chic way to transform your venue to another place and time.

Saying *"Cheers!"* is a celebratory way to toast another when beginning a celebration together. It's nice to learn the appropriate way to say *"Cheers!"* for whatever event you are hosting. Here are a few translations to get you started:

- Dutch: Proost
- Filipino/Tagalog: Mabuhay
- French: Sante
- Hebrew: L'Chaim
- Italian: Cin cin
- Irish: Slainte
- Polish: Na zdrowie
- Portuguese: Saude
- Swedish: Skal
- Thai: Chok dee
- English: Cheers!

Jennifer Levene Bruno is the publisher of *Veranda* magazine and is someone who really lives the brand. She has hosted many memorable parties at her gorgeous home. Here are a few of her entertaining tips.

Q: What's the best supplement to a party?
A: Three things: the right mix of people, good food, and lively music.

Q: What makes a party a memory for you?
A: Good, memorable conversations. Or, playing Catch Phrase!

Q: Who are some of your favorite guests or types of guests?
A: I love hosting people who are engaging, good storytellers, and have multiple passions in life.

Q: What is your favorite thing to do when preparing for an event?
A: I love to clean and organize my kitchen and main floor for entertaining.

Q: What has been your favorite event to attend or host, and why?
A: Surprise milestone birthdays. I love to celebrate others. I love the element of surprise (when it is positive). I am very collaborative, and I enjoy reaching out to the friends and family of the person being celebrated to gather single words to describe them, or testimonials of why they are so special.

Q: What is your secret to unwinding when the party is over?
A: Cleaning. It's therapeutic.

Q: What's your Rule of Fin?
A: As the host, you should not spend too long talking with any one person. Work the room, and make sure everyone always has a drink in hand.

chapter nineteen

The Classic Cocktail Party

"Is it a cocktail, this feeling of joy? Or is this what I call the real McCoy?" —**Song lyric from "At Long Last Love," Frank Sinatra**

IF THE AFOREMENTIONED parties are all about the theme, a *classic* cocktail party should be just that—classic. To host a true cocktail party, you don't need much to capture the right energy. When I think of the stuff of really great ones, I always tend to go a little retro. I might imagine sipping a gin martini on a rolling great lawn, watching a bustling crowd have a great time, with hundreds of white paper moons and twinkle lights strung up in the trees—a big band in the near distance. Or, mingling in a dark, smoky clubroom with the modern likes of Frank Sinatra and his Rat Pack crooning at the piano. When hosting my own cocktail party, a background of jazz standards and the musical notes of a cocktail shaker are a must.

Cocktail parties are great for entertaining a variety of people—for introducing new groups of friends to each other, hosting business colleagues, or inviting guests to your place after an afternoon recital or concert. You can even host a cocktail party before a late-night dinner celebration at a restaurant.

The drinks really are the stars of the menu at cocktail parties, so have fun creating the beverage menu. Mermaids & Martinis hosted a thirtieth birthday party where all of the martinis were inspired by the 1930s: for instance, "Bathtub Gin Martinis" and the "Prohibition on the Rocks." If you can't hire a bartender and full bar service for your event, keep it cheap-and-chic by offering one or two signature cocktails alongside a red and a white wine, a prosecco or champagne, and one type of beer. Always have a mocktail and a selection of water and sodas available for guests who will not be imbibing.

Refer to the "Bar" section in the first chapter of this book if you are going to set up a full bar at your party. Remember to have cocktail napkins, stirrers, and garnishes readily available.

Keep your décor clean and classic. One or two beautifully appointed flower arrangements and lots of white votives with dim lighting will set the appropriate tone. Finally, add your "sugar on top!" This is a surprise element that is in keeping with a classic cocktail party. For example, I planned a cocktail party for a couple, and we hired a magician to work the party with magic tricks. He did this in a quiet manner for the different couples and groups who were mingling. It was very unobtrusive to the overall party, but it made the night that much more memorable for each guest. A cheap-and-chic idea is to buy tons of black, white, and silver balloons and let them float up to the ceiling—guests will feel like they are sipping under a moonlit piano.

Cheers to many classic cocktail parties in your future. And to "Ol' Blue Eyes," thanks for the songs that always get us in the mood for great conversation over a cocktail.

chapter twenty

The Big Game Night

"It is not how big you are, it's how big you play."

—**Unknown**

I LOVE A GOOD Super Bowl party—personally, I'd prefer to be in the kitchen or serving cocktails instead of actually watching the game, but that always works well for my guests! One of the best things about having a Super Bowl party is the classic dishes that go along with the party; after all, everyone loves to indulge in comfort food on a cold winter's day while huddled around the flat screen cheering for their team. Let's face it—food really is one of the most important parts of a Super Bowl party, so why not build your party around the food you are going to serve? The following are some of the dishes I suggest serving during the big game, and the party ideas they've inspired. Trust me, you will score a lot of points with these!

Tomato Soup Tureens with Grilled Cheese. Create mini grilled-cheese sliders with different flavor combos, like brie and avocado, English cheddar and apples, or the always classic American cheese on great sourdough bread. Wrap them in craft paper and write the team letter or draw the team logo for an extra special touch. Serve tomato soup in little black steel tureens (all the better if you happen to be a Steelers fan and they are playing in the Super Bowl) and place cheese graters full of folded napkins and cutlery on your table. This is a great way to organize and display utensils. Lay pieces of green AstroTurf on the table for a fun tablecloth or use a row of team pennants as a table runner. Daisies, or another festive flower, placed in empty tomato soup cans make pretty centerpieces at this party. Hang oversized team jerseys on the backs of chairs. For extra effect, consider baking and icing a cake in the shape of a football or a football field (or ordering one from your favorite bakery!).

"Pigskins in a Jersey." This recipe is a twist on the classic pigs in a blanket. Wrap hot dogs in crescent rolls and bake in the oven according to the crescent roll package directions. Once your "Pigskins in a Jersey" have cooled, use mustard or ketchup in a squeeze jar to write little team initials on each piece. The truly artsy Mermaid can even try to incorporate the team symbol. Display each team's "Pigskins in a Jersey" on separate trays alongside small ramekins of ketchup, honey mustard, and spicy mustard for individual dipping. Football-inspired paper plates and napkins complete the look.

Pizza and Champagne. There is something about pizza that just makes people happy. And it really does go well with every occasion, but especially on game days. Serving pizza with champagne dresses up your event in just the right way. Delivery pizza is usually a home run, but to really impress your guests, whip up a few homemade pizzas. My friends in California love to grill their pizzas outside. You can purchase pizza dough at any grocery store. Pick up some shredded mozzarella and parmesan cheese, tomato sauce, and your favorite toppings—no matter how plain, exotic, or decadent you want to go. I've been served pizza with potato chips and rosemary baked on top, and I've even had Nutella pizza pie. Guests can get in on the fun and create their own pizzas from a toppings bar you set up in your kitchen. If you opt for delivery, serve your pizza on real platters or pizza stones to complement the dressy champagne. Then, use empty pizza boxes lined with brown craft paper as makeshift trays for napkins, paper plates, forks, and knives.

Soup's On. Chili is so easy to prepare (or buy!), and it always hits the spot on a chilly winter day. Think about providing both meat and vegetarian versions. Add a toppings bar to really wow your guests. Your toppings bar could include shredded and block cheeses, sliced and diced onions, scallions and a variety of hot sauces, crackers, fresh baked bread, sour cream, and chopped jalapenos. Guests will love customizing their bowl of chili and pairing it with a seasonal craft beer to watch the game.

Chinese Food: My friend, and fellow Mermaid, Vanessa says that no matter where you are in the entire world (and she's been almost everywhere), there is *always* a Chinese restaurant nearby. And, what's more, Chinese food is always a winner. Order a huge spread and lay it out buffet style so everyone can create his or her own plate. Fortune cookies are a great treat made more fun when you customize the fortunes with game predictions and plays. String a few paper lanterns (perhaps in the colors of the teams) throughout your home, and you will have the perfect Chinese-infused football party.

Omelets. Treat your guests to unexpected cuisine with an omelet bar for cozy game fare. All you need is a couple of skillets, some eggs, a cook top, and, of course, a variety of mixers like different cheeses, meats, and vegetables. Eggs and a lovely bottle of Pinot Grigio go together like Mermaids and martinis! Pair the

eggs and wine with some crusty bread, and guests will feel like they've gone to heaven. Breakfast is great served any time of day.

Sandwiches: Sandwiches are an American classic, and the variety they offer is inimitable. From the child-like peanut butter and jelly to a manly meat-lovers supreme, the types of sandwiches you can serve run the gamut. Most delis will be glad to cater, and having one of

those crazy foot-longs is always fun at a game party. But if you feel like doing it yourself, don't fret. It's easy to offer some delicious, filling, and unforgettable sandwiches to your guests. Head to your local bakery and select two or three unique, fresh breads, then head to the grocery or deli to purchase a variety of meats, chicken and/or tuna salad, cheeses, vegetables, spreads and sides. Let guests get creative and make their own sandwiches. You can even have a contest to see who creates and names the best sandwich based on their favorite team player. Don't forget the selection of chips and pickles. Emptied ketchup, mustard, and mayonnaise bottles can make cute vases for flowers.

Touchdown Tumblers: It's easy to theme a signature cocktail on Big Game night. You could choose a favorite beer or cocktail and serve in large tumbler glasses, or offer a variety of beverages in "branded" soft drink cups with team names or logos pasted or hand-written on the cups.

Here's a *fin*Tastic Idea: Some friends of mine recently hosted a "Super Commercial" party that just focused on the commercials since they are so good that day! Guests voted on their favorites, and everyone looked forward to commercial breaks. No matter what foods or themes you choose for this event you are bound to have a great party. Go team!

Ariane de Bonvoisin is the author of *The First 30 Days*. Here she shares some of her thoughts on entertaining.

Q: What's the best supplement to a party?
A: Food makes a big difference, especially for folks like me who are vegetarian. I also like inspirational quotes, cards, and happy, feel-good things around.

Q: Who are some of your favorite guests or types of guests?
A: People I don't know, or people from different walks of life who I wouldn't normally meet—a Buddhist monk, a painter, a teacher, etc.

Q: What is your favorite thing to do when preparing for an event?
A: I like to invite many diverse people and friends who I know would benefit from knowing each other. Also, I love to look for a great party favor—something uplifting, like a lucky charm.

Q: What has been your favorite event to attend or host, and why?
A: I like book signings. It's such an achievement, and the end of a long road for the author, and the people there are usually interested in the book. I think the general vibe of book signings can be improved, but the purpose behind it is lovely.

Q: What makes a party a memory for you?
A: The people I met, how comfortable I felt there, and how easy it was to find the drinks, food, people, and bathrooms.

Q: What is your Rule of Fin?
A: Make sure you are wearing something you feel amazing in, and eat something before, especially if you have dietary restrictions.

Q: What is your secret to unwinding when the party is over?
A: Drinking a bottle of water and taking a shower before hitting the bed.

part seven:
THE MERMAID MANUAL

chapter twenty-one

Wine Down with Mermaids

"Wine is bottled poetry."
—Robert Louis Stevenson

A FEW YEARS AGO, I was given a beautiful, and unexpected opportunity of a lifetime. Summer had just begun, and I had sublet my West Village pad in order to flee the city for a couple of months of warm weather and travel. The journey kicked off in the South of France with three of my best Mermaids. Then, I met up with friends and traveled throughout Europe, spending time in London before I went solo to volunteer in Portugal on an archaeological dig. (I actually dug up the tooth of an extinct female bull that is in a museum!) The trip finally wrapped in Paris, my favorite European city. While I was there, I was treated like a princess by an incredibly gracious French couple, hosts Darlene and Bahram, who introduced me to a lovely gentleman who was a French restaurateur.

Like any good Mermaid, one of the first things my new friend and I did together was host a cocktail party at his Parisian pad where each guest brought a bottle of wine. I felt fairly sure I knew enough about wine to co-host the party, but I also knew I wasn't exactly *sommelier* status. After the party was under way, a magnum of red was produced. My glass was poured, and naturally I took a sip. The other guests looked a bit, well, *shocked.* Apparently I had just broken some unspoken protocol. Oops. Thankfully, the charming British man who brought the wine came to my rescue and said, "Hilary, the Prime Minister gave this to me as a gift. Would you like to do a formal taste first, before you drink it?" Later I learned that this bottle of wine cost the equivalent of $1,800 American dollars. Whoa. It was a great glass of wine, but I'm not sure it was worth a month's rent, no matter how you drink it.

From that experience, I decided it might be worth my while to learn more about wine. Mermaid Jen Frank, author of *Wine at Your Fingertips,* was gracious enough to share some of her wisdom with me about the basics of wine, how to entertain with wine, and how to get the very best for your dollar! So, here's Wine 101.

The Formal Taste

You might be asking yourself, *what exactly is a "formal taste" of wine?* Basically, it's the motions that wine geeks go through to assess the wine before tilting it back and drinking it. But, as silly as it may seem, the formal taste will help you to appreciate what's in your glass, particularly if it is an $1,800 wine!

The first aspect of a formal taste is the swirling of the wine in the glass. The key here is not to fill your glass too high as the wine just might swirl on to your friend's sweater. Gently swirling a small amount of wine releases the aromas in the wine as it mixes with oxygen.

After swirling, stick your nose into the glass and see what aromas come to mind for you. You might smell floral notes, woodsy notes, fruity notes, or a combination of some, or all of them. These notes will alert you to what flavors you can expect when you taste the wine. They can also alert you to a bad wine if you detect "off" odors.

The next step is undoubtedly the most fun: sipping the wine! This may sound simple, but in a formal tasting there is a protocol to it. You want to take a pretty good swig and swish it around in your mouth a little bit before swallowing it. Many professional tasters spit the wine into a designated bucket, but that usually only happens when countless wines are being tasted in succession, and the taster wants to stay sober enough to enjoy the last of them. While the wine is in your mouth, concentrate on how it feels and tastes. After you swallow it, focus on how long it lasts on your palate. If you are indulging in this tasting with friends, discuss what you noticed about the wine and evaluate it. The most important thing is that you enjoy the wine and want to continue to drink it. Once you make it through this tasting process, it's safe to sip to your heart's content.

Grapes & Places

The best way to learn about wine is to taste it, lots of it. Discovering which grapes you like best and what wine regions you prefer will enhance your enjoyment of wine, and put you at ease when entertaining with it. So where to start? It helps to know the major grapes and where to find them. There are over 10,000 different grape varieties out there, but you'll run into six of them time and time again. Familiarize yourself with the following red grapes: Pinot Noir, Merlot, and Cabernet Sauvignon. Get acquainted with these white grapes: Riesling, Sauvignon Blanc, and Chardonnay.

Below is a handy chart that gives you the basics about a wine's body, key aroma, and flavor characteristics. The simplest way to think about the body of a wine is in terms of milk. Think of light-bodied wine as skim milk, medium-bodied wine as whole milk, and full-bodied wine as half & half or cream. The aromas and flavors listed here are typical to the grape. You will get better at identifying aromas and flavors the more you taste. The most critical thing to remember is that there is no wrong or right when it comes to identifying flavors; it's just an impression you get from your own personal palate.

Here in the US, we label wines by grape name, but in many other countries wines are labeled according to the region in which the grapes are grown. Knowing which wine regions produce the major grapes, and what they are called there, will help you when shopping for wine or ordering in a restaurant.

Riesling is an easy one because it is labeled by the grape name, whether it's from the state of Washington, Germany, or France. One thing that can be tricky about Riesling is its level of sweetness. Wine labels, which are required to display alcohol levels, can help you here. If you're looking for a sweet Riesling, go for a bottle with less than 10 percent alcohol. If you

Type of Grape	Body	Aroma and Flavor
Riesling	Light-bodied white	Fragrant, peach, honey, refreshing
Sauvignon Blanc	Light-to-medium-bodied white	Citrus, herbal, grassy, zippy
Chardonnay	Full-bodied white	Buttery, rich, tropical fruit, nutty
Pinot Noir	Light-bodied red	Cherry, strawberry, earthy, silky
Merlot	Medium-bodied red	Blueberry, black cherry, chocolate, soft
Cabernet Sauvignon	Full-bodied red	Black currant, blackberry, cedar, plush

prefer dry Riesling, choose one with at least 12.5 percent alcohol. Anything in between 10 percent and 12.5 percent will have just a hint of sweetness. Sweetness should not be confused with fruitiness. When wine people talk about sweetness it means there is residual sugar left in the wine after most of it was turned into alcohol during the fermentation process.

Sauvignon Blanc is popular in California, New Zealand, Chile, and South Africa, where it is identified by grape name. It does, however, masquerade as Pouilly-Fume and Sancerre in the Loire Valley of France, and as "White Bordeaux" in the Bordeaux region of France.

Many important Chardonnay-producing regions classify the grape by name, including California, Australia, and Italy. In France, Chardonnay is the grape used to make white burgundy, veiled under such labels as Chablis, Mersault, Corton Charlemagne, and Chassagne-Montrachet. Chardonnay is also the white grape used in making champagne from France and many sparkling wines from other regions around the world.

Pinot Noir is the grape found in red burgundy and in wines labeled with names like Cote de Nuits, Volnay, Pommard, and Gevrey-Chambertin; it's also the main red grape used to make champagne in France. California, Oregon, and New Zealand are other popular areas for Pinot Noir, where it can be recognized by its grape name.

Merlot is grown all over the world, but is at it's best in California, France, and Italy. Except for in France, where it is one of the major red grapes in Bordeaux, Merlot is known by grape name. Cabernet Sauvignon, which is the other major grape in Bordeaux wines from France, is also widespread—but much admired when from California and Italy where it is recognized by grape name. The wines known as "Super Tuscans" from Italy are made using large percentages of Merlot and Cabernet Sauvignon as well.

Other white grapes you should recognize by name are Pinot Grigio/Pinot Gris, Chenin Blanc, Gewürztraminer, and Viognier. Other reds to keep in mind include Syrah/Shiraz, Zinfandel, Malbec, and Sangiovese.

Party Time!

Now that you are familiar with the classic grape varieties and where they're made, it's time to break out the party planner in you. If you're throwing a dinner party, you're going to want to match wines with the foods you'll be serving. We've already talked about the body of wines, which is the single most important factor in pairing wine and food. A light-bodied wine will be overwhelmed by a heavy dish, and a full-bodied wine will overpower lighter foods.

There are all sorts of specific principals when it comes to pairing wine and food, but if you want to make your life simple and keep your guests happy, just remember these tips:

- Light-bodied wines pair well with light dishes and delicate sauces (i.e., Pinot Noir with salmon in mustard broth).

- Medium-bodied wines work best with medium-weight dishes (i.e., Merlot with grilled lamb chops).

- Full-bodied wines complement heavy dishes and rich sauces (i.e., Chardonnay and lobster pot pie).

- Crisp wines balance crunchy or fried foods (i.e., Sauvignon Blanc and fried chicken).

- Regional wines match up nicely with foods from that same region (i.e., Sangiovese/ Chianti with pasta in meat sauce).

- Some go-to, versatile food wines include sparkling wine or champagne, Sauvignon Blanc, Pinot Grigio, Pinot Noir, and Sangiovese. These wines complement a wide variety of foods.

- Foods such as asparagus, artichokes, and vinaigrettes are difficult to pair with wine. Serve beer instead.

Now it's time to tackle the question of how much wine you will need for your get-together. Each regular-sized bottle (750 ml) contains about five glasses of wine.

> **RULE OF FIN:**
> On average, people consume two to two-and-a-half glasses of wine (some more, some less). So, if you're having ten guests for your dinner party you should plan on having at least five bottles of wine. It's fun to start the affair with a sparkling wine, followed by a white, and then a red as the dinner courses progress.

If you go this route, you and your dinner guests will consume at least six bottles of wine. Of course, you probably know your friends pretty well, so plan accordingly based on their potential to drink wine. Some wine stores offer discounts on cases (bottles), and it might be worth it to buy a mixed case to have on hand, especially since you can always enjoy the leftovers at a later date.

If you're throwing a bash and entertaining a

sizeable crowd, the calculations get a little trickier. Use this cheat sheet, based on a 4–5 hour party, to help you figure out how much wine to order. Again, it helps to size up your crowd's party quotient; are they light, average, or heavy drinkers?

cut the foil that is found around the neck of the bottle below the lower lip; this will help avoid any foil getting into the wine and, besides, it looks nicer that way.

Opening and pouring sparkling wine and

Type of Drinks	# of Revelers	Wine to Buy (1 case = 12 bottles)
Just Wine	20	2 cases
Just Wine	50	4-5 cases
Wine, Beer, Booze	20	1-2 cases
Wine, Beer, Booze	50	2-3 cases
Wedding Wine	100	10 cases
Wedding Wine & Beer	100	5-6 cases
Wedding Wine, Beer & Booze	100	3-4 cases

It's a smart idea to have two different whites and two different reds available for a big party. For instance, if you offer a Sauvignon Blanc and a Chardonnay for the whites, and a Pinot Noir and a Cabernet Sauvignon for the reds, you should make everyone at the party very happy.

Serving It Up

If you're going to be the hostess with the mostest, you are going to have to learn how to serve wine properly as well. Get yourself a suitable wine opener (the waiter's corkscrew is best), and you'll be ready to go. A practical tip is to

champagne is different. The cork, which is most easily removed by turning the bottle and *not* the cork, should make a slight hiss when it comes out, not the giant "pop" that has become the usual "it's a party" routine. Pouring sparkling wine as you would beer, with the glass slightly tilted, which helps to keep the froth, or the head, from overflowing. Champagne flutes should be filled three-quarters of the way to the top.

Proper glassware and serving temperature are important when presenting wine to your guests. That said, as Hilary mentioned before, you don't

> **RULE OF FIN:**
> *Seven to success! It should take approximately seven turns of the corkscrew to successfully pull the cork out of the wine. Once you have the cork out, or have unscrewed the cap, wipe the top of the bottle with a clean cloth and pour yourself a small taste to ensure the wine is not faulty. Pour your guests' glasses one-third to one-half full. At a dinner party, pour in a clockwise direction around the table, pouring your glass last.*

need to invest in many different shaped glasses for every type of wine. Offering one glass for still wine and another for sparkling wine is sufficient. Make sure the still wine glass is large enough to allow for some air and some swirling room, and that the sparkling wine glass has a tulip shape to concentrate the bubbles and keep the wine chilled. Thin crystal is best for bringing out the flavors of wine, and stemware with an actual stem to hold the glass by, helps to avoid changing the temperature of the wine, which happens when holding the glass by the bowl.

Many people serve white wines too warm and red wines too cold. Room temperature fluctuates quite a lot from home to home, so the best

estimate of the correct serving temperature, short of buying a wine chiller with temperature settings, is to chill wines in the refrigerator before serving.

> **RULE OF FIN:**
> *Whites should be chilled for forty-five to sixty minutes, and sparkling wines should be chilled for sixty to ninety minutes before drinking. Even reds can benefit from chilling in the refrigerator for twenty minutes if you have an unusually warm home or apartment.*

If you do have a wine chiller for storing wines, it is much easier to keep wines longer without danger of them becoming cooked from too-warm temperatures, or damaged from fluctuating temperatures. If you don't have one, do your best to keep your wines in a cool, dark place with a steady temperature and no vibrations.

Desperately Seeking Value

Once again, if you are purchasing wine for a large event or party, some wine stores offer volume discounts; most retailers at least offer regular discounts by the case. This can really add up when you are buying multiple cases; but even if you're only buying one case, a 10 percent or 15 percent discount can amount to a free bottle or more. And who doesn't love free stuff?

You certainly don't have to spend a month's rent on wine in order to get a great bottle, even if you're merely picking up a bottle to drink with your girlfriends or enjoy with dinner. One of the best ways to unearth values is to locate a good wine store and get to know the people who work there. If it's a reputable store that cares about its inventory and its customers, the sales people will be able to point you towards wines that give you the most bang for your buck. If you trust your wine merchant, you can also shop the sales they feature in the store. If they stand by their inventory, they're likely trying to move one wine out to bring in the new vintage, and not just trying to unload something that is of poor quality.

Another way to discover values is to look to lesser-known wine regions and less-familiar grape varieties. Countries such as Chile, Argentina, and Portugal still present very reasonable prices on wonderful, well-made wines. Less adored wine regions within France, such as Provence and the Languedoc, and up-and-coming regions in California, such as Paso Robles and Lodi, also offer relative values.

The major grapes we talked about are no doubt very useful to know; but there are many less common grapes out there that don't demand the high prices of varieties like Chardonnay and Cabernet Sauvignon. Try searching out white wines made from Verdeho from Spain, Torrontes from Argentina, and Grüner Veltliner from Austria. Deals can be found amongst red grapes, including Carmenere from Chile, Aglianico from Italy, and Malbec from Argentina.

Good buys can sometimes also be found with smaller brands. Quite often, when a wine brand becomes a household name and the wines can be seen in advertisements in magazines and online, you are paying more for the brand than for the actual wine in the bottle. Give small family wineries and less-recognizable producers a chance and odds are you'll get some premium juice for less.

Cheers! Great wine can do a lot to personalize a party and make it fun. Here's hoping these wine basics and tips will help you throw a memorable get together without breaking the bank.

> **RULE OF FIN:**
> *Wine can seem intimidating, but the more you taste, the more you know. The cost of the wine is not the measure of the wine.*

chapter twenty-two

Fabulous Flowers and Creative Centerpieces

"Arranging a bowl of flowers in the morning can give you a sense of quiet in a crowded day—like writing a poem or saying a prayer."

—Anne Morrow Lindbergh

MERMAIDS KNOW that centerpieces are more than just floral arrangements. The centerpiece is one of the most important aspects of the party: it can set the tone for the event, it highlights the theme, and, best of all, it has big potential to wow guests. Done well, centerpieces become conversation pieces. We've talked about several centerpiece ideas

in previous chapters, but here's a breakdown of some of the best centerpieces I've ever encountered. They can be tailored to fit any budget. Feel free to replicate them for your party, or, in true Mermaid fashion, use these ideas as a starting point for your own creative centerpieces.

Fashionista. If your friend is a fashionista, why not create arrangements in beautiful boxes from her favorite stores? We did this for our friend Carol, who loves everything Hermes! Just make sure you place a watertight container in each box.

A Few of His, or Her, Favorite Things. Draw inspiration for your centerpiece from something the guest of honor loves. For instance, if your dad loves playing pool, fill a large hurricane glass vase with multicolored pool balls and place two long pool sticks parallel to each other down the center of the table. Display white pool chalks so that guests can write their own place cards on colored papers, or leave notes for the hosts. Use wooden pool triangle racks as raised "placemats" at all of your seats. In addition to being a centerpiece, the pool sticks can be used as one long trivet to hold platters of hors d'oeuvres.

If your mom loves reading, use double-sided glass frames to showcase the covers of her fa-

vorite books, which can be copied on a color copier and enlarged to fit the frames. Line the center of the table with the frames so everyone can enjoy looking at them. Mom's book club pals will love talking about the book covers on the table, they're sure to inspire conversation on other books they've read. You could also create personalized "bookmarks" as place cards.

Farm to Table. A variety of fresh vegetables from the farmer's market will look beautiful when arranged in a glass or wooden bowl. Fresh herbs also make for an eye-catching (and fragrant!) centerpiece. Fill Mason jars, or plain old water glasses, with a variety of fresh herbs, like basil, dill, or cilantro. These centerpieces are especially fitting when the food being served is laden with the herbs on display.

Hollowed Be Thy Name. Hollowed fruits and vegetables are simple centerpieces that can be customized for any event, any season, and any budget. The best fruits and veggies for hollowing are apples, pears, pumpkins, squash, artichokes, watermelon, cantaloupe, and honeydew. Each of these items can be easily hollowed with a knife (or an ice cream scoop or melon baller), and then used to hold just about anything: flowers, candy, candles, dips, more food—you name it. Imagine a Thanksgiving table set aglow by hollow squashes and pumpkins, of all colors, sizes, and shapes, some filled with little tea lights and others with stuffing or gravy. Be creative!

Non-Traditional Centerpieces. You don't have to stick to flowers and candles when it comes to creating your centerpieces. Any of these ideas will make an excellent addition to your next party.

- **Photos:** What better way to celebrate someone special than by enlarging photos of that person to be displayed in the middle of the table?

- **Sweet towers:** Macarons or penny candy, chocolates or cupcakes, they all look deliciously sweet in the middle of a table. Sweet towers are simple to accomplish with three-tiered trays. Remember an easy way to make a three-tiered tray? Take two glass vases and place three different-size plates in between each one and on top (largest plate on the bottom, smallest on top).

- **Clear glass vases filled with different items based on the occasion:** From tall, skinny vases filled with a colorful mix of drugstore and designer lipstick tubes for a bachelorette party or bridal shower, to small square glass vases filled with aromatic coffee beans for a brunch buffet, the vase centerpiece is easy to pull off, and has a big wow quotient.

  - **Fish bowls.** One of the most beautiful centerpieces I've encountered featured incredibly exotic fish in round vases set on gorgeous Asian-inspired lattice holders made of bamboo. But even if your affair doesn't have Asian flair, a fish bowl centerpiece can add a unique accent to your event. Even inexpensive goldfish from your local pet store

will delight young and old alike. As a bonus, the fishbowl centerpiece can also make a great party favor or prize at a kid's event.

Remember, your centerpiece should start conversations among your guests and set the tone for your party. Whether you are working with pennies or millions, I hope you feel inspired to create lovely, original, and unique centerpieces for your next event. These elements are the "sugar on top" of your table!

> **RULE OF FIN:**
> *Bowls piled high with just one colored fruit such as lemons, limes, or oranges make for a clean, monochromatic look and are an easy and inexpensive centerpiece to create.*

When sending flowers to someone for a special occasion, make sure to add a personal touch, like a handwritten note or a small trinket incorporated into the arrangement. You can drop these things off to the florist before the delivery or overnight them to the floral shop if you live in another town. Incorporating the recipient's favorite flower or color in the bouquet will also make their day.

I asked one of the most creative floral designers in the world, James Francois-Pijuan of Francois-Pijuan Design, for his advice on flowers and centerpieces. Here's what he said:

Q: How can I help my flowers last longer?
A: Add one teaspoon of bleach and one half a can of 7-Up to the water in the vase or container. Bleach keeps the water clean and free of bacteria, and 7-Up gives flowers a sugar fix, which they love. If you don't have any 7-Up on hand, vodka and corn syrup work, too. Change the water every day (or at least every 1–3 days) and cut the stems every 3 days if your flowers are being kept at room temperature. For wooden stems like you find on hydrangeas and cherry branches, one or two good hits with a hammer on the stems helps the plant absorb more water.

Q: What are some tips for making floral arrangements?
A: Start with a good base. This is the key. Arranging flowers is like putting on clothes: you have to start with a base and build from there. What that base looks like all depends on the colors, texture, and the mood of the party. But having a good base is essential to a great arrangement. For example, if you were working with a base arrangement of all white Calla lilies, one pop of color could work nicely by adding just one beautiful amaryllis flower. Also, when building flower arrangements, it's best to work from the "outside in." For example, first add the filler (i.e. green leaves, bear grass, lemon leaf) to the water, then start filling in the arrangement with the "highlights," i.e., the beautiful flowers, berries, and whatever else you are working with. The "highlights" should always be added to the arrangement last.

Q: What kinds of colors and styles of flowers make great centerpieces?
A: Colors and styles are personal choice and taste, but a general guideline is that monochromatic is best for a clean look, and multiple colors of flowers will add more of a fun, spicy flair.

RULE OF FIN:
If you are working on a smaller budget, buy lots of "filler" like greens and branches, and then add the flowers you want to stand out. The filler will frame the arrangement and make the flowers "pop." This is a great way to save some money while still showcasing a rich, lush, beautiful look.

chapter twenty-three

Gifts with Meaning

"The ornament of a house is the friends who frequent it."

—Ralph Waldo Emerson

Hostess Gifts

GRATEFUL GUESTS always make the best guests. When you have the great fortune to be invited to a party, bring a token for the host or hostess and personally hand it to him or her in a quiet moment. You can always send flowers or a gift of gratitude after the party, if that suits the event better. Or, if you are looking for a cheap-and-chic way to give one of the greatest gifts of all, offer to stay and help clean up, and stay anyway when the host refuses. Another cheap-and-*very*-chic way to express your gratitude is to take the time to send a handwritten card after the party.

Should you want to bring a gift for the hosts, here are some *fin*Tastic ideas from cheap-and-chic to spec-and-swish:

- Candles with a box of personalized matches

- A vintage or personalized apron to add some flair to kitchen attire

- Stationery or monogrammed note cards

- A nice dossier to help your traveling pals stay organized; consider customizing it with initials or a message

- Gift certificate for a spa treatment or in-home massage

- Cleaning service (or, if it's the holiday season, a month of cleaning services!)

- Personalized or engraved journal

- iPod with a pre-loaded mix of party music and engraved with a message on the back— my favorite message is "Swim the Room!"

- A beautiful serving tray for the hosts to use at future events

- Gift basket of treats or drinks that go along with the party's theme or the host's favorite things

- A nice set of napkin rings paired with a great set of linen napkins

- Plant or flowers. If you choose a plant, select something easy to maintain, like bamboo or a peace lily. Hand paint or spray-paint the pot to personalize this gift.

- Kitchen towels tied up in twine and wrapped up with olive or lemon soaps

- Holiday ornaments

- Cocktail ring for the hostess to wear at her next cocktail party

- Relaxing bubble bath, oils, or bath salts for the Mermaid to unwind and visualize her next big event

- A bottle of wine is a standard hostess gift, so why not get creative with the packaging? If it's a summer party, wrap a bottle with netting, shells, and raffia or pair with a great themed wine stopper. I've found stoppers in the shape of boats, golf balls, and even high heels for the fashionista host.

- Something regional, like a case of Boston beer or a Maine lobster kit

- Vintage cookbooks are beautiful and unique. I find great ones at my favorite bookstore in NYC, Bonnie Slotnick (bonnieslotnick.com). I treasure an antique wooden cocktail recipe book my friend Angie gave me for my birthday—I love leafing through it for ideas and inspiration.

- Magazine subscriptions—either hard copy or for the tablet

- Engraved Merriam-Webster dictionaries, these are now manufactured in different leathers, crocodile and even patent. Talk about both practical and pretty!

Don't have a big budget for gifts? Offer to help the hostess design her party invitations or create and wrap party favors. Sometimes this is the gift that means the most.

Gifts for Every Occasion

"Every gift which is given, even though it be small is in reality great, if it is given with affection."

—Pindar, Ancient Greek poet

No matter what the event or occasion, a Mermaid always tries her best to give the right gift. If the recipient has a registry (bridal or baby), then stick to it. There's nothing boring or predictable about getting a person exactly what they want and need. But if you are looking for some ideas outside of the registry, or want to combine an item on the registry with your own gift idea, then read on.

Baby Showers. An expecting couple I know had lived in Boston for many years, so I sent them the book *Make Way for Ducklings* along with a sterling silver frame with an embossed mama duck and her ducklings waddling across the top. They loved that the gift reminded them of their favorite city and the famous duck statues at the Boston Common. It was a precious way to celebrate their new baby. You can easily tailor this idea to your friend's hometown or favorite city. Another creative idea is to buy the mama a traditional straw Moses basket and fill it up with goodies! For a couple that had lived in multiple cities, I lined the basket with a baby blanket and then filled it with travel books written for kids and families based on each of the places they had lived.

Breakfast in Bed. Get a large wicker basket and fill it with a beautiful wooden breakfast tray as the centerpiece. Add a great cookbook on breakfasts, a French coffee press, tins of coffee or tea, and delicious jams and spreads, and wrap the whole basket up with a colorful tablecloth.

A Sweet Pair. An ice cream maker paired with an ice cream scooper and glass ice cream sundae dishes makes a sweet gift for any occasion. Include some fun toppings like hot fudge, caramel, or butterscotch, and a great recipe book on homemade ice cream.

Captured Memories. For newlyweds, order leather-bound photo albums with dates inscribed on the binding. Start with the year they got married and progress five or ten years into the future. The newlyweds will love thinking about filling these albums with great memories in the years to come.

Engrave the Experience. Another great newlywed gift is to have the couple's wedding invitation engraved on a beautiful crystal keepsake box. Ask the engraver to mimic the font and nuances of the invitation. I did this for my friends, the Bradys, who were married at the Planters Inn in South Carolina. I brought the invitation to Tiffany and Co., and their engraver actually recreated a very unique southern plantation tree that was on their invitation. It turned out beautifully.

Stress No More. Planning a wedding, preparing for a baby, or just growing older can be taxing, right? Treat the celebrant to a day at the spa, or, for the budget-minded, to a single spa treatment to help him or her unwind—alone!

A Park Bench. In some cities you can purchase a park bench relatively inexpensively. Look up your local park's governing board and see if they offer such an option. How great for a newly married couple, or a newly retired couple to have a special bench where they can sit and enjoy each other's company! And, it's a nice gift for the community, too.

Honeymooning. For the newlyweds, why not call ahead to the hotel where they are staying on their honeymoon and do something special? Friends of mine were thrilled, after all the excitement of their wedding, to arrive in Bali and discover that their honeymoon suite was decked out with flowers,

champagne, and a private "table for two" dinner waiting for them. You might consider purchasing an ocean excursion for two, or a day at the hotel spa.

Around-the-World. For the gourmet, consider giving a pizza stone, a pasta maker, an Italian cookbook, and a great bottle of red wine wrapped in a classic red and white checked tablecloth. With any luck, the recipient will invite you over to enjoy the gift with him or her. (Tailor this idea to any country whose cuisine strikes their fancy.)

Housewarming Gifts

"Where we love is home— home that our feet may leave, but not our hearts."
—**Sir Oliver Wendell Holmes**

Simple Souvenirs

With a little creativity, you can make a meaningful gift from the simplest of souvenirs. I asked my friend Nicole to bring back a handful of coins from Ireland for me so I could use the coins to make a bracelet for another friend who has a love for all things Irish.

Nothing shows your love better than helping a relocated friend or family member settle into their new digs. Most folks are always grateful for a helping hand when it comes time to move, so if you are looking for something cheap-and-chic, consider offering your time. If you want to spend a little money instead, consider one of the following ideas.

- My all-time favorite housewarming gift is a "Gurgling Cod" pitcher from Shreve, Crump & Low (shrevecrumpandlow.com). This is a whimsical and beautiful jug, and when you turn it over to pour water, it actually makes a "glug-glug" sound which is entertaining and also looks chic on a table.

- Engraved door-knocker

- Hammock to relax in their new yard

- For my friends Jen and Scott (who love to surf and recently moved to Santa Monica from England), I gathered a bunch of items from the Santa Monica  Pier and delivered them in a beach pail.

- A one-week pass to the local gym or yoga studio

- Mailing address labels with their new address (you can make these on a computer for free!)

- A great framed photograph of a memory together at their old house

- A gift certificate to a local restaurant

- A "delivery" box, which is a cute box or binder that can store and organize restaurant take-out menus. This is great for people who live in urban areas and like to order delivery a lot.

- Forget-Me-Not! This basket holds all of those pesky things one might have forgotten to pack or buy for their new home in case of a power outage or storm, like flashlights, a mini first aid kit, batteries, fuses, light bulbs, LED lanterns, and, of course, Mapquest directions to your house from their new home.

- A set of monogrammed cocktail napkins paired with a spirit and stirrers

- A subscription to the local newspaper

- Flowers by the month—sent on the day of the person's birthday every month

- A bottle of champagne to "christen" their new home

- Give a good friend a nudge and purchase a class for something they have always talked about wanting to try—like a cooking course or learning a new language.

RULE OF FIN:

Sending a monogrammed gift? For a couple, modern etiquette is for the monogram to feature each person's first initial along with the surname initial (so, for Ty and Annie Bailey, the monogram would be TBA). For an individual, like Hilary Susanne Pereira, the monogram would be HSP.

Anniversary Gifts

"A successful married life requires falling in love many times, but always with the same person."
—**Mignon McLaughlin**

Mermaids celebrate anniversary traditions with our own twist. Below are some ideas for treating your partner extra special on your next anniversary.

- 1st—Paper. Write a poem for each other, or, for something spectacular-and-swish, how about plane tickets to someplace special to celebrate a year of being together?

- 2nd—Cotton. Celebrate your anniversary at a great restaurant where he can wear that cute button-down shirt you just bought him, and you can dress up in the flirty sundress he just bought you!

- 3rd—Leather. An engraved leather datebook for him, and a fabulous handbag for her.

- 4th—Silk. Start the anniversary magic sensually with his-and-hers silk boxers and lingerie, and keep it going outside the bedroom with a keepsake silk tie for him and a special silk scarf for her.

- 5th—Wood. How about a great piece of furniture for your house?

- 10th—Tin or Aluminum. Cheap-and-chic: an engraved ice bucket for a 10th anniversary toast. Spectacular-and-swish: a new car.

- 15th—Crystal. A weekend away to a glamorous hotel filled with chandeliers will really make a spectacular-and-swish memory. Beautiful crystal toasting flutes are a cheap-and-chic way to say, "Here's to us!"

- 20th—China. Reinvent your partnership! It's never too late to purchase fine china.

- 25th—Silver. Go with Tiffany and Co. silver by Elsa Peretti for her, and silver cufflinks in the little blue box for him.

- 30th—Pearls. A classic string of pearls is sure to be treasured by any woman. A catered dinner, featuring an oyster-laden raw bar and champagne, is also sure to make a splash.

- 35th—Coral. A deep-sea fishing or scuba diving excursion, or a romantic trip to an ocean resort will please you both.

- 40th—Ruby. A ring for her, and a trip to Vegas for him.

- 45th—Sapphire. Anything with a sapphire for her! A vintage Bombay Sapphire bottle of gin and monogrammed barware set for him.

- 50th—Gold. Engrave your wedding bands.

- 55th—Emerald. If you have made it this far—travel to your own special "Oz," that dreamy vacation you've always longed to take with each other!

- 60th+—Diamond. Everything comes full circle in time. Propose all over again, renew your vows, and celebrate each other and how special it is to find a lasting soul mate in this crazy world.

Mermaid Musings

"I believe in pink. I believe that laughing is the best calorie burner. I believe in kissing, kissing a lot. I believe in being strong when everything seems to be going wrong. I believe that happy girls are the prettiest girls. I believe that tomorrow is another day, and I believe in miracles."

—Audrey Hepburn

The Mermaid's Language

THE MORE YOU CHANNEL your inner Mermaid, the more you might find yourself speaking Mermaid! While your better half, friends, and family might look at you like you're crazy, other Mermaids will understand. Here's a quick glossary of some of a Mermaid's favorite terms and phrases, just in case you want to give a non-Mermaid a cheat sheet.

*fin*Tastic. It's better than fantastic; it's better than fabulous; it's *fin*Tastic!

Hurts My Feelings. This one *always* means something good, which might be why you get confused looks when you say it. This phrase is inspired by only the best finds, the most beautiful flower arrangements, the most chic décor, and truly the things that touch your soul deeply. For example, "You mean so much to me, you hurt my feelings!" Or, "That flower arrangement is so stunning it hurts my feelings." If you hurt my feelings, you are probably a friend for life.

Nana-Yo. Nana-Yo is used to describe anything wild or out of control. It pretty much means "crazy town and the land of fruits and nuts." This expression is inspired by Mermaid Tara's two-year-old son.

He used to crave bananas and yogurt, but couldn't say either word properly. So, he would yell "nana-yo, nana-yo, nana-yo" over and over. He can say both words perfectly now, but we still love "Nana-Yo" as our go-to expression for things that are just out of this world.

When celebrating out on the town or on the road, look for word-of-mouth recommendations from people you trust. It could save you and your traveling companions money, and potentially a bad experience. Here are a few places I am inspired to recommend!

- The Ivy, Los Angeles (theivyrestaurant.com). Great for celeb spotting and dining, their signature cocktail, the Ivy Gimlet—is ah-mazing.

- Shutters on the Beach, Santa Monica (shuttersonthebeach.com). This hotel immediately brings me to my happy place. For me, it represents everything I love about the West Coast but sprinkled with classic East Coast charm. It's right on the Ocean with a great view of the Santa Monica Pier, and the lobby always promises a roaring fire and over-sized leather chairs to curl up and read a great book. The rubber ducky dolphins placed in the bathtub in your room add the perfect touch of whimsy.

- The Waldorf Astoria, (waldorfastoria.com). I've done a few events at this iconic hotel and they have always been stellar to work with. PS: Did you know that they invented Red Velvet cake? The recipe originated at this hotel and the cake's main ingredient was beets which gave the cake its dark red tint.

- The Tides, Miami (www.kingandgrove.com/tides-south-beach). A few years ago, my friends and I were celebrating a bachelorette and had an 8-hour layover in Miami. We were not staying overnight at a hotel but decided to stop and eat lunch at the Tides. The service went above and beyond when the maître d' offered to bring all of our luggage to an empty suite and let us hang out at the hotel all day, including lounging and swimming at their pool. Later, the concierge even called a car to take us to the airport!

- Loews Hotels (loewshotels.com) I spent a lot of time at this hotel for a Food & Wine Festival. Service was wonderful, the gym was superb and the room service even had a "spa" menu. I still think about getting free shuttles to Target to pick up supplies and how amazing the concierge treated us.

Merman. This is the male version of a Mermaid, and he is a dream on ice. Enough said!

Dream on ice. Speaking of the aforementioned, when we say that you, or something is *"a dream on ice,"* it's exactly how it sounds and seems . . . perfect!

Stop! What this really means is, "Keep going!" because whatever you are saying or doing is amazing.

PGH: Mermaid shorthand for "Party Guest of Honor." When used in a sentence, it might go something like: "Well, what did the PGH specifically request from the bar menu so we can make sure those items are overstocked?"

I can't. I only put this here because you will very rarely hear this come out of a Mermaid's mouth—in the literal sense. Simply put, there's nothing a Mermaid can't do. If she says, "I can't," she really means, "I won't." If you find this phrase ready to roll off your tongue, keep your mouth closed and count to ten. Now, do you still want to say it? (In some scenarios, "I can't" can also mean something is just too good. For example, "I just CAN'T handle it, I love it so much.")

Heartbroken. Mermaids never use this word in response to something romantic in nature, like an actual heartbreak or break up. Rather, "heartbroken" describes how we feel when something doesn't go quite as planned for our party, or when something goes just too perfectly. Yes, heartbroken can signify something tearful OR something wonderful. The context tells the story. For example, we could be heartbroken about not securing the florist we love, or be sincerely heartbroken by how beautiful a bride looks.

A Mermaid's Treasure Chest

A Mermaid always keeps some simple treasures on hand to create her next party. Whether it's impromptu or has been planned for months, if you have just a few items at your disposal, your next party will really stand out. Of course, the most important tools for your treasure chest are these: your Mermaid attitude, the Mermaid Mantra, and a bright smile! Here are some items to keep in your treasure chest:

- Twine, ribbon, raffia, fishing line
- Wine keys
- Bottle opener
- Plain white cardboard coasters (for personalizing with conversation starters, quotes or messages)

- A pack of cocktail napkins; have a few packs in different colors or patterns and prints. Invest in a pack with your monogram.

- Ink and rubber stamps, for personalizing napkins, coasters, and anything else you desire.

- Something that is capable of being projected (maybe it's a laptop or your favorite tablet), or invest in a quality projector. You can find some deals online if you search.

- Candles: tea lights, votives, pillars, and tapers. Also, stock up on glass holders for candles. And, some LED tea lights. Most important, always have a box of birthday candles!

- Permanent markers—black and multicolored

- Package of white printable labels for mailing invitations and for labeling gifts or party favors.

- A stash of place cards themed with different motifs. A stack of blank place cards for extras in a pinch.

- Cloth kitchen towels

- Hole punch, stapler, glue gun, and tape

- Scissors and craft scissors

- Post-its (These are great for labeling your serving platters, mocking up place settings, and labeling the clothes you are packing in your suitcase.)

- Floor pillows (These can be re-covered for different occasions.)

- Large, medium, and small glass hurricane vases

- Matches or a long butane lighter

- Karaoke machine (I'm serious.)

- Blender

- Ice bucket and/or wine cooler

- Gold and silver spray paint

- Portable speakers for an iPod, CD player, or karaoke machine

- A beautiful journal (These make taking notes during a party-planning meeting more fun, and they're a great tool to carry with you for jotting down inspirations.)

- A great pen that you love and that will inspire you to send more thank-you notes.

- Measuring tape

- An oversized black chalkboard. This can lean anywhere and is an easy and fun way to invite people into your party with a message—and it can be accessorized with varied colors of chalk, depending on the event. Mini and medium sized chalkboards can make great additions to parties as well as using chalkboard paint.

- Paper "moons." Stock up on these lanterns in white and various colors, as well as the LED battery-operated type.

PS: The Mermaid's Treasure Chest can be filled with as much or as little as you can store! Some hosts I know dedicate an entire room, a closet, or just a simple drawer.

The Portable Treasure Chest: Don't Leave Home Without It!

When you are traveling to your venue, pack a mini treasure chest in a medium-sized pouch or cloth toiletries bag. Personalize it with a monogram or icon to make it uniquely yours. You never know when it might come in handy!

I remember a time when I was helping my friend Samantha pick up the catered food for her baby shower. We were stuck in major traffic and we were on schedule to be very late for her own shower! She had all the materials for the place cards and décor in the car, so I climbed into the backseat and started assembling. I'll never forget the shocked look on Sam's face in the rear-view mirror when I produced a hole punch, a pair of scissors, a stapler, and a ball of twine out of my purse.

Here's what should go in your mini "traveling" treasure chest:

- Hole punch
- Scissors
- Mini-stapler
- Measuring tape
- Permanent markers (black and colored)
- Twine or string
- Fishing line
- Glue stick
- Birthday candles
- Matches
- Tape, regular and double-sided
- Extra place cards
- A bottle of aspirin or ibuprofen (I've had many a client or friend ask me!)
- Stain remover stick
- Extra battery pack for cell phone

Overnight Guests

"Guests bring good luck with them."

—**Turkish Proverb**

With many celebrations comes travel and family time. You might find yourself in the guest room, on the couch, or on an air mattress next to your cousin from Ohio. No matter where you are, here are some tips for being a good overnight guest.

- Always bring a token of gratitude. You can refer to the ideas in chapter 23 to help you get creative and personal. Even if you are visiting close friends or family, a small gesture of gratitude for their hospitality is appropriate.

- If you are traveling by plane and can't easily pack a gift, consider leaving fresh flowers or a bottle of something for the hosts to enjoy after your stay. Alternatively, you might think of sending a gift certificate to a local restaurant or spa to pamper your hosts after your departure.

- Offer to help out around the house, but recognize that your hosts may sincerely just want you to relax and enjoy your stay. If that's the case, then politely thank them and make one last offer of your services, or you could help out by setting the kids up with a game or movie in the next room or taking their dog out for a quick walk instead.

- Don't be too difficult. It's fine if you are a vegetarian, if you have animal allergies, or if you don't like children. But remember, you are the guest in *their* home. So, if the pillows are too hard, the shower water isn't hot enough, you slept poorly every night, and you have just declared yourself a vegan, you are officially hard to please! And that's OK, just keep it to yourself.

If you find yourself on the other side of the equation—the hostess of overnight guests—there are some small gestures you can make that will really enhance your guests' stay. Remember, just like Mermaids know how to throw a party with creativity, flair, and class, they also know how to host overnight guests with creativity, flair, and class.

- Don't hover! A guest never feels comfortable if you are a helicopter. They are more likely to break something, or forget to wipe down the sink every time they use it if you are hovering and making them nervous.

- Whether you are inviting friends into your urban studio apartment, or your fifty-room lakeside compound, there is no excuse not to make someone feel welcomed. The day your guests arrive, place fresh flowers in the bedroom and a pitcher of fresh water by the bedside with clean glasses. Little chocolates left on the pillow officially make you the hostess with the mostess!

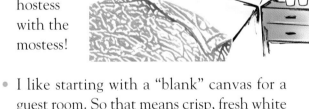

- I like starting with a "blank" canvas for a guest room. So that means crisp, fresh white sheets and coverlet. Keeping it simple, neat, and basic can give you the canvas to "paint" any guest room to fit any guest.

- Welcoming friends to the beach? Why not dress up their bed for fun with bright, pat-terned beach towels laid at the foot of the bed? Toss an inflated colored beach ball on the bed, and set out a straw tote or plastic beach pail filled with suntan lotions, magazines, and bottled water.

- Hosting a weekend in the country? Lay out thematic magazines like *Garden & Gun*, *Town & Country*, and *The Oxford American*. Place a tin thermos filled with water or a bedtime tea in the guest room. (Guests not a fan of tea? A leather flask filled with something a bit stronger might be appreciated.) Drape a plaid wool blanket on the bed, and in lieu of a flower arrangement, place a bowl of pinecones on the nightstand. They will make the room smell amazing and keep with your country theme.

- It's always welcoming to have a book about your region available for guests to peruse. My friend, Mermaid Maura, keeps a copy of Edith Wharton's *Hudson River Bracketed* in the guest room of her country house in the

Hudson River Valley, as well as a copy of Truman Capote's *A House on the Heights* in the guest room of her place in Brooklyn Heights.

- Turn your bedroom into a boudoir for your uber-chic girlfriend visiting from out of town. Drape a faux fox throw or a vintage fur coat along the bottom of the bed and pair with a mirrored tray that hosts a bottle of champagne, a spritzer of Chanel No. 5, and a glam book like *Valley of the Dolls* for her to get lost in. Place a pair of Maribou slippers next to her bed for a decadent trip to a bubbly bath (and glass of bubbly) that awaits her in the guest bathroom—courtesy of her Mermaid host, of course!

- In the guest bathroom, hang hotel-style robes on the door, roll your plush towels instead of folding them for a polished look, and lay out a pair of new slippers for your guests. Create a little "beauty bar" or a personal care kit for guests. This can include basics like mini "hotel-style" bottles of shampoo, conditioner, toothpaste, bath gels, lotion, shave cream, fresh packages of toothbrushes, and razors. A cheap-and-chic way to achieve this is to stock up on some pretty mini-sized glass bottles and create your own labels for them—you can buy oversized bottles of shampoo and conditioner, etc., and refill them every time new guest visits.

- In the morning, leave a wicker basket outside of the guest room filled with warm towels straight from a tumble in the dryer, the morning paper, and a small tray with a French press of steaming hot, fresh coffee.

- If you really want to be a spectacular-and-swish overnight hostess, consider preparing a great welcome bag filled with fun and local items, like some local honey or jam from your town's farmer's market, a good book about the region you live in for guests to enjoy during downtime, cashmere slippers, bottled water, and local magazines. These little treats will make your guest's stay much more enjoyable. My friend Alyssa hosted a girl's weekend in Saratoga Springs and she greeted us with welcome bags that included Saratoga Springs's namesake bottled water, a jar of Saratoga salsa, and a spa certificate to visit the famous Saratoga Springs Spa for a soak in the magic of the baths. We all had a great time at the spa that weekend and had goodies to take home and remember our meaningful time together!

- Old is very chic! My Grandmother used to give me all of her old perfume bottles—anything vintage, or little samples that she would get at the department store, everything from Chanel to White Linen! I love the way they all looked clumped together on a dresser; it was so romantic and pretty. Dress up your guest's room with old, vintage items.

- If you don't have a guest bedroom, transforming guest spaces can take just a little creativity. My friend Chris created a mini "theater" in his finished basement for his daughter. The space included a stage and a proper curtain on a rod that could be pulled back and forth. So, he decided to also include a Murphy bed for guests, and they had instant privacy with the curtain.

- Summer sleepovers. These can be so fun, and they don't have to be stressful. Invest in a few tents, or refer to our teepee making strategies in the last chapter and you have an immediate transformation of any outdoor spot into a mini campground for guests. Of course, you'll send them to bed with a bonfire and S'mores!

- The Attic. A space normally used for storage, the attic, or a finished garage or basement can make for a great guest room. Why not clear it out and really put it to work when you want to throw the party of the year and invite a guest list that includes out-of-towners? You can create an entire bedroom suite in one of these spaces with air mattresses dressed up in chic bedding, covered floor pillows, and a couple of rugs. Mini teepee hideaways and temporary decals will brighten the space.

Here's A Tip . . . Leave One!

"Manners are a sensitive awareness of the feelings of others. If you have that awareness, you have good manners, no matter which fork you use."
—**Emily Post**

Mermaid Memory
Mermaid Hilary

When I was a college student in Boston, I moonlighted a couple of nights a week as a singing waitress . . . on a boat. At first, I was a terrible waitress and a pretty good singer. I eventually became a decent waitress, but I never forgot my first day on the job—it was Mother's Day. I was a nervous wreck, and, needless to say, my service was subpar. I had never waited tables before, much less in a restaurant on a boat—that was moving! The absolute low point was when I managed to spill a frozen strawberry daiquiri on the lily-white silk jacket of one of the celebrating moms. So, you can imagine my bug-eyed surprise when the woman approached me after brunch, handed me a big tip, and said, "Oh Hilary, I just loved your song."

RULE OF FIN:
When tipping, it's always better to be too generous than not generous enough.

Sometimes a tip can go beyond the service you receive and can reward the server for the attention, humor, and care he or she provides your group. So what makes for a great tip? Here are some basic guidelines on tipping everyone from your tailor to your taxi driver.

Tipping is a custom that expresses your gratitude for a job well done. Legend has it that the word "tip" came from a pub owner who used the acronym on a box "To Insure Promptness." Now, whether that myth is true or not, tipping could be thought of as a reward for prompt and attentive service.

I once witnessed a move that was the stuff of Sharon Stone in the film *Casino*, and I have copied it many times. Slip the bartender, hostess, or valet a wad of bills at the beginning of the night and you and your pals will be taken care of *all* night. Trust me, it works!

Coupons and Gift Certificates
How do you calculate the tip if you're redeeming a coupon or gift certificate? Base the tip on the normal price of the goods or service. Remember, whether you are getting a service at a discount or for free, the amount of work done by the server is not reduced just because you paid less.

Mermaids On-the-Go
Whether you hail a cab or cruise in a limousine, consider offering a gratuity between 10-20 percent

of the fare. If you use valet service at a hotel, restaurant, or shopping area, offer the driver a 10 percent tip on the charge. If the valet service is free, a tip of several dollars is appropriate.

Holiday Tipping Etiquette

The holidays are a great time of the year to remember those people who serve you on a regular basis. To make it special, try sending a gracious card with the tip inside. Make sure you send it early enough to ensure holiday delivery.

- **Cleaning services:** The tip should be the equivalent to the cost of one cleaning session.

- **Gardener:** Tip between $25 and $50, depending on the size of your yard.

- **Mail carrier:** If you have a relationship with your local postal service employee, remember they can't accept cash. Instead, give them a gift certificate valued up to $20.

- **Beauty services:** Consider tipping your stylist at the end of the year with a minimum of the cost of a service she provides you. I've been devoted to my hair stylist for over ten years, so I like to get her something meaningful in addition to a cash tip.

- **Teachers:** Whether it's a teacher, tutor, or coach, consider tipping between $50-150. You might also think about giving them a gift card to a bookstore or office supply store. My best friend from high school, Robin, has been a school teacher for years and she always tells me how she never expects gifts and then is so appreciative of thoughtful ones that she can share with her family, like restaurant gift certificates or movie vouchers.

- **Mermaids & Milk & Cookies:** The person who handles milk & cookies duty (babysitters) when you're not able to should receive a tip equivalent to one night's pay, as well as a small gift from your child. Full-time help (nannies or au pairs) should get one week's pay or more, based on their tenure.

- **Personal trainer:** Upon reaching your goal, consider tipping $60-100.

- **Staff/hired help at an event:** At least 20 percent, but I have also had clients who gave much more if they were thrilled with our service.

Mermaids Dining Out

When dining out, make sure you have a good handle on the service before deciding on a tip. If the service isn't what you had hoped for, speak to the manager. The manager cannot correct the situation if they do not know about it, and skipping the tip won't accomplish anything except for ensuring that the next customer who gets that server will get worse service than you did.

- **Food server:** Tip 15–25 percent of the pre-tax total, depending on the *service* and not the *meal.*

- **Cocktail server or bartender:** Tip 15–25 percent of the bill total. If a bar has a cover charge, you do not tip on it.

- **Busser:** It's not necessary to tip the busboy or busgirl unless they did something extra special, such as cleaning up a huge mess. If so, then tip $2–5.

- **Host/Hostess:** Tipping a hosts is not necessary unless that person went above and beyond to get you a special table. However, if you have no reservations, considering tipping $5 or more to secure a spot.

- **Coat check attendant:** A $2-5 tip is courteous.

- **Restroom attendant:** A $1-5 tip is courteous.

- **Musicians:** If a musician visits your table, tip $2–5. At a lounge, tip the musician $1–5 on your way out.

Mermaids Getting Married

When planning a wedding, remember that many contracted services include tips within the final bill. Review each contract carefully so you do not double tip.

- **Officiator:** Whether this person is a priest, rabbi, or friend, tip the officiator a minimum of $100. If travel is involved, considering covering the officiator's travel expenses and offering a larger tip. Give the gratuity to the best man, who will pass it on to the officiator following the ceremony.

- **Limo driver:** Tip 20 percent of the total fare.

- **Florists, Photographers, Bakers, Musicians, and DJ's:** A tip is only necessary when the service is beyond expectations; consider up to 15 percent.

Remember, being generous pays! Proper tipping is a gracious gesture of appreciation for services rendered.

> ### RULE OF FIN:
> For any service provided to you at your home (i.e., yard work, pool cleaning, in-home grooming services), plan to provide beverages and snacks. Serve breakfast, lunch, and/or dinner if the crew is there for the whole day and into the night. If it is very hot or very cold and the crew is working outside, set up a little table with cold refreshments or a hot coffee/cocoa urn, paper cups, and lids.

Mermaid vs. Non-Mermaid

What defines a Mermaid is not something that can be easily described. It is in who she is, and you know it when you see it. For example, a Mermaid always roots for another Mermaid, and she shows her support, no matter if her own life is going perfectly peachy, or if she has recently taken a trip to Slump City. A Mermaid isn't perfect, but she is gracious and charming, and even if a Mermaid Mishap occurs, she reminds herself to *just keep swimming!*

Trying to figure out if you're a Mermaid or a Medusa? Check out these scenarios.

Mermaid Bestie is in Trouble. Your best friend just found out her boyfriend has another girlfriend he met online. Although we can't help that he is a very little man (maybe in more ways than one), well, he is who he is. Still, Mermaids know that this kind of news can be devastating to any ego. A Mermaid will cancel plans and race over to her friend (she may be toting a bottle of tequila, a box of tissues, or both). A Non-Mermaid would just brush her friend off, tell her to get over it, and go sign up for match.com too.

Memory Like an Elephant . . . Sometimes. Something important is today and you can't put your finger on it? Between birthdays, anniversaries, holidays, and various events, it can all be difficult to manage. Mermaids aren't always perfect, but they make up for their mishaps. Forgot your friend's birthday? Make a delicious picnic lunch to enjoy while you catch up, or celebrate by presenting a cupcake complete with a candle and heart-felt written card. Non-Mermaids would tell her the cards in the mail and catch ya' next year!

RULE OF FIN:

Set up an interactive calendar and fill it out with all your important dates. Have birthdays, holidays, and anniversaries set to "reccurring," and set up some type of alert system so you never have to worry about it again!

Social Media Savvy. Mermaids always know to keep their personal issues *personal*. If you're having a rough day, take a break from the Internet and post an inspirational quote (for yourself and your friends) instead of broadcasting your woes in a public status update. Be conscious of the pictures you post or are "tagged" in—would you want your boss or grandmother seeing them? Think twice, fair Mermaid, and only post the "good side" of your profile for the whole world to see. Keep the other stuff for your inner circle.

Above and Beyond. Mermaids always swim the extra mile. A Mermaid who is heading to a birthday dinner for a pal and realizes no one has made plans for a cake will dash into the nearest store and pick up a dessert and candles. A Non-Mermaid hopes someone else remembers to pick something up. A Mermaid will also be the one at a restaurant to excuse herself to whisper to the maître d' that there is something very special to celebrate that night. When the cake and candles arrive at the end of dinner, her friend is surprised *and* happy someone remembered her recent promotion.

Gratitude Goddesses. A Mermaid always says thank you. Even if she doesn't have time to sit down and write a formal note, a Mermaid will send a paperless post (paperlesspost.com) or an email within two weeks of the occasion.

Thoughtful and Generous. A Mermaid is thoughtful. She remembers that it's the little things that mean the most. She will bring "buckeyes" because she knows they are her Ohio friend's favorite dessert, or she will gift a bottle of organic wine to her host because she knows it's the only wine that doesn't give her a headache.

Thank-You Notes

Say thank you! Send a note to your guests after an event to thank them for sharing their time with you. As the guest, nothing beats a hand-written note to express your gratitude to your host, especially if you want to be invited to future parties. Keep a stash of beautiful stationery in your treasure chest just for this purpose. If you just can't find the words, send a quote or a line from a movie that captures the way you feel. Your host will be touched by your thoughtfulness.

Tasteful Toasts

Mermaid Memory
Mermaid Hilary

I went with my friend Alvina to Paris during Fashion Week one year. We went to the Hotel Coste for a lovely Parisian dinner (and we sat near Karl Lagerfeld, which was a thrill!). During the dinner, my French friend Bahram made a toast to our table that I now use all the time. It is, "May the best moment of your past be the worst of your future." I wish that for you and hope you enjoy these tips on toasts!

Practice your toast in front of a mirror and a friend a few times before you deliver the toast. It's okay to bring your notes with you when you go up to deliver a toast, but memorizing is always best. When it's time to deliver your toast, stand up and try to look at the person or people you are toasting! And always follow these guidelines:

- Make your toast short and meaningful. As Franklin Roosevelt once said, "Be sincere; be brief; be seated."

- Ask friends and family for great anecdotes or stories about the toastee when you are preparing your toast.

- Include in your toast a bit of wit and wisdom.

- Your toast should also focus on the occasion or event you are celebrating.

- Incorporate a great quote, if appropriate.

- Jokes are great, but not if they are "inside" jokes. You risk losing the crowd.

- Raise your glass at the end of your toast and take a sip.

- Don't forget to say "cheers" in the proper language if you are celebrating in another country!

If you are terrified of making a toast, consider taking a public speaking class or ask a friend who is a great public speaker for some coaching. You will probably feel better stretching yourself and trying something new, it's better to face our fears then let them win!

When the Party's Over

"I am thankful for the mess to clean after a party because it means I have been surrounded by friends."

—Nancie J. Carmody

The morning after, in the bright light of day, things can look quite different than they did the night before. If you awake to a minor (or major) mishap, follow these guidelines.

- Wax melted on your tablecloth? Freeze the tablecloth, and the candle wax should peel off (using a butter knife or even the edge of a credit card should work). If wax remains, take out two brown paper lunch bags, place one under the spot on the cloth and the other bag on top. Heat your iron to medium (judge carefully based on your iron and the fabric of your cloth) and gently iron the top bag. The bag should peel off the cloth with the remainder of the wax stuck to it.

- Need to get rid of the "mean reds"? (And not the kind Holly Golightly speaks of.) I remember inviting three friends over one night for hors d'oeuvres and wine. All three were guys, and I had just bought a brand new white rug to compliment my new white couch. I announced to the guys before pouring a single drop, "Careful, please! This is an all-white zone." I naturally assumed one of them would make a slip-up. Well, guess who spilled HER entire glass of Malbec? My friend Ian immediately ran to the kitchen and grabbed a box of salt. We covered every inch of that stain with the salt and didn't rub or touch the area of the rug. I let it sit for twenty-four hours and vacuumed the spot the next day. My rug was white as pure snow!

- Another product I love is Wine Away, which really works for the "mean reds."

- If you spill red wine, tomato sauce, or a dark liquid on wood, try immediately pouring baking soda on top of the stain and let sit for an hour before wiping up.

- Kitchen smells? Light a candle. Or, follow my mom's advice. She swears if you put a few lemons down the garbage disposal and then turn it on, smells disappear.

Perhaps the mishap you awoke to wasn't a stain or a mess, it was *you*. Here are some hangover remedies.

- Sleep! It is important to get lots of rest after a big night out. This is the best way to let your body recover and repair.

- Drink plenty of water. Many people swear by coconut water, which is a great way to hydrate.

- Drink a detox smoothie for breakfast. Frozen

blueberries, acai, and strawberries are all great detoxifiers. You can blend these with water or milk and ice for a fresh start to your day.

- Take a vitamin C tablet before bed and you will feel much better in the morning. My friend Jennifer swears by this one.

- As a last resort, indulge in the *"hair of the dog that bit you."* Bloody Mary's all around, and/or an order of bacon and eggs.

How Do You Gracefully Kick Guests Out?

Gently!

Please don't start cleaning up, or stop serving abruptly and turn off the lights. And please don't leave the room and go to bed. (Yes, that has happened. It was gruesome!) You can gracefully end your evening in a polite way by saying, *"This was so much fun. Let's do it again soon. I'll call you next week to set up our next get-together!"*

Lessons Learned

"Treat people as you would like to be treated. Karma's only a bitch if you are."

—**Author Unknown**

If there is a universal Rule of Fin, I would think it is that *everyone* makes mistakes. They are rarely fatal, and are almost always a great learning experience. A Mermaid always shares her lessons learned with her friends. Here are some I'd like to share with you:

- If you are hiring a caterer, ask them in advance what appliances they will need. Then, check to make sure all of yours (or those at your venue) are working. It won't be fun when the convection oven you haven't used in years isn't working properly and you don't find out until it is time to make soufflés for dessert. (This happened to me at an event and just thinking about it, well, let's move on!)

- Measure your room before you decide what size tables to order. A floor plan of your event space with exact measurements will be your best friend. Some rental companies will be willing to send along two sizes of everything so you can test them in the space.

- Send a day-before reminder to guests. It's great to send out a save-the-date and a formal invitation, but people are so over-scheduled that it's smart to send a quick email, text, or pick up the phone (remember that old device?) to leave a message about how thrilled you are to be seeing that person the next day.

- Communicate well. Be really clear with your vendors, from the very first conversation, about timing, pricing, and especially the details of your event. You will minimize any day-of surprises if you have clear, concise communication from the start. Aim for only happy surprises—not scary shocks!

- When having things shipped for an event, never trust online-only orders. Always call to speak to a human so that you can be sure every detail is communicated correctly, from the shipping address to the drop-dead date you need the products delivered by.

- How many times have you said something and instantly wished you could take it back? Gossip is dangerous: it really is like playing with fire. As a guest at someone's event, if you are going to complain that the caterer's sliders taste more like hockey pucks, best wait until you are no longer at the party. Likewise, you never know who may be sitting inside of a bathroom stall at a wedding, and if you have said some ugly things about those bridesmaids' dresses, well, it won't be pretty when the host or bride hears about your wagging tongue.

- If a guest has had a little too much to drink and it's starting to be very disruptive to the event (falling down, slurring words, breaking glasses and gosh forbid—starting a fight), well, this is neither cute nor sophisticated. Pull the guest aside and quietly tell the guest you'd love if they would switch to water. They should get the hint. If not, enlist another friend to help get them in a taxi for home.

- Be prepared for weather woes by having a back-up plan. Umbrellas, a pop-up tent, and slickers for guests are a must. White kitchen plastic bags can double as "slickers in a pinch" by cutting holes in the tops for guests to slide over their head. Use the extra pieces of the plastic bags that you cut off to hand to guests and they can tie as makeshift head-kerchiefs.

- Spilly Sally. Yikes. It happened. You accidentally spilled merlot or chocolate sauce on one of your guests. Offer to pay for a steam clean or a dry clean, immediately. If the accosted refuses, send them a heartfelt note the next day with a solution to the mishap! You could include directions on how to remove the stain or another offer to make it up to them.

- Wardrobe malfunctions: It has happened to the very best of us . . . we arrive at the party to discover we are wearing the exact same evening heels as the hostess, or, worse yet, halfway through the evening, we find the tag to our dress has been hanging out of the back all night. Well, when someone (finally!) alerts us to the oversight, smile a really big smile and graciously say something like, "Well, of course, I wouldn't dream of wearing any old thing in my closet to a party of yours—obviously I bought this brand new dress!" Always have a pedicure the day of a party and, if need be, kick off your heels—let the host be the star of her party. Plus, you never know when a neat-freak host may demand you leave shoes at the door!

- Be nice to people. In the heat of the moment of an event, the host can feel pressure and can be grouchy at staff, or those helping out without even realizing it. If you find yourself acting in an unbecoming manner during your event, take the time at the end of the event to apologize to the offended, and if the offended is hired help, giving an extra tip is in order for your less-than-Mermaid-like behavior.

Anchors Away, Mermaid!

"Don't cry because it's over, smile because it happened."
—Dr. Seuss

THANK YOU for taking the time to read this book and for sharing with others what it means to be a magnificent Mermaid! But let's not stop being friends and co-hostesses at the turn of the last page. Log onto MermaidsandMartinis.com to plan your next fabulous fete!

Until then, dive into that big, beautiful ocean of life. Enjoy every minute, and remember to celebrate the people who mean something to you. Don't be afraid to let them know! But first, let's raise a glass to that beautiful reflection in the water . . .

YOU.

The Mermaid's Rules of Fin

Rules of Fin: For the Hostess

- Energy is contagious. A positive host is a magnet for positive guests. Whatever you are doing, do it with energy! A small dose of enthusiasm will cover up any imperfection. If you get lost along the way, don't be discouraged. Instead, recite the Mermaid Mantra— *"There's a star in my eye and the room is alight. They don't want to be anywhere but here tonight"*—and you'll be back on track in moments.

- Create a vision board—a great way to inspire ideas for your next event.

- Big budget or no budget, every party can be priceless! Create a budget spreadsheet before your event to help keep you on track.

- The Mermaid Motto is: *"It's the Small Things That Make Life Big."*

- A Mermaid always keeps some simple treasures on hand to create her next party. Whether it's impromptu or has been planned for months, if you have just a few items at your disposal, your next party will really stand out.

- Set up an interactive calendar and fill it out with all your important dates. Have birthdays, holidays, and anniversaries set to "recurring," and set up some type of alert system so you never have to worry about missing an important date again!

Rules of Fin: Flowers & Centerpieces

- Start with a good base. When building flower arrangements, it's best to work from the "outside in." For example, first add the filler (i.e., green leaves, bear grass, lemon leaf) to the water, then start filling in the arrangement with the "highlights," i.e., the beautiful flowers, berries and whatever else you are working with. The "highlights" should always be added to the arrangement last.

- When sending flowers to someone for a special occasion make sure to add a personal touch like a hand-written note or a small trinket incorporated into the arrangement. If you are sending flowers from afar, no problem. Incorporating the recipient's favorite flower or color in the bouquet will make her day.

- If you are working on a smaller budget, buy lots of greens and branches and then add one or two buds that you want to stand out. The filler will frame the arrangement and make the flowers "pop" This is a great way to save some money while still showcasing a rich, lush, beautiful look.

- Check out local gardens and farmer's markets for some "fresh" ideas and inspiration on how to create your own floral centerpieces or event decor!

- Bowls filled with lemons, limes, or oranges make colorful and easy centerpieces.

Rules of Fin: Décor

- Well-placed splashes of color, pattern, texture, and even temporary decals will transform a space—instantly.

- Invest in or rent a tent or canopy if you are hosting a party outdoors. Dress them up with with different fabrics and festive décor accents.

- Cheap and chic mood makeovers to any room are simple to do before a party. Add one or two bouquets of flowers. Dim your lighting and light lots of candles. Place stacks stacks of 2-4 "coffee table" style books around the room with an artful object on top. The nature of these books could change out to reflect the theme of your event.

Rules of Fin: The Right Invite

- The right invite should include the 5 W's: What, Where, When, Who and Wear—i.e., What to Wear!

- Focus on the people who showed up, not the ones who didn't. Typically, 20-30 percent of people will cancel, decline, or call at the very last minute with an excuse.

- Always invite your neighbors when you are hosting a party—this will eliminate any potential grudges and also provide a heads-up about any noise disruptions the evening of the party.

Rules of Fin: Lighting Up A Party

- "One scent per event." Stick to just one scent during an event because you don't want competing scents to overwhelm your guests. When hosting a dinner, only use unscented candles at the dinner table so as not to compete with the aromas of your food.

- Before lighting a candle, trim the wick to about 1/4 inch from the wax. Finally, light your candles no earlier than thirty minutes before "show time" to ensure they last throughout the evening.

- You can change the mood of your room in a flash with colored light bulbs. Head to your local hardware store or home improvement warehouse and let lighting inspiration strike!

Rules of Fin: A Mermaid's Party Look

- The 80-minute rule! When planning a party, give yourself an hour and ten minutes before the event begins to get ready. The extra ten minutes allows for any last-minute duties you might have forgotten about and still leaves you with a full hour for prepping yourself.

- Dress the part, but don't overdo it. One or two statement pieces speak volumes. Any more, and you are no longer wearing an outfit; you are wearing a costume.

- When you wear classic styles and outfits to events, you will never age in photographs.

Rules of Fin: The Bar

- When planning your bar and beverage service, a good estimation is 2-4 drinks per guest at a party. Mermaids usually estimate at least one drink per person per hour of the event, so plan accordingly.

- When making your "Ice with a Twist," make sure to prep with enough time. Twenty-four hours is a good guideline to ensure the ice creations will be thoroughly frozen for the event.

- If you don't want to use jiggers, for the perfect pour count, *"One Mississippi, two Mississippi, three Mississippi, four"* and then stop pouring.

- Mermaids love to infuse our own vodka at home. This is super easy. Take a pitcher or glass container and add vodka and whatever else you want to infuse it with, like pineapple, lemon, mango, or all of the above!

Rules of Fin: Food & Wine

- The fresher and more in season the food is, the better it's going to taste and the more you are going to look like a "Top Chef" in the kitchen. Get to know your local purveyors and Farmer's Market.

- An inexpensive way to dine in at your party is to hire a private chef by calling your local culinary school. Students are always looking for an opportunity to practice their craft, and usually will do so at a greatly discounted rate.

- Food looks much better when served on white plates and platters.

- Wine can seem intimidating, but the more you taste, the more you know. The cost of the wine is not the measure of the wine. If you like the taste of the wine, then it's good for you, no matter what the cost.

- On average, people consume two to two-and-a-half glasses of wine at a dinner party. So, if you're having ten guests for your dinner party, you should plan on having at least five bottles of wine.

- When setting up a bar at home, start with a 6 or 8 foot table with a draped linen. Renting glasses? One simple stemmed glass can be used for wine, beer, soft drinks and water. Rent 3-4 glasses per person because people will not always re-use their glass.

Rules of Fin: Mixing & Mingling

- Swim the Room! A hostess makes introductions so that others can mingle. In mixed company, it is polite to address the female first.

- Be mindful of your guests' conversations, and try to be respectful of interruptions. Even if you haven't had the chance to talk to a certain person, it's still rude to cut off a conversation he or she is engaged in with another guest.

Rules of Fin: Themed Parties

- Birthdays: Remember to personalize. Don't forget whom the birthday celebration is for!

- Engagement: An engagement party should reflect the couple. Focus on what makes them the perfect pair and use that as the inspiration for all the party elements.

- Bachelorette Party: The bride-to-be shouldn't spend a dime at her bachelorette party, or feel any pressure to do something she might regret the next day.

- Wedding: There is nothing worse then sending guests home with another trinket to be stuffed in a junk drawer. Instead, think about making a donation in everyone's honor to an organization that is meaningful to the bride and groom.

- Baby Shower: At a baby shower, make sure the Mer-mama has a comfortable chair close by and a mocktail in her hand at all times. Also, assign a couple of Mermaids to help her unwrap gifts and get around the room to say hello to everyone. It could be her last social outing for a while!

- Mermaids & Milk & Cookies—Kids Parties: Give your littles guidelines to follow, but let them be creative and free to plan the party of the year!

- New Year's Party: Kick off the New Year surrounded only by people who lift you up, not bring you down. It's the perfect time of year to commit to a new philosophy: *"Out with the old and in with the new."*

- New Year's Day: Host an at-home spa party or other healing modality for friends. Honor the place that is *exactly where you are*.

- Valentine's Day: Entertain with love. Whether you are part of a couple or are single, remind yourself that there are only three things that last: faith, hope and love. And LOVE is the most important.

- St. Patrick's Day: If you are lucky enough to be Irish, ask your parents or grandparents how your family has traditionally celebrated this holiday and incorporate some of those ideas in your next St. Patrick's Day party. Do the same for any heritage you have and see how easy it is to top your next party with tradition.

- Easter: When egg decorating, make sure not to overcook hard-boiled eggs. Overcooked eggs are more likely to crack. Also, wait until the eggs are completely dry before decorating with colored dyes, glitter, stencils, stickers and fabrics.

- Fourth of July: No matter where a Mermaid's birthplace is, she doesn't pass up a chance to celebrate a fun tradition. Ask friends or people you meet during your travels to share their patriotic pastimes—and you will have new ideas for celebrations!

- Halloween: Keep in mind a Halloween party for all ages: Not too scary, racy or boring.

- Thanksgiving: Be thankful for the traditions that you share with others, and make sure to tell at least one person at your Thanksgiving party why you are thankful for them.

- Destination Celebrations: Whatever country you are celebrating, pick up a travel guide that lists the country's traditional meals and celebrations.

- Cocktail Parties: A cocktail party is typically 2-3 hours in length, and guests are served a mixture of light and/or heavy hors d'oeuvres (stationary or passed). This type of party is the perfect opportunity to introduce new people to each other. Always serve a signature cocktail!

Rules of Fin: For the Guest

- Don't be a flat tire on another's party! If you can't be a best guest, then *guest on outta there, sister!*

- Be on time or let the host know if you will be late.

- Swim the Room! Beware of being a party "latcher" or the host's shadow.

- Bring a hostess gift, something that adds to the theme or send flowers or a meaningful item or note the next day.

Rules of Fin: Party Inspiration

- When a wave of inspiration comes rolling in, a Mermaid grabs her surfboard (or at the very least, her notepad!)

- Enjoy the process of designing your party.

- If you go to a flea market at the end of the day—right before the stalls are packing up—sellers will be much more willing to barter and unload, and you'll walk away with some deals and steals. Don't feel like you'll miss all the good stuff if you get there late. Remember, if it's meant to be, that piece will find you *any* time of the day.

Rules of Fin: Gracious Gift Giving & Fun Party Favors

- To wrap gifts in a cheap-and-chic way, use craft paper, newspapers, or even construction paper and tie with twine. Draw a message or stamp something on the packaging. For spec-and-swish wrapping, dress it up! Anything from tying a necklace or bracelet around a smaller gift as "ribbon" to finding beautiful pieces of printed papers, wallpaper, or even pieces of fabric will make a big hit.

- The "Plan-Ahead" Mermaid will shop right after the holidays when décor and gifts are 50-75 percent discounted, and she will save these items in her treasure chest for the rest of the year.

- Sending a monogrammed gift? For a couple, modern etiquette is for the monogram to feature each person's first initial along with the surname initial. So, for Ty and Annie Bailey, the monogram would be TBA. For an individual, like Hilary Susanne Pereira, the monogram would be HSP or HP.

Some of a Mermaid's Favorite Brands, Stores, and Sites

Resources

Magazines
- *Coastal Living* (coastalliving.com)
- *Food & Wine* (foodandwine.com)
- *House Beautiful* (housebeautiful.com)
- *Lonny* (lonnymag.com)
- *O: The Oprah Magazine* (oprah.com/omagazine)
- *Real Simple* (realsimple.com)
- *Travel & Lesiure* (travelandleisure.com)
- *Veranda* (veranda.com)

People
- Alvina Patel (vancleefandarpels.com)
- Amanda Middlebrooks(sohohouseny.com)
- Ariane de Bonvoisin, The First 30 Days (first30days.com)
- Bonnie Slotnik (bonnieslotnickcookbooks.com)
- Brittany D. Costa, Health & Wellness (brittanydcosta.blogspot.com)
- Chef David Lapham (chefdavidlapham.com)
- Chiera King, Kismet Cards (kismetcards.net)
- David Aronson, Lighting (davidmitchellaronson.com)
- Dominique Love, CEO and co-founder of the Atlanta Food & Wine Festival (atlfoodandwinefestival.com)
- Elizabeth Bauer (elizabethbauerdesign.com)
- Gabrielle Bernstein (herfuture.com, spirit junkies, add more ing to your life, gabbyb.tv)
- Jen Frank, author of Wine at Your Fingertips and founder California Wine Merchants (cawinemerchants.com)
- Jennifer Edwards Milam, founder of Reveal Event Style (revealeventstyle.com)
- Karla Lightfoot and Stella Grizont from "Ladies Who Launch" (ladieswholaunch.com)
- Leanne Shear, *New York Times* writer and author of *Cocktail Therapy* and *The Perfect Manhattan* and founder of Rogue Female Fitness Fitness (leanneshear.com)
- Peg Samuel, founder of Social Diva (socialdiva.com)
- Tracey Toomey, co-author of *Cocktail Therapy* and *The Perfect Manhattan*

The Bar
- Boston Cocktail Shaker Set (williams-sonoma.com/products/double-walled-boston-cocktail-shaker/)
- Flex Ice Cube Trays (worldwidefred.com/home.htm)
- Midori (midori-world.com)
- Patron (patronspirits.com)
- Sofia Coppola (franciscoppolawinery.com/wine/sofia/blanc-de-blancs)
- Ultimat (ultimatvodka.com)
- VeeV vodka (veevlife.com)
- Wild Hibiscus (wildhibiscus.com)
- Wine Away (wineaway.com)

Food
- Abington Farmers Market (abingdonfarmersmarket.net)
- Balthazar Bakery (balthazarbakery.com/home.php)
- Chelsea Market in NYC (chelseamarket.com)
- David Lapham, Personal Chef (chefdavidlapham.com)
- Dominique Love, Co-founder, Atlanta Food & Wine Festival (atlfoodandwinefestival.com)
- Eataly in NYC (eatalyny.com)
- Macaron Towers (laduree.com)
- Nancy Wall, Founder, Flour Child Kitchen (flourchildkitchen.com)
- Tracie Turinese, Founder, The Cake Bar (thecakebaronline.com)
- Trader Joes (traderjoes.com)
- Victoria Donnelly, Founder, Cakeology (cakeology.com)

Décor
- Anthropologie (anthropologie.com)
- Brooklyn Flea Market (brooklynflea.com)
- Candles by Odin (odinnewyork.com)
- Century Novelty (centurynovelty.com)
- Crate and Barrel (crateandbarrel.com)
- Dollar stores (dollartree.com, dollargeneral.com, familydollar.com)
- Fishs Eddy (fishseddy.com)
- For Your Party (foryourparty.com)
- Jo Malone (jomalone.com)
- NO-Stick hanging hooks for paper lanterns (command.com)
- Oriental Trading (orientaltrading.com)
- Pearl River (pearlriver.com)
- Pottery Barn (potterybarn.com)
- R.D. Chin, Feng Shui Architect (rdchin.com)
- Sabon Lavender Diffuser Bottle (sabon.com)
- Shreve, Crump & Low (shrevecrumpandlow.com)
- Target (target.com)
- Taylor Creative (taylorcreative.com)
- West Elm (westelm.com)
- Williams-Sonoma (williams-sonoma.com)

Florals
- James Francois Pijuan (francois-pijuan.com)
- Sarah Tallman, Sarah Tallman Design (sarahtallmandesign.com)

Theme Elements
- 1st Dibs (1stdibs.com)
- Alameda Pointe Antiques Faire, San Francisco, California (alamedapointantiquesfaire.com)
- Anthropologie (anthropologie.com)
- Brimfield Antique Show, Brimfield, Massachusetts (brimfieldshow.com)
- Brooklyn Flea, Brooklyn, New York (brooklynflea.com)
- Century Novelty (centurynovelty.com)

- Costco (costco.com)
- Coste Hotel (hotelcostes.com)
- Cost Plus World Market (costplusworldmarket.com)
- Ebay (ebay.com)
- Etsy (etsy.com)
- foryourparty.com (foryourparty.com)
- Gilt Groupe (gilt.com)
- iTunes (itunes.com)
- Krispy Kreme Rental Truck (krispykreme.com)
- Lucky Break Wishbone (luckybreakwishbones.com)
- Luna Bazaar (lunabazaar.com)
- Marburger Farm Antique Show, Marburger, Texas (roundtop-marburger.com)
- One Kings Lane (onekingslane.com)
- Open Sky (opensky.com)
- Oriental Trading Co. (orientaltrading.com)
- Pandora (pandora.com)
- Pearl River (pearlriver.com)
- Photo Booth (photoboothless.com)
- Red Carpets, Step & Repeat, and Photo Booths Rentals (redcarpetrunway.com)
- Santa Monica Airport Outdoor Antique & Collectible Market, Santa Monica, California (santamonicaairportantiquemarket.com)
- Solar System Star Registry (starregistry.com)
- Sundance Film Festival (sundance.org)
- Union Square Greenmarket (grownyc.org/unionsquaregreenmarket)
- Wellfleet "Flea" in Cape Cod (wellfleetcinemas.com/flea-market)
- West Palm Beach Antiques Festival, West Palm Beach, Florida (festivalofantiques.com)
- Zelo.com (zelo.com)

Gifts

- Chasing Fireflies (chasingfireflies.com)
- Dogeared (dogeared.com)
- FAO Schwarz (faoschwarz.com)
- Hermes Scarves (Hermes.com)
- Merriam-Webster Dictionaries (merriam-webster.com)
- Red Envelope (redenvelope.com)
- The Monogram Shop (themonogramshops.com)

Photography

- Abby Liga Photography (ligaphotography.com)
- Brian Friedman Photography (b-freed.com)
- Daniel Movitz (movitzphotography.com)
- Jamie Betts (jamiebettsphoto.com)
- Kellie Sliwa Photography (kelliesliwaphoto.com)
- Michael Paniccia (michaelpaniccia.com)
- Nina Choi (ninachoi.com)

Illustrations

- Anna Yakhnich (annayakhnich.com)

Graphic Design

- Mary Sue Englund (bludesignconcepts.com)
- Anna Yakhnich (annayakhnich.com)
- Vibha Sahel (vbadesigns.com)

Styling and Wardrobe

- Dale Sudakoff, Stylist (dalestyle.com)
- Dean Banowetz, the Hollywood Hair Guy (hollywoodhairguy.com)
- Mala Elhassan, Hair Stylist/Makeup Artist (malany.com)
- Odin & Pas de Deux (odin.com, pasdedeuxny.com)
- Rent the Runway (rentherunway.com)
- Whydidyouwearthat.com (whydidyouwearthat.com)

Party Venues

- Decidio (decidio.com)
- Loews Hotel (loewshotels.com)
- Party Pointers (partypointers.com)
- PartyReservations.com (partyreservations.com)
- Peninsula Hotel and Spa in New York City (peninsula.com/New_York)
- Shutters on the Beach, Santa Monica, California (shuttersonthebeach.com)
- Soho House, London, NYC, Miami Beach (sohohouse.com)
- The Ivy, Los Angeles (theivyrestaurant.com)
- The Waldorf Astoria, NYC (waldorfastoria.com)

Budget Estimator Tools

- http://www.evite.com/app/party/calculator/view.do
- http://www.oprah.com/money/jeanchatzky/groups/guide/guide_party_f.jhtml
- http://www.party411.com/budget.html

Drink Calculator

- http://www.evite.com/pages/party/drink-calculator.jsp

Invites

- BeforeYourParty (beforeyourparty.com)
- Evite (evite.com)
- Paper Presentation (paperpresentation.com)
- Paperless Post (paperlesspost.com)
- PAPYRUS (papyrusonline.com)
- Party Essentials (party-essentials.com)
- Tiffany Engraved Invites (tiffany.com)
- Wedding Paper Divas (weddingpaperdivas.com)

Acknowledgments

" . . . Life is a red wagon rolling along . . . You pull for me and I pull for you."
—Lyrics by Jane Siberry

Jamie Colangelo Malkin: You are the Mermaid with the Most-est. My gratitude is boundless. How do I write the words "THANK YOU" big enough? Your beautiful ideas and invaluable collaboration and contribution on *Mermaids & Martinis* (and to my life) will forever be appreciated. You are the definition of *fin*Tastic. I love you.

David Dunham: The ultimate Merman and one class act — and my publisher, along with Joel Dunham, Associate Publisher. I'm so glad we brought this book to life. Thank you for your creative vision, support and savvy. And, huge thanks to your wonderful family, Katy, Emily and Debbie for sharing ideas over a long lunch and becoming Mermaid fans.

Emily M. Prather: You were one of my greatest gifts! Your contribution was immense. You always seemed to "get" what I was writing and believed in every word. Thanks for being a brilliant editor and such a gracious Southern *dream on ice* all at once.

Mary Sue Englund: Is it really possible to be this talented? Your gorgeous design is as beautiful as your gorgeous singing voice I will see you at the Bluebird one day soon in Nashville and then who knows where!

Paul Birardi: If you travel to "The End" on a really perfect day, with a really perfect view of the sunset—that is how big my gratitude is. All of the doors you opened, the stellar advice and constant support—I thank you so much. And, "Life is GOOD."

Candi Maher: The Mothership of all Mermaids. You are missed. You are loved. You were the most thoughtful person on the planet. We all miss your confetti cards and I miss your NYC visits. Every holiday, I raise a glass to you Candi—I know you are having a ball wherever you are.

Nicole Brady: I love you, Mermaid! And, Kevin, Caitlin, Joe, Michele (and the aforementioned Paul), and Jenny! And, of course, Elizabeth, Nicholas and Michael (and the belated Pierre). I've learned many of my tricks from you, your thoughtfulness rivals the best of 'em and you continue to be a wonderful friend year after year after year . . . .

Peter and Samantha Arcari: Peter, your cocktail prowess is amazing, thank you for helping create some magical Mermaid-tails. Sam, I've learned so many creative event tips along the way from you, Mermaid!

Vanessa Colombo Rahman: Thank you for being such a genuine friend and sister over so many years. Anything you have given me, I boomerang right back with LOVE to you, Asad, and the Lady Bug. We have had a pretty good run in this city, haven't we? Here's to many, many more!

The Colombos: Elsie, Bob, and Alex, you have made a profound difference, and I thank you for your kindness and generosity throughout the years.

Brooks Betts Dibble: OH, the original Little Mermaid. Thank you so much for EVERYTHING. Again, the Universe has no accidents, and I knew we were destined from the minute I saw that "508" phone number on your resume. So proud of all you have accomplished since, and I love you, Brooksie.

Ian Thurston: Ianno—I know I am so blessed, connections are so rare and we have such a beautiful one. Thank you for understanding and "getting" me, always. I hope to host you and Jason at a million more Mermaid memories—and please, feel free to spill the red wine next time!

Mala Elhassan: My savior of all things beautiful. Thanks for waving your pretty wand on me. The conversations in your chair have meant more than the hair, darling.

Alvina Patel: It all started over sangria with you, lady! I'm so happy you are always full of such bright ideas! We have seen a lot along this winding way and I simply cannot wait to make many more memories together! I appreciate your support, candor and humor—and, love you, always.

Brittany Costa: Thank you for being a cousin who sometimes feels like a little sister that I can guide along and help—and sometimes like a younger and much wiser version of me! I so appreciate your love, support, and constant "YES"es. Can't wait to watch you hit the sky, you STAR.

David Lapham: Whether doing a demo together at Williams-Sonoma, catering for a client, or practicing my "lines" in your kitchen, I'm always learning something from you. I'm so grateful for the delicious recipes you contributed to this book and all those nights of inviting me over for dinners to "discuss business." You were one of my very first friends in New York, and I know you will be one of my last in this lifetime (oh, and according to my "astrology" retreats, there will be many more lifetimes!) ;-) Thank you, Merman, you are the tops!

Clark Mitchell: The ultimate Renaissance man, you do it all! Thank you for the beautiful photographs you contributed and for co-creating all of those "business dinners" too. You are the best!

Raye Lynn Mercer: Thanks for being such a great example of having a dream and going for it.

Annie and Ty Bailey: If only I could have Annie's Amagansett dressing with a side of Baileys every day… thank you both for being so terrific. Ba-nannie, I will always want to borrow something from your closet until the very end of time.

Joy Marcus: You have been the most amazing Mermaid over the years. Thank you so much for believing in this brand. It has been my absolute pleasure to collaborate with you on so many events. Especially the ones that involve your lovely family.

Megan Maguire Steele: Thank you for all of your creative ideas and showing the Mermaid-love.

Dennis Pereira: If I look up "Best" in the Mermaid dictionary there is a picture of you. Best advice-giver, best recipe tester, best teepee builder, best cocktail maker, best corny joker, (apparently best woodsman, now?) best photo-taker and most of all, best Dad and best friend! I love you Denny P., thanks for all of your support.

Michele Pereira: I appreciate your lovely sense of style and your passion for finding the perfect swatch of wallpaper. Also, I celebrate your creativity and determination for reaching goals—but mostly, I admire your appreciation for the *small things that make life big.* You are so excellent at turning a mundane moment into a very funny, meaningful memory—I love that about you, *"Snowgoose!"*

Margy Thurber: You are so special. Not many people are born with your natural, easy, loving way. Your energy attracts fun, light and lots of love. I'm so lucky to call you my favorite aunt! Earle, I am lighter every day from the grace of your amazing art on my walls. Thanks!

Kirsten Mitak: You are really not from planet earth—you are heaven sent. I don't know if I've ever met anyone as nice as you. I feel blessed for your friendship, and the fact that we are related is a bonus. Thanks for your love and I have so much for YOU!

Tracy White: You and me, kid…only the only's know. You are a beautiful 'nerd' and I really can't fit all the reasons to thank you here. But, know that every gesture meant the world to me.

Valery Thurber: Val, what can I say but, "Keep living the theme lady!" And, thank you for always being so Mermaid-a-licious over the years at all of our family events. I heart you so much!

Cat Markman Berman: (aka, S.S.)—Thank you for being more than a friend, an "evolutionary partner" on this journey. We are stronger than the ghosts in our heads and the monsters beneath our beds. Thank you for the mirror, and all of those around-the-world memories, Kitty. I love you!

James Francois-Pijuan: You make everything prettier. Thank you for being such a great partner in design crime! The way you think makes my head spin—and, I love it!

Tilly Markman: You were definitely born under the sea. I am so grateful for the thoughtful gestures over so many years.

The Atheys: Thank you for all of the great support over time and for my beautiful Godchildren, Jason and Michaela, the cutest!

Melissa Gray Washington: Thank you for being such a wonderful friend and including a Mermaid on your beautiful wedding day. We've celebrated a lot together over the last few years—just the beginning!

Anne Marie Steward: Thanks for being the aunt who loves tearing up the Big Apple as much as I do. I look forward to our next adventure…you are hilarious, thoughtful and very loved.

The Tucceris: Thank you Robin, for being the longest, loyal, and true friend to me. Kevin, thank you for being such a wonderful friend to me over the years. And, to Princess Grace and my gorgeous Goddaughter Harper, I love you, Mer-babies!

My Broadway Lights: Kim, Mel, Hol, Alyssa…love you guys so much and so glad we are still in each others lives.

Ariane De Bonvoisin: I have so much to thank you for, especially giving me the best idea of my life—stay true to what we *know* is right, not what we *think* is right. And, thank you for introducing me to David! I love you, A.

Michael Hall: Merman. And, really great dresser. Thank you for co-climbing the ladder and your endless support and kindness.

Stefi Spodek Fleischer: Babyia! What can I say but I just love you—my partner in all good ideas. Thanks for being in my life in such a positive and accepting way all these years. And, thanks to John and Brody for making you so happy.

Allison Falkenberry: Always a believer, I love you so much, Al! Thank you for inspiring me and being such a funny, sweet, beautiful pal.

Sarah Tallman: Sarah, you are a creative soulmate. Collaborating with you on *Mermaids & Martinis* events always adds so much beauty! And, there is always a spot at my house for Miss Rosie.

Aisling McDonagh: Irish Goddess! You are so incredibly thoughtful, it's ridic! I am so grateful for Organic Style, because of this beautiful friendship born. Thanks for everything, Ais.

Jennifer Levene Bruno: JLB—I LOVE YOU! To pieces. You are the epitome of Superwoman. I'm SO proud of you. You inspire me to want to have it all and still be as graceful, kind and warm as you.

Janna Robinson: What a blessing to meet you. There are no mistakes in the Universe, right? I'm so glad to have become friends with such a wonderful, talented, determined lady like you.

Alethea and Alex Sibois: Thank you for hosting me in your home in Paris (and London!). I found many inspirations in those cities, and of course, in your amazing home-cooked dinner parties.

Leslie Picard and Monique Manso: Thank you for having a taste level that makes me want to work harder every day! And, thank you for your support over the years.

Meg Doperak: I feel lucky to be around your intelligence and kindness day in and day out. Thank you for making work creative and meaningful.

Rebecca Farber: Thank you for giving me a job (many times!) I've learned so many valuable lessons from you over the years—especially about maintaining a sense of grace and composure regardless of what is happening around you. You ARE Southern charm.

Mary Haskin: Gracefully leading our ship, you are a true Mermaid—with many party ideas that I stole! With your permission, of course. Thank you for being you!

Kristen O'Hara: Thank you for encouraging me to 'take a detour' and figure out what really lights me up. And, thanks for those ladies lunches at Nello, complete with quick trips to the Hermes store across the street. For inspiration, of course!

Karla Lightfoot: Thank you for your sisterhood, friendship, guidance, and love. Your depth and self awareness are inspiring. You truly are a dream on ice.

Stella Grizont: Thank you for that electric smile and energy that can light up the whole city of Manhattan. Woop-ah, lady!

Stella Araya Weil: Thank you for sharing Valentina, and your tips on: "Waste not, want not." Your spirit is so bright, and your generosity and thoughtfulness are contagious! I can't wait for more weekends with your little and the Grill Master!

Liz Ritzcovan: Thank you for being wrapped up in a bow with a Mermaid Batik block print. You are a reason to say "STOP! I just can't take it!"

Claire Kaye: My British Broadway Buddy! Thank you for listening to a lot over the past couple of years. You have the best ideas and deserve all of the success and happiness on the way to you.

Vic and Tara Silvestri: Tara—you have been so important to me over the years, and the contributions you have made to *Mermaids & Martinis* are uncountable but the ones to my spirit and life—I am changed. Thank goodness there was a "Roommate Finders" before Craigs List! Vic, thanks for being a favorite-friend-fan of mine over the years. Right back at you!

Jennifer & Scott Harris: Jenny and Scotty! Thank you for all of the support and love over the years and rolling out the welcome mat for me in London and Santa Monica.

To Ronni Kolotkin: Thanks for loving Shanti all year long, every year! She is blessed to have found you—me too!

Ron Young: You are amazing.

To Amanda Middlebrooks and the whole crew at Soho House: Thank you for your support, kindness, and often doubling as my "office" to create this book. Those spicy margaritas didn't hurt our creative thinking either, right Jamie?

Katherine Woodward Thomas and Claire Zammit: Thanks for your wisdom on evolutionary partnership, and holding a space for all can only make life sweeter.

Shelley Baer: The crystal rock garden? I love your shimmer and soul, Shell. Thanks for leading by example. I can't wait to plan that wedding!

Darlene and Bahram: You taught me how generous people can be, especially to a stranger in a foreign country.

The Rezendes: Bunnies! Thank you both for your great tips on kid-hosted parties. Kim and Guy—see you in NYC! And, thanks for being so *fin*Tastic!

Dane Smith: Thanks for always making me laugh no matter what is going on in my life. Your strength inspires me, your humor slays me.

Lauren Zerboulis and Vibha Sahel: You two are a match made in heaven! LZ, for all the mechanical pencil-ship, I am forever grateful. Vibha Las Vegas—your beautiful invites make this book so much better.

Aaron Webber: Thank you so much for your excellent photo skills and easy going spirit along the way. I can be a handful, I know!

Kristin Moshonas: Thanks for taking a chance on me. It was wonderful finding a gal who loved the pretty in life as much as me. And, we sure did have some fun hosting film parties in Wine Country!

Dale Sudakoff, Leanne Shear and Tracey Toomey McQuade: You three have it all—beauty, brains and continue to make me belly laugh every time I see you. Thank you!

Anna Yakhnich: Oh, if only we had met two years ago…what might we have done? I'm so lucky you came along, you drew the Mermaids better than I could ever have imagined! (And, you made me look hot!) Thank you.

To all of the contributors and photographers to this book, thank you for your generosity, time and talent.

To my Grandparents and Jim McLoughlin: Thanks for seeing your grandchildren, nieces and nephews as extraordinary people. Now, they are!

To all of our clients: Thank you for inviting us into your vision. We have loved every minute of turning parties into memories and feel blessed to have worked with such dynamic, creative and kind people along the way.

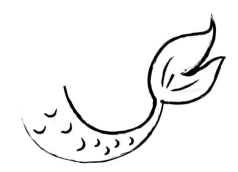

About the Author

I HAVE A RECURRING DREAM. It is light and loose and lovely. It's the dream of the perfect party. Watching everyone around me have a good time. Seeing a room light up. Enjoying a great cocktail and even greater conversation.

If there is one thing I've learned, it's that we can learn much more from our clumsy missteps than from our soaring successes. One of the best tips I ever received was to pay attention, to realize what's important to you, and to remain true to the path that feels right to you. I learned to follow my "gut"—my G.U.T., *Great Unedited Truth*. Many times I should have, or could have done what seemed to be the "right" thing, but straying from that road, while not always easy, has led me to, truly, the right thing for me. It's pretty simple: dream little or dream big, but always have your own dream.

One of my dreams led me to New York City, and it was there I received one of the most important invitations of my life—an invitation to a "reality" party. When I first arrived in Manhattan I remember swimming through a sea of people before getting on the M31 bus each morning to go to work. I would sit down (when I was lucky enough to get a seat) and stare out the window, wide-eyed and wondering, *how did I ever end up on this bus?* The city seemed so enormous, so overwhelming, and I thought I would never catch up and find my way into the pulse of it all. Here I was in this amazing fairytale of a city, where it seemed people could magically turn dust into dollars, and I felt like I was swirling around in the center, trying to figure it all out.

At the time, one of the best aspects of my job was to create big, "buzzy" ideas and events for clients. Along with those big events came even bigger budgets—sometimes so big I would have to pinch myself: $25K to spend on tents? $500K to spend on a roundtable luncheon? The expansive funds helped when it came to limitless creativity, but the irony was that in my personal life, my yearly salary was less than my neighbor's bills for doggy daycare. But hey, just like living in a tiny New York apartment, you learn to compartmentalize and you start to comparmentalize your thinking too! As Dorothy put so well, "There is no place like home." And New York City is my scarecrow.

Throughout my time growing and learning in this incredible city, one thing I never let go of was my dreams. Finding my inner Mermaid and writing this book is a little dream come true with some big rewards—I've met and interviewed the most amazing people, hosted memorable Mermaid events all over the country (and the world), and have learned so much along the way. *Mermaids & Martinis* is meant to share a few tips from my own personal experiences, lessons from other brilliant Mermaids and Mermen and also from this delicious big apple—New York City. This city can be compared to the perfect cocktail: one part sweet, one part sour, sometimes stirred, but never shaken.

I always think that with big dreams, the right approach, a little help from friends, and a lot of faith, life will be something to celebrate—every day.

Celebrate and swim lightly,

Hilary